VAJPAYEE

ADVANCE PRAISE FOR *VAJPAYEE*

'A fascinating account of Vajpayee's life as prime minister and a bold statesman. Shakti Sinha comes across as a keen observer and an able narrator'—General V.P. Malik, former Chief of Army Staff

'The most challenging period in India's most difficult decade has been amply captured by the author who had the ringside view that was the envy of many'—Manvendra Singh, veteran journalist

'Those interested in a fascinating period of India's recent political history will glean much from a careful perusal of this compelling first-hand account'—Sumit Ganguly, professor of political science, Indiana University

'Atal Bihari Vajpayee was one of India's finest prime ministers. Shakti Sinha's wonderful book offers us a deeper understanding of one of the key architects of the golden economic growth period that marked India's coming of age, both as a promising global economic power and a confident nuclear power with continental reach'—Vijay Kelkar, chairman, Thirteenth Finance Commission, and chairman, India Development Foundation

'Prime Minister Atal Bihari Vajpayee ended India's prolonged handwringing on nuclear policy, rolled back Pakistan Army's aggression in Kargil, and made a bold new effort to promote peace in Kashmir and reconciliation with Pakistan. A close associate of Vajpayee, Shakti Sinha offers deep insights into Vajpayee's leadership in those turbulent yet transformative years'—Professor C. Raja Mohan, Institute of South Asian Studies, National University of Singapore

VAJPAYEE

THE YEARS

THAT CHANGED

INDIA

SHAKTI SINHA

VINTAGE
An imprint of Penguin Random House

VINTAGE

USA | Canada | UK | Ireland | Australia
New Zealand | India | South Africa | China

Vintage is part of the Penguin Random House group of companies
whose addresses can be found at global.penguinrandomhouse.com

Published by Penguin Random House India Pvt. Ltd
7th Floor, Infinity Tower C, DLF Cyber City,
Gurgaon 122 002, Haryana, India

Penguin
Random House
India

First published in Vintage by Penguin Random House India 2020

ISBN 9780670093441

Typeset in Adobe Caslon Pro by Manipal Technologies Limited, Manipal
Printed at Replika Press Pvt. Ltd, India

www.penguin.co.in

Dedicated to the memory of my parents, Hemprabha and Shivaji Sinha

The love of books, curiosity and eclecticism that all four of us siblings, Nalini, Ranjan, Kiran and I, gained from you is the best inheritance any child could hope for

Contents

1

Swearing-in

The morning of 19 March 1998 was unusually calm at 7 Safdarjung Road, the home of Atal Bihari Vajpayee. It seemed time had stood still. The new day after a long night seemed almost surreal when I reached the place at around 7.30 a.m. The swearing-in ceremony was to be at 9.30 a.m., still some time away. This silence was in sharp contrast to the atmosphere I had witnessed on 15 May 1996 at 6 Raisina Road—where Vajpayee lived then—as he was sworn in for the first time as prime minister. It was all rather unreal, as the first Vajpayee government did not have any meaningful chance of surviving. The atmosphere was joyful, even riotous, with hundreds streaming in and out of the house, a genuine Indian tamasha in full flow.

My mind went back to when I first saw and heard Vajpayee. It must have been November or early December 1970 in Ranchi. It was an early-evening election meeting, and the mid-sized Kutchery ground was quite full. Indira Gandhi, who ran a minority government with the support of the Communist Party of India and Communist Party of India (Marxist), had called for early elections. The leading Opposition parties, Congress (O), Jana Sangh,

Swatantra Party and the Samyukta Socialist Party, had formed a mahagathbandhan (Grand Alliance). It seemed to pose a very formidable challenge to the ruling Congress (R) of Mrs Gandhi. Just as Vajpayee began to speak, it started drizzling. Naturally, he interpreted it as the blessing of Lord Indra. The crowd loved it; the speech was mesmerizing and we all felt elated. But that feeling did not last very long, as Indira swept the elections, including Ranchi, where the Jana Sangh candidate, Rudra Pratap Sarangi, lost. The mahagathbandhan was created with the sole motivation of 'Indira *hatao*' (remove Indira). It had developed no coherent vision, no alternative point of view; it was hobbled together only to get rid of her. It had learnt no lessons from past defeats and assumed that if the parties got together, then, mathematically, their polling numbers would stack up enough to defeat her. Indira Gandhi was relatively alone and all she said was, '*Garibi hatao*' (remove poverty). The people gave her a crushing mandate—330 MPs out of 536 in the Lok Sabha.

FOR DECADES, VAJPAYEE HAD BEEN paving his path towards electoral success. Finally, twenty-eight years later, he assumed the position of India's thirteenth prime minister. It was a long journey that began in 1957, when he was elected to Parliament for the first time, a member of the Lok Sabha from Balrampur, Uttar Pradesh.[1] This was not his first electoral foray, having unsuccessfully contested a Lok Sabha by-election from Lucknow a couple of years before. This time, his party, the Bharatiya Jana Sangh (Jana Sangh for short), asked him to contest from Lucknow, Balrampur and Mathura. Vajpayee was a familiar face in Lucknow, having

---

[1] This section on Vajpayee's political journey is partly based on a 1999 hand-written essay ('I Recollect') that he wrote for his friend and long-time chronicler, Dr N.M. (Appa) Ghatate, who was editing a book of Vajpayee's speeches. The book, *Decisive Days*, edited by Dr Ghatate, was published by Shipra Publications, New Delhi, in 1999.

begun his journalistic carrier there in 1948. Balrampur was seen as a relatively safer seat, and there were no volunteers to fight the elections from Mathura. Vajpayee won Balrampur, narrowly lost Lucknow but failed badly at Mathura, where he lost his security deposit since he got less than one-sixth of the votes polled. The Jana Sangh won only four seats in a Lok Sabha of 494 members, and none of the four had ever been members of any legislature. Initially, the Jana Sangh members, being few in numbers and seated on the backbenches, rarely got opportunities to speak, and Vajpayee even had to stage a walkout, protesting against the non-allotment of time to speak. Yet he soon made his mark. His first speech in 1957 was on foreign policy, which remained his favourite subject throughout his public life.

Jawaharlal Nehru had retained the foreign ministry portfolio even as he was prime minister. During the 1958 debate on the budget of the foreign ministry, Nehru, in his reply to the discussions, addressed the points raised by Vajpayee in great detail. Nehru began in English, but when he came to Vajpayee's points, he switched to Hindi. Even as Vajpayee was critical of Nehru's policies, he seemed overawed by the latter. After Nehru's death, Vajpayee's eloquent eulogy in the Rajya Sabha, of which he was then a member, was that of an admirer.

Vajpayee lost his seat from Balrampur in UP in the next general election in 1962. He said that he had looked after his constituency well and had a good reputation because of his scathing criticism of the government. (In those days, elections for the Lok Sabha and state assemblies used to be held together, with ballot papers of different colours.) Money power and the manipulation of caste and communal sentiments have been used by political parties over decades to win elections. On the day of polling, a communal incident of stabbing was staged to frighten away Hindu women from the polling booths. But what tilted the balance was the message that was spread by his opponents, asking people to vote for Vajpayee, to stamp that Jana Sangh symbol (*deepak* or lamp) on the pink ballot papers used for assembly elections. As a result, the Jana Sangh won in four of the five assembly constituencies of Balrampur, but Vajpayee lost his Lok Sabha seat. Even after thirty-seven years, this defeat rankled Vajpayee.

He entered the Rajya Sabha soon after, since by now the Jana Sangh had enough legislators in state assemblies to send its representatives to the Upper House of Parliament. And a few years down the line, in the 1967 general election, Vajpayee won back his seat from Balrampur—this was the last time he would contest from that constituency.

The 1967 election was the first time that the monopoly of the Congress party was challenged, both at the union level and in many states. One of the most interesting features of this election was an informal understanding between the Jana Sangh, led by Deendayal Upadhyaya, and the socialists, under the leadership of Ram Manohar Lohia. Prime Minister Indira Gandhi, who was seen as a puppet in the hands of the Congress high command until that time, decided to take matters into her own hands. She adopted pro-socialist policies, like the nationalization of private banks and the abolition of privy purses. She also forced a split in the Congress party and then went on to run a minority government for one and a half years.

The '70s was an eventful decade for India and for Vajpayee in various ways. Late in 1970, Indira Gandhi called for midterm elections in order to establish her authority. As mentioned earlier, four leading Opposition parties came together and formed a mahagathbandhan but failed to stop her from sweeping the elections. The liberation of Bangladesh in December 1971 and the Congress party's landslide wins in the elections to the state assemblies in 1972 made Indira Gandhi's position extremely dominant. Her mishandling of the economy, which led to high inflation, and her political dominance made her very unpopular and increasingly authoritarian. The JP Andolan, a strong movement that started in Bihar and Gujarat but then spread all over north India, challenged her politically.[2] Faced with the prospect of losing power after a judicial verdict set aside her electoral win as a member of Parliament, she imposed a state of emergency, suspending Fundamental Rights in June 1975. Vajpayee, like most Opposition leaders and tens of thousands of others, was arrested and kept in detention. His health deteriorated in custody in Bangalore, and he was shifted to the All India Institute of Medical Sciences (AIIMS) in Delhi.

Then, in a sudden move in January 1977, Indira Gandhi announced the holding of elections and most political prisoners were freed. Having grown wiser through their jail experience, the Opposition parties instead of forming a loose alliance decided to come together as a single party, the Janata Party, which received an overwhelming mandate from the people. Morarji Desai became the prime minister and Vajpayee, the foreign minister, something that he had prepared himself for over his two decades of parliamentary life. Unfortunately, this government did not last long and fell in less than two and a half years, in August 1979.

Contrary to assumptions, Vajpayee ensured broad continuity in India's foreign policy at the time, but he also showed an inclination to make bold moves. He went to Pakistan (1978) and to China (1979), the first ministerial visits to these countries since the wars of 1965 and 1962 respectively. He also hosted the Israeli defence minister, Moshe Dayan, whose visit was initially kept under wraps. The Morarji Desai government fell in August 1979;

---

[2] The JP Andolan, named after Jayaprakash Narayan, the veteran Sarvodaya leader, who brought the students and then the Opposition parties on a single platform against corruption and authoritarianism and for political change.

Vajpayee's next stint in office, of a fortnight, was to come only in May 1996, when he was sworn in as prime minister.

Mrs Gandhi came back to power with a large mandate in the elections of January 1980. But she got embroiled in the troubles in Punjab and was tragically assassinated on October 1984. The parliamentary elections of December 1984 held after Indira Gandhi's death and the subsequent large-scale massacre of the Sikhs resulted in a total sweep for the ruling Congress (I). Her son Rajiv Gandhi succeeded his mother as prime minister. Vajpayee, who had successfully won the elections from New Delhi in 1977 and 1980, was shifted by his party to his old seat of Gwalior, his hometown, where he had spent his youth and which had sent him to Parliament in 1971.

This time, Congress (I) sprung a surprise by fielding Madhavrao Scindia, scion of the former princely family of Gwalior. Vajpayee lost, and his party, the Bharatiya Janata Party (BJP)—formed in 1980 from the ruins of the Janata Party, which self-destructed in 1980—won only two seats in the 1984 parliamentary elections.

THE 1984–96 PERIOD SAW CONSIDERABLE political and economic turmoil: Rajiv Gandhi's mishandling of the Shah Bano case; the banning of Salman Rushdie's novel *The Satanic Verses*; the re-opening of the locks of the Babri Masjid–Ram Janmabhoomi structure; and the serious allegation of corruption, in the Bofors case, against the Congress. Due to all this, Congress (I) badly lost in the 1989 elections.[3] V.P. Singh, who had been a minister

---

[3] Shah Bano, a Muslim woman, had been divorced by her husband. Since Islamic law did not have a provision for maintenance, she filed a petition under Section 125 of the Criminal Procedure Court, which provides that a magistrate may allow a monthly maintenance of up to Rs 125. Her ex-husband contested this and went all the way to the Supreme Court, which dismissed his claim that maintenance was against the Sharia. After initially welcoming the judgment, Rajiv Gandhi went back on his word and, in a

in Rajiv Gandhi's government before resigning and leading the Opposition campaign, became the prime minister. His Janata Dal had won only 140 seats but received support from the BJP, with its 86 MPs, and the left parties.

The BJP's long match to power was now coming into view. L.K. Advani emerged from Vajpayee's shadow and, with his championing of the Ram Janmabhoomi movement, changed the contours of Indian politics. V.P. Singh did not last long, but his decision to implement the long-forgotten Mandal Commission's recommendations on the reservation of government jobs for Other Backward Class, was another game changer. Chandra Shekhar, who succeeded V.P. Singh, did not last long as well. He had split from the Janata Dal and was supported by the Congress (I), but his efforts to sort out the Ayodhya dispute were nipped in the bud by Rajiv Gandhi, who withdrew support.

As the 1991 midterm elections were underway, the country got a jolt with the brutal assassination of Rajiv Gandhi. The polling was even halted for some time, with later rounds held after a gap of a couple of weeks. Sonia Gandhi rejected the Congress's request to lead the party. The responsibility then fell upon P.V. Narasimha Rao, whose political career seemed to be over at that time and who was therefore not contesting elections. Vajpayee had decided to contest these elections to the Lok Sabha. His constituency of choice was Lucknow.

Even though Vajpayee was in the Rajya Sabha then, his first home in Parliament remained the Lok Sabha. At the last minute, the party asked him to file his nomination from Vidisha as well.

---

bid to placate conservative Muslims, had the provisions of Section 125 amended to exempt Muslims from its purview. This led to a backlash among a section of the Hindus. So in order to placate them, the doors of the Babri Masjid, sealed by a magistrate to prevent the breakdown of public order till the civil dispute was adjudicated, were opened by the government.

He felt this was hardly fair. Since L.K. Advani was also contesting from two seats, Gandhinagar and New Delhi, the party wanted to justify that decision, and so it made Vajpayee follow suit. Vajpayee won from both the constituencies, and the BJP crossed the three-figure mark, ending up with 119 MPs in a house of 542. The Congress won 221, and though well short of a majority, Narasimha Rao became the prime minister and appointed Manmohan Singh as his finance minister. The rest, as they say, is history.

Advani became the leader of the Opposition in the Lok Sabha, a development that disappointed Vajpayee. Years later, he was to tell a visitor that if a secret ballot of BJP MPs were to be held to determine the position, he was confident that he would have won the election. Vajpayee became very active in Parliament, and though the BJP welcomed economic reforms, on specific details there was enough space to take on the government.

Advani became the face of the party; Vajpayee, even when he disagreed with the party, went along, as was his wont. He had opposed Advani's Rath Yatras but also flagged off one. Similarly, while he never encouraged the *kar sevaks* to build the temple—the idea, in fact, disturbed him—he never said anything that would embarrass the party. A video has been doing the rounds that shows Vajpayee addressing a group of kar sevaks in Lucknow a day prior to the demolition of the Babri Masjid. His language is ambiguous; he did not ask them to demolish the disputed structure but, in a play of words, spoke about the land being levelled before the construction could begin.

The unexpected turn of events at Ayodhya on 6 December 1992 started the process of the shifting of the BJP's focus away from Advani and towards Vajpayee. The fact that the demolition took place in Advani's presence, despite the UP BJP government's assurances to the SC that the structure won't be demolished, diminished his standing. The demolition meant that a potent symbol that had been used to rally people was gone. Then, the resultant communal violence across the country that took thousands of lives, and especially Dawood Ibrahim's bombings in Mumbai that left 300 dead, unnerved the country. In response to the demolition, Advani resigned as leader of Opposition, Kalyan Singh resigned as chief minister, the UP government was dismissed, President's rule was imposed and the Rashtriya Swayamsevak Sangh (RSS) was banned. Advani was arrested and kept in a government guest house in Jhansi. After a few days, the BJP state governments in Madhya Pradesh, Rajasthan and Himachal Pradesh were also dismissed.

Upset and hurt at the turn of events, Vajpayee rose to the defence of the party and the RSS. When Parliament reconvened, he moved a no-confidence motion against the Narasimha Rao government. Vajpayee said that he was unhappy at what happened, expressed regret and even called Ayodhya a tragedy. His basic point was that the BJP and RSS were not behind the demolition. He blamed the politics propagating a distorted version of secularism and asked that the culprits be punished. It was often said of Vajpayee that he was the 'right man in the wrong party', but he dispelled such thoughts.

The Ram Mandir issue had delivered for the BJP, but it had to move beyond this issue if it wanted to become India's ruling dispensation. When Advani was appointed the party president in 1994, after Murli Manohar Joshi's single term, Vajpayee became the leader of the Opposition in the Lok Sabha. The same year, when Pakistan put Kashmir on the agenda of the UN Human Rights Commission, at Narasimha Rao's request, Vajpayee led the official Indian delegation and successfully countered this move. On 13 November 1995, when the BJP National Convention was being held in Mumbai, Advani announced at a public meeting at Shivaji Park (Dadar) that Vajpayee would be the party's prime ministerial candidate for the 1996 general elections. This announcement sent shock-waves through the

Indian political system, catching even Vajpayee by surprise. It was the first time any Opposition party had said that it had a prime ministerial candidate, and it was a sign that the BJP was going to make a serious bid for power. Who better than Vajpayee to reach out beyond the base to the larger electorate?

The BJP's isolation, post-Ayodhya, is often forgotten. Going into the elections, it had only two allies, the Shiv Sena in Maharashtra and the Samata Party in Bihar, the latter more as an anti-Lalu front than any ideological compatibility. The Shiv Sena thought that the BJP was not pushing the Hindutva agenda aggressively enough, now that Bal Thackeray was Hindu Hriday Samrat.

THE HOUSE ON SAFDARJUNG ROAD was quiet for various reasons, the least of which was that there was no novelty attached to the idea of Vajpayee becoming PM any more. The consensus among the workers and supporters of the BJP and among most political analysts was that Vajpayee deserved, or at least was expected, to become the prime minister after the 1998 midterm polls. The BJP-led National Democratic Alliance (NDA) was on the threshold of a parliamentary majority when the final results came in, something no political party or alliance had managed since 1984, when the Congress overwhelmingly swept the elections in the aftermath of Indira Gandhi's tragic death.

The enhanced security detail guarding Vajpayee since May 1996 had made it much more difficult for anyone to walk in and out of his house, and this was another reason for the relative absence of people at his swearing-in ceremony on 19 March 1998. But these were minor issues that paled in comparison to the hectic political drama of the previous two weeks. If a marathon could be run like a combination of a sprint and an obstacle race, with a hint of Greek drama thrown in, this was it. The joy of victory, of achieving what you set out to be, had been considerably watered down. In fact, there was a lingering bitter taste that would not go away for the entire thirteen months of the government. It wasn't sombre all the way; there were many highs, some unbelievably so, but it mostly felt like skating on thin ice.

I had left 7 Safdarjung Road only a few hours earlier, around 3 a.m., after ensuring that all the ministers-to-be had been tracked down and the invitation cards for the swearing-in ceremony for their families, friends and supporters handed over to them. Luckily, the function was to be held in the forecourt of the Rashtrapati Bhavan. Earlier, such functions were normally held in the Ashoka Hall of the Rashtrapati Bhawan, but it could hardly accommodate a couple of hundred people.

The list of ministers had been finalized late the previous evening—a moment in which I was extremely nervous. Even though I had been with Vajpayee since May 1996, I was not expected to attend political meetings and had only recently started interacting with so many big leaders—L.K. Advani, George Fernandes, Jaswant Singh, Ramakrishna Hegde, Surjit Singh Barnala, Pramod Mahajan and others. Even after the names had been checked and re-checked, the cards distributed, and it was time to go to bed, there was a last-minute rethink: the name of Jaswant Singh was withdrawn, since he had lost the election and it was not considered proper to make him a minister, yet.

This did affect the composition of the government, as had been slotted for finance, a key portfolio. He had been the chair of the parliamentary standing committee on finance and had come across as a big-picture person, a genuine liberalizer with his Swatantra Party background. Of all the leaders, I knew him the best, as he would frequently drop into Vajpayee's parliamentary office. He was then co-writing a book on battles fought in India since the sixteenth century and used the office to read and write occasionally.[4] (It was another of his books, the one on Jinnah, that got him into trouble with his party, but that was still many years away.) The staff called him Major Sahib, for he had been one until he quit the army for public life. We would exchange a few desultory words on the challenges facing the economy.

Vajpayee was the epitome of grace whenever he ate his breakfast of papaya and toast, completely unhurriedly, as if it were just another day. Little did I realize then that it was this ability to face adversity that was among his greatest strengths. The newspapers read, the galabandh in place, we set off for Rashtrapati Bhavan. Before I got into the car, Namita, Vajpayee's foster daughter, embraced me as only a sister-in-law, who was a strong pillar of support, could and wished me luck. As I got into the car with Vajpayee to drive to Rashtrapati Bhavan, I felt overwhelmed by thoughts and emotions. I recall being told in June 1996 that continuing with Vajpayee could mean jeopardizing my career in bureaucracy. After the expected fall of the first Vajpayee government, in May 1996, I could have gone back to my regular job as a director in the commerce ministry but chose to continue with Vajpayee as secretary to the leader of Opposition in the Lok Sabha, a first for any member of the higher civil services.[5] I actually didn't think too much about continuing with him despite his losing office. If I had worked with him when he was prime minister, it was only natural that I would do so when he was not. Did I expect him to become PM? Yes, but the 'when' of it did not seem relevant.

We rode to Rashtrapati Bhavan in silence as usual. Somewhere on Rajaji Marg, he asked me, 'Finance *ka kya hoga*?' My instinctive, immature response was that he should keep it with a good minister of state to handle routine matters. I said that we would

---

4   The book was 'Sauryam Tejo' which he co-authored with a retired army officer, Suraj Bhatia.
5   Pulok Chatterjee subsequently held the position when Sonia Gandhi became the LOP.

manage until a regular finance minister was found. One minister of state had already been decided upon. It was to be R.K. Kumar, Jayalalithaa's point person in Delhi. No more words were uttered during the rest of the short journey.

The almost unnatural quiet of Safdarjung Road was replaced by the cacophony of the Rashtrapati Bhavan. The sun was much higher and it was getting warm. The swearing-in ceremony was impressive. The council of ministers was a mixture of those who had made a name for themselves in public life and those who were representing important state leaders. From the BJP, there was L.K. Advani, Murli Manohar Joshi, Sikander Bakht, Madan Lal Khurana, Yashwant Sinha, Rangarajan Kumaramangalam and Ram Jethmalani among others. Important leaders from other parties included George Fernandes, Ramakrishna Hegde, Surjit Singh Barnala, Buta Singh, Nitish Kumar, Naveen Patnaik, Suresh Prabhu, V. Ramamurthy, etc. Ministers of State included Ram Naik, Uma Bharti, Maneka Gandhi, Sukhbir Singh Badal, Babulal Marandi and R.K. Kumar.

It was an interesting group. Two ministers, Nitish Kumar and Naveen Patnaik, and two ministers of state, Uma Bharti and Babulal Marandi, would go on to become chief ministers of their respective states. At the time of writing, Naveen Patnaik is the longest-serving chief minister of Odisha by a mile, and Nitish Kumar is the second longest-serving chief minister of Bihar. (Of Sri Krishna Sinha's seventeen years as premier/chief minister of Bihar, three and a half years were pre-Independence; so Nitish Kumar is catching up with Sri Babu, as he was known, as the chief minister for the longest tenure post-Independence.)

Sikander Bakht and Sushma Swaraj came to the BJP after the Janata Party self-destructed. Neither had been with the Bharatiya Jana Sangh (BJS), BJP's precursor. Nor did they have any RSS connection. The Janata Party came about with the merger of the leading non Congress (I) parties: the BJS, Congress (O), Bharatiya Lok Dal and the Socialist Party. Bakht was a former Congressman, while Swaraj had a socialist background. Swaraj, in fact, had been a minister in Haryana in the Janata Party government in 1977, when she was hardly twenty-five, but quit her position on grounds of principle when she felt that Chief Minister Devi Lal was autocratic.

Rangarajan Kumaramangalam, who regrettably died so young, was a third-generation minister. He had joined the BJP from the Congress and had been a minister of state in the Narasimha Rao government but had had to quit, having asked the party high command to introspect after some electoral losses. His father, Mohan Kumaramangalam, who died in a plane crash in Delhi, was among the group of communists who had joined the Congress and rose to become a minister in the Union government.

Besides Bakth and Rangarajan Kumaramangalam, there were a number of other long-term Congressmen, among whom V. Ramamurthy still regarded himself as a Congressman. A veteran Congress leader from Tamil Nadu and a former union minister, he had formed the Tamizhaga Rajiv Congress (TRC). Another was Buta Singh, a former union home minister in Rajiv Gandhi's government who had a played a major role in the post-Operation Blue Star reconstruction at the Golden Temple in 1984–85, for which he was temporarily excommunicated from the Sikh Panth. He apparently courted controversies, or at least they followed him, as his subsequent career would show. At this moment, he was out of Congress but was to return to it soon. Jayalalithaa had her two representatives in the cabinet, senior leaders S. Muthaiah and M. Thambidurai, and her point person in Delhi, R.K. Kumar, as minister of state. BJP's need to accommodate the allies was so great that even a senior leader like Ram Naik was sworn in only as minister of state.

The swearing-in ceremony passed in a blur. Vajpayee did mention to some presspersons that he would be holding the finance portfolio for the time being. This time, Vajpayee's entry into the prime minister's office seemed natural. N.N. Vohra, the outgoing principal secretary to the prime minister, and Brajesh Mishra, the incoming one, received the prime minister as we alighted from the car. Little did I realize that over the next year and a half, I would accompany Vajpayee in all car journeys, except when ill or really tired. In the prime minister's room, photos were taken and the first order signed, appointing Brajesh Mishra as the principal secretary. Somewhere down the line, my appointment order was also signed. I was technically an interloper till that moment, since I had been posted at the Delhi Vidyut Board as member (administration).

The previous day, Mishra and I journeyed to South Block to get a feel of the place and be briefed about its functioning, upcoming crises, etc. While Vohra and Mishra secluded themselves, I met with other officers. I got a detailed briefing from C. Phunsog, then a joint secretary in the PMO and, later, chief secretary of the Government of Jammu and Kashmir. I really benefited from my interaction with Phunsog, an outstanding officer, who introduced me to other officers, told me who does what and so on. It was important to know the processes and persons, since it seemed quite easy to step on toes, which I did fairly soon, but that story can wait.

One of Vajpayee's clear instructions was that other than the principal secretary, there would be no change in the PMO. All officers from the secretary down would remain. Vacancies would be filled in by normal means, unless some specific expertise was required. Then we could tap persons trusted and needed, but not by pushing out somebody. The principal secretary and private secretary serve the same term in office as their boss, unless sacked without notice.

Appointing Brajesh Mishra was a stroke of genius, though it did not feel that way then. When Vajpayee became prime minister in 1996, Bishan Tandon, an extremely competent and straightforward officer had become the principal secretary. He had worked in Indira Gandhi's PMO as a joint secretary and had written about it. Vajpayee and Brajesh Mishra had known each other for a long time. This, presumably, was from the days Mishra was the Indian representative to the United Nations (UN), and Vajpayee regularly went to the annual session of the UN General Assembly as a member of the Indian delegation. Mishra quit the government after Indira Gandhi treated him unfairly. He later joined the BJP and became the convenor of its foreign policy cell.

Vajpayee's first major parliamentary intervention was on foreign policy in 1957, and since then he had developed a deep knowledge and expertise on the subject. He was the foreign minister in the first non-Congress government in 1977, headed by Morarji Desai. Vajpayee's understated personality and his silences at meetings, discussions and conversations meant that most people underestimated his grasp of the subject and his powers of observation and recall.

In the interregnum between his two terms as prime minister, Vajpayee was the chairman of the parliamentary standing committee on external relations. The country faced many external challenges, like the negotiations on the Comprehensive Nuclear-Test-Ban Treaty and the signing of the Chemical Weapons Convention. There were many occasions when the BJP issued press notes, and finally, there was the matter of writing the BJP election manifesto and the particular language on India exercising its nuclear options. Mishra's interactions with Vajpayee went up considerably during this period. They broadly held the same views, bonded well and developed a smooth working relationship.

Since Mishra agreed with Vajpayee's broader thrust on foreign policy and with his clear intention to exercise the nuclear option, he became a natural choice for principal secretary. I felt bad for Bishan Tandon, and when he asked me why Vajpayee had not appointed him, I really had no answer. In retrospect, it was clear that at the top, emotions must be kept in check and not be allowed to come in the way of decision-making. And contrary to popular impression, Vajpayee was an iron hand in a velvet glove.

Even before portfolio distribution and negotiations that took much of the working day got underway, Prime Minister Vajpayee was on his way to the National Stadium for an India–Pakistan hockey test. I can justifiably claim credit for it. A couple of days before, journalist and sports administrator Lokesh Sharma had approached us about Vajpayee inaugurating the hockey test series. This was discussed with Vajpayee, Brajesh Mishra and others. The general response was non-committal. I thought it would send the right message, besides being good optics, and made the point that the invitation should be pushed. A BJP prime minister's first act in office: attending an India–Pakistan match. What could be better!

When Vajpayee walked on to the turf, there was a roar from the crowd. The spectators were in such a good mood that they cheered with gusto for the Pakistan team. Arguably, the bilateral relations between the two countries were not as bad as they are at present, but they weren't good either. The 1993 bomb blasts in Mumbai, the terror in Kashmir, even the Khalistan mayhem was not that far away, but on 19 March 1998, the people of Delhi had forgiven and forgotten. India won the match 3–2.

The rest of the day passed in meetings at the prime minister's office in South Block, sorting out portfolios for the ministers who had been sworn in. This was made infinitely more complicated by the occurrences of the past two weeks, which suddenly empowered many political players into bargaining better positions for themselves and their interests, even if it meant a weak government. In fact, the elections to the Lok Sabha were not due until May 2001, but the fractured verdict of 1996 meant that a stable government could not be sustained. The developments of 1996–97 became an important factor contributing to the results of the February 1998 midterm polls to Parliament and to the process of government formation subsequently.

2

A Hung Parliament

A new term entered the lexicon of Indian politics after the 1996 elections: a hung parliament, which aptly described the 'neither here nor there' state of affairs of our political system. The BJP emerged as the largest party in Lok Sabha with 160 seats, and its pre-poll allies picked up another twenty-six, including eighteen for the Shiv Sena and eight for the Samata Party. The Congress (I) had 140 seats, down a hundred from its strength when Parliament had been dissolved just before the elections. The National Front (NF), a loose grouping of the Janata Dal and Samajwadi Dal, had sixty-three members.[1] The Dravida Munnetra Kazhagam (DMK) and the Tamil Maanila Congress combined took all thirty-nine seats of Tamil Nadu as well as the lone seat of Pondicherry. The Left Front had fifty-two members. The Bahujan Samaj Party (BSP) had eleven MPs, the Akalis had

---

[1] The Telugu Desam Party of Lakshmi Parvathi, a constituent of the National Front, was wiped out. The other Telugu Desam Party, led by Chandrababu Naidu, which ran the state government of Andhra Pradesh, won sixteen seats. It then duly took its place in the newly formed United Front, which was nothing but the NF and Left Front coming together.

eight, the Asom Gana Parishad (AGP) had five and the Tiwari Congress won in four seats.

Although the BJP was the largest party, it polled just over 20 per cent of the votes, much less than the Congress (I), which was supported by over 28 per cent of the electorate. The BJP's strike rate was better because its support was not dispersed all over the country but concentrated in UP, Bihar, Madhya Pradesh, Maharashtra, Gujarat and Rajasthan.

India had seen parliamentary elections before without a clear winner but this one was different. Though the 1989 election is identified with V.P. Singh and the after-effects of the Bofors scandal, it was actually the Congress (I), led by Rajiv Gandhi, which won the most seats—194—in that year. The Janata Dal won only 140 seats, but since Rajiv Gandhi had lost the psychological battle, with the Congress's tally having steeply fallen from 415 in 1984, he did not even attempt to form a government. In any case, he would have found it difficult to get support from any party. V.P. Singh went on to become the prime minister with outside support of the BJP and the left parties. Similarly, the Congress (I) was the largest party in 1991, but even after the sympathy wave occasioned by the assassination of Rajiv Gandhi in Sriperumbudur, Tamil Nadu, it was still fifty short of a majority. There were no other claimants, and P.V. Narasimha Rao went on to form a minority government. He liberalized the economy and gained a majority in Parliament using *sama*, *dana*, *bheda* and *danda*.[2] But the 1996 result was different in that neither psychologically nor numerically was any side naturally positioned to form or not form the government.

---

[2] *Sama* (discussion), *dana* (gift), *bheda* (dissension) and *danda* (use of force) are the four *upaya* (methods) of handling external threats. According to the Arthashastra, these must be applied sequentially in the order indicated here.

Narasimha Rao was smart enough to realize that with the kind of depletion the Congress (I) had been subjected to, it would be better for it to not attempt to form the government. This did not mean that the Congress was reconciled to sitting it out. It just wanted to exercise power indirectly. The Jain hawala scandal—which, with the Supreme Court intervening, came out in the open in 1993, purportedly exposing the bribes that had been paid to politicians and recorded in diaries—had weakened both the BJP and Narasimha Rao's internal rivals, like Arjun Singh. L.K. Advani, the BJP party president, and Madan Lal Khurana, Delhi's chief minister, also had to step aside. Arjun Singh, N.D. Tiwari and Madhavrao Scindia left the Congress (I) to fight separately. The stalling of economic reforms and the cynicism bred by perceived rampant political corruption went against the Congress (I) and helped the BJP— but only up to a point.

The President's invitation to Vajpayee to form the government was seen as an act of constitutional propriety, since the BJP was the largest single party and part of the largest pre-poll alliance. (It remains a matter of debate whether the largest party, or pre-election alliance, should automatically be called to form the government in the absence of a confirmed majority. This principle was, in any case, given a go-by just two years later by a different President.) The newly formed United Front (UF)—consisting of the NF minus Lakshmi Parvathy's TDP, N. Chandrababu Naidu's TDP, DMK–TMC, AGP and the left parties backed by the Congress— emerged as a viable alternative that had the numbers. However, it was still to get its act together when the invitation to Vajpayee arrived. The wording of the letter from the President was simple and direct. It read something like, 'I shall swear you in as Prime Minister tomorrow, 15 May, at 11 a.m. You should prove your majority by 31 May.' Fortunately for Vajpayee and the BJP, no letter from the Congress (I) president and the outgoing prime minister, Narasimha Rao, pledging support to the UF reached the President in time. Apparently, Narasimha Rao was resting.

The UF's delay in staking a claim to form the government was because it could not decide on its prime ministerial candidate. This was partly because the UF was itself a strange political creature. The leaders of the mainly one-state parties—DMK, Samajwadi Party, TDP, AGP and Tamil Maanila Congress—did not really want to move to Delhi. There were three national parties, but these were basically limited to two or three states. The Janata Dal had its presence in Karnataka and Bihar, where it ran the state governments, and in Odisha. The Communist Party of India (Marxist) ruled West Bengal and Tripura, with Kerala rotating between rival fronts led by them and the Congress (I). The Communist Party of India was the junior partner of the CPM in West Bengal and Kerala, and had residual presence in Bihar. Both the communist parties had some presence in Andhra and Tamil Nadu, but could only win seats in these states occasionally, and that too in alliance with others.

The CPM leader and consummate backroom dealmaker Harkishan Singh Surjeet was instrumental in stitching together the UF. He was on very good terms with those Congress leaders who saw themselves as left of centre. The UF agreed on Jyoti Basu, the long-serving West Bengal chief minister, as their prime ministerial candidate once former prime minister V.P. Singh had ruled himself out. However, though both Jyoti Basu and Surjeet were in favour of the idea, the CPM as a party did not go along with it. Basu was later to characterize this rejection as a 'historical blunder'. Mulayam Singh Yadav and Lalu Yadav were also interested but did not find enough takers. It was only then that H.D. Deve Gowda, the Karnataka chief minister, was chosen.

COMING BACK TO THE FORMATION of Vajpayee's first government in 1996. I reached his house at 6 Raisina Road early in the morning of 15 May. It was not an ordinary day, and I obviously could not take my car in, so I parked it next to the Press Club. When I left the house, close to midnight, as the private secretary of the prime minister, my car was missing. It had been towed away to the Parliament Road police station. An interesting way to begin a new job.

There were a lot of people. Everyone was happy. There was sloganeering; there was crying. The enthusiasm was contagious, but the feeling that it wouldn't last did not leave me. However, for the ordinary BJP worker in me, it was a dream come true, and I did not want to be woken up.

I had two credentials for the job: One, my track record as a bureaucrat was decent. Two, there was no time to look around for another candidate, and I was right there. But how come I was there to begin with? Mrs Kaul, my mother-in-law's elder sister, was the pillar of the Vajpayee household. She was very fond of me and remained so till she passed away. Leaving personal relations aside, rarely have I come across somebody who would strain so much to help people who approached her. A legion of people could get treatment at AIIMS because she had built up excellent relations with the doctors there over the decades. Though Mrs Kaul had no role to play in my selection as private secretary to the PM, it was because of her that my wife, Surabhi, and I became regular visitors to 6 Raisina Road. That Vajpayee was an Opposition politician did not deter me from openly visiting his place.

Since I was new to the job, particularly to the top levels of bureaucracy, I was nervous—a greenhorn actually. More so, though I had known Vajpayee for years, I was not on chatting terms with him. This, as I realized, was because he was naturally a shy person, not at all a backslapping sort and slow to open up. For a person who had achieved so much, without any godfather in politics, and who resonated so well with the public at large, he also seemed strangely very conscious of his limitations. Again, as

I later realized, this quality was what made him very successful. It was so easy to underestimate him, for people never understood how observant he was, how conscious of using the correct word at critical times and how much effort he could put into things that he found important. His pauses while speaking were not just for effect but for precision, even when scoring a debating point.

Vajpayee had an amazing sense of humour, which was self-deprecating and came from a very high degree of self-confidence. He knew how to use words to bring a smile on people's faces. I am reminded of two incidents that best illustrate this facet of his personality. The year was 1998. The BJP-led Delhi government had invited him to be the chief guest at the inauguration of the flyover at Yamuna Bazar. The master of ceremonies kept referring to him as the '*bhootpoorv pradhan mantri*'. When it was his turn to speak, Vajpayee said that he knew he was the *poorv pradhan mantri* but had no idea where the *bhoot* came from.[3]

On another occasion, Vajpayee was on a trip to New York when he experienced some inflammation in his gums. The dentist he went to started asking questions about the infection, when it began, etc. As Vajpayee described to an audience in Delhi, 'Doctor *itihas ki jankari lay raha tha aur mera chehre ka bhugol badal raha tha* (While the dentist was finding out about history, the geography of my face was changing).' As was typical of him, he would never joke at somebody else's expense; his jokes were mostly directed at himself.

Even as the government was settling down, trying to find its feet and gather support, minor crises kept cropping up. President Shankar Dayal Sharma sent a draft of a short speech that he said he would deliver when Parliament would meet for the first time. This was completely against constitutional and

---

[3] *Poorv* means past, as does *bhoot*. The two terms are often joined together to mean the same thing, but bhoot also means ghost.

parliamentary propriety as the President is not supposed to
read his own speech to Parliament but one that the Council of
Ministers sends him. When the President of India or the Queen
of England says, 'My government would adopt such and such
policy', the policy in question is obviously that of the elected
government. In fact, until the budget speech became the primary
instrument of making policy announcements of the government,
it was the annual address of the President at the first sitting every
year that was used for such announcements. Pre-liberalization,
the budget was limited to being the annual statement of accounts
and listing of taxation proposals. Many would wish that it once
again became just that.

Once this hurdle was behind us, and the Council of Ministers
discussed and finalized the speech and sent it to the President, he
expressed his unhappiness at the phrase 'license-permit raj' and
sought its deletion. Discretion being the better part of valour,
this request was accepted and a substitute phrase was put in its
place. To me, it seemed like in both these instances the President
was asserting his position—though to what avail, I wonder. The
coming into office of the Vajpayee government was no doubt due
to Presidential discretion, but it did not seem that the government
would last. So what was the need for these actions?

There were many such legal or technical issues, but leaving
those aside, the one incident I remember best was the search
for A.P.J. Abdul Kalam. Vajpayee called on Narasimha Rao as
propriety demands, a few days after assuming office. The two
had a history of getting along rather well. While Vajpayee was
away at 7 Race Course Road, Mother Teresa landed unannounced
at Vajpayee's residence with a retinue. I ushered her in. When
Vajpayee returned, he spoke at length with her and after she left,
he asked me to invite Dr Kalam to meet him urgently.

It was a holiday, and Kalam's home and office numbers went
unanswered. I put Venkat, one of the PMO staff attached to the

residential office, on the task of locating Kalam. This was early afternoon, and it was only after 9 p.m. that Venkat located Kalam at a DRDO guest house in Kolkata. I spoke to him and requested him to take the early-morning flight back to Delhi to meet the PM. We only had Indian Airlines back then, and there were probably only two flights a day between Delhi and Kolkata.

But Kalam did reach Delhi the next day, around noon, and met Vajpayee. What transpired between the two can only be guessed, though people have written about it, something we shall come back to later.

THE FIRST ORDER OF BUSINESS was the convening of Parliament and the swearing-in of the elected members. Parliament cannot meet without somebody presiding over it, and since the speaker cannot be elected till members are sworn in, the senior-most parliamentarian is sworn in as speaker pro tem. The President swears in the speaker pro tem, who would then administer the oath of office to all the newly elected members.

Indrajit Gupta, the veteran Communist Party of India parliamentarian, was the senior-most MP, other than possibly Vajpayee. But before a formal proposal could be sent to the President, Vajpayee desired to speak to Indrajit Gupta and take his consent—a simple formality. When Gupta came on line, and before the call could be transferred to Vajpayee, Gupta asked whether the call was about asking for his support. He was assured that it was not. Was his question a joke? Or did it reflect the tense, early stage when it was still unclear whether the government would succeed in gathering enough support to survive. It would be clear soon.

The Vajpayee government conceded defeat even before the battle started, or so I thought. The Congress–UF put up Purno Sangma as their candidate for speaker. The BJP, seeing the numbers stacked up against it, did not put up a candidate. Should

Vajpayee not have resigned then, after publicly acknowledging that he did not have the numbers?

The two-day debate on 27–28 May was electrifying. Even though he did not have the numbers on his side, Vajpayee got his moments of vindication. Murasoli Maran, senior DMK leader and nephew of M. Karunanidhi, informed Parliament that though the DMK was approached, the BJP did not resort to money-bag politics. One could see Vajpayee's face glow when this compliment was paid.

Narasimha Rao pointed out that non-alignment was not mentioned in BJP's election manifesto. Somebody scanned through the Congress manifesto; it had nothing on non-alignment as well. Vajpayee's reply to the debate was magisterial. He pointed to India's inherent secularism and how the first mosque was built in Kerala, very early in Islam's history, when the Prophet was still alive. A Hindu king had gifted the piece of land, to Arab traders who frequented the Malabar Coast, on which this mosque was built. The unnaturalness of the coalition that wanted to prevent the largest party from taking office was his key message that day to Parliament, and to the nation. For days after this debate, the speech was the talking point across the country. The campaign for the next election had begun.

Deve Gowda was sworn in three days later, on 1 June. Lalu Yadav, president of the Janata Dal, at once suspended Ramakrishna Hegde from the Janata Party. Deve Gowda and Hegde were rivals in Karnataka but this was unexpected. Unknown to Deve Gowda, the expulsion laid the seeds of his own marginalization in less than two years. In the discussion on the vote of confidence, Deve Gowda took on Vajpayee and said that oratory was no substitute for governance. Obviously meant to cover up for his own lack of felicity in English, Deve Gowda's remark, as time would tell, was quite off the mark. It is extremely unfair that Vajpayee is remembered for his public speaking, which was outstanding but represented just a small part of his persona.

Stuck as he was with many criminal cases that the CBI was either investigating or prosecuting, Lalu Yadav hoped to get his favourites appointed to important posts in the CBI—so Deve Gowda implied when he called on Vajpayee some weeks into his term. He kept referring to Vajpayee as 'sahib' throughout the conversation and was extremely deferential. I was touched when Deve Gowda turned to me and said that in case I wanted any posting, I should inform Mahendra Jain, his private secretary, who had come along for the meeting. The offer was genuine but one I could not take up. Deve Gowda came out as an old-style politician, who believed in good relations outside the legislature, irrespective of all the name-calling inside.

The UF was a government of generally low-key ministers. To compensate for the fact that they had no Sikhs on their side, a minor Akali politician, Balwant Singh Ramoowalia, was inducted into the government as a full cabinet minister. Similarly, most of the parties deputed relatively junior members as their representatives in the Council of Ministers. This was not incidental. The party leaders back home in their states did not want rival power centres. Yet it did not always work out that way. Renuka Chowdhury of the Telugu Desam Party was flamboyant and was noticed. The result was that Chandrababu Naidu did not give her a ticket to contest the 1998 Lok Sabha elections or the Rajya Sabha elections. Ultimately, she left the party and joined the Congress. Naidu in turn was unwilling to nominate any representative to the government in the Centre and did so reluctantly in 2014.

I had a small role to play in the selection of one of the ministers of the UF government. Goa had elected two non-Congress MPs, both first-timers in Parliament. Churchill Alemao was the South Goa MP. The Directorate of Revenue Intelligence (DRI), the preventive arm of the customs department, ended up shooting dead one of Alemao's brothers, a former sailor, as part of an anti-smuggling operation. Alemao had been chief minister of Goa for less than a month in 1990 when the then Congress (I) government of long-time CM Pratapsingh Rane was brought down through defections. The speaker of the Goa Assembly, Luis Proto Barbosa, was to become the CM, but this had to wait until the deputy speaker could be removed through a no-confidence motion. The man who masterminded this toppling operation was Ramakant Khalap, leader of the Maharashtrawadi Gomantak Party (MGP), who was to be elected the north Goa MP in 1996. Though much senior to Alemao in politics, he became the deputy chief minister in the former's government. In any case, the bulk of the MLAs propping up the government were from the MGP.

One afternoon in late-May 1996, must have been a Sunday, as I was relaxing at home with the artist Subodh Kerkar, Khalap dropped in. He told me that he would be happy to support the Vajpayee government, but his one vote would not make a difference. He felt, and I also admire politicians for their ability to sense developments much better than the rest of us, that the incoming UF government would make one of the Goa MPs a minister. His fear was that if Alemao beat him to it, it would be a terrible loss of face back home. I enjoyed the irony of the situation. Khalap had made Alemao Goa's chief minister for a short period and worked as his deputy, if only in the formal sense.

An uncle of mine was a long-time Tata Steel employee based lately in Patna with a mandate to keep relations with the Bihar government on an even keel. He was reported to be close to Lalu Yadav, so on a lark, I gave him a call. He spoke to Lalu Yadav. Khalap was summoned and when the UF government was expanded, it had a law minister from Goa. Khalap is an outstanding lawyer and, according to all accounts, acquitted himself very credibly of his tasks as minister.

After Vajpayee's government fell, and there was little for him to do, he took off on a short holiday for Manali with his family. I, too, was relatively idle. So taking advantage of the presence of my artist friend Subodh, we decided to go off to the hills. It was not until we had left my home early next morning that we decided where to go, and ended up driving to Manali. We reached at around 8 p.m., and when he saw us, Vajpayee expressed his surprise and said that he felt bad that I drove fifteen hours to reach Manali when I could have flown with him. His concern was palpable. The next evening, as we sat down for dinner in the lovely house that Namita and her husband, Ranjan, built at Prini, just outside Manali, I got an excited call on my mobile phone, a rarity in those days. It was from Khalap, thanking me. He had been sworn in as minister of state with independent charge.

Khalap had to bear the brunt of Pramod Mahajan's joke in Parliament, which the latter used tellingly to demonstrate the strange creature that the UF was. According to Mahajan, at one of his official visits to China, during which Khalap too was present, the Chinese communists wanted to know how India's parliamentary democracy functioned. Mahajan said that he explained to them that his party, the BJP, was the largest party but sat in the Opposition. The Congress (I) was the second-largest party and also sat in the opposition but supported the government. The third-largest party, the CPI (M), was in the ruling front but not in the government. And Khalap, whose party had one MP, was the government.

MY LEARNING CURVE WAS IN its nascent stage. Since Vajpayee's family was away to Manali for the summer holidays, I was the only constant company he had at home from 8.30 in the morning to 6.30 in the evening. Fortunately, there were enough people trying to meet him, but I had to otherwise handle him all alone. This included fixing appointments, sorting out the mail received, preparing replies and giving him company at lunch. The last was the easiest—two people silently eating their meals. Fortunately, the food at the Vajpayee–Kaul household has always been outstanding.

Running a small office without a hierarchy or files being 'put up' for orders was a novel experience. The leader of Opposition was entitled to a small office, equal to what a deputy minister had. There were three incumbents who had all retired from Parliament, having reached levels of the lower bureaucracy.[4] They had been with Vajpayee ever since he had become leader of Opposition in the previous Lok Sabha. I occupied the vacant post of secretary to the leader of Opposition. In the residential office, I had a room next to Vajpayee's, while the others shared a larger room nearby. My room also functioned as the waiting room for guests who had come to meet Vajpayee.

Vajpayee soon moved house, back to 7 Safdarjung Road, the house he had occupied as the external affairs minister in the Janata Party government (1977–79). Here, the office block was small and compact, with three rooms slung together. When Parliament was in session, a large room was given to the leader of Opposition in Parliament House, and attached to it was another small room (actually, a veranda turned into a room). The four of us sat here. But the trouble with this room, which also functioned as the waiting room, was that it could only be accessed through Vajpayee's room, which opened into the circular corridor running around the building. The whole setup could not have been more different than what I'd been used to as a senior member of the permanent civil services. There was no fancy office with attached bathroom or an antechamber to relax, no staff car, no personal

---

[4]   One of them, T.N. Makan, died many years later in terrible circumstances. He used to live in Malviya Nagar. Having stepped out of the house one evening, he went missing, and his body was found in a pit dug up by the municipal authorities.

attendant to handle phone calls, no peon to bring tea and files or run errands.

For me, the most difficult thing in that job was to deal with the letters received. In the beginning, these ran into hundreds every day. Later, we received several dozen daily. Most were requests for favours and complaints, which we passed on to the relevant government departments 'for appropriate action'. Many people sent books, especially of poems, while others sent their best wishes. They all received a reply, signed by Vajpayee, thanking them. The real difficulty was with the letters sent by political and other leaders. I used to place those in a folder, seen in all government offices, called the 'dak pad'. These are marked for the relevant officer by the boss, sometimes with a message on what is to be done. I realized that the letters mostly remained in the dak pad, though occasionally Vajpayee would call one of the assistants and dictate a reply. Later, when my confidence grew, I started writing out the replies myself, which he would generally sign or make minor modifications to. I obviously could not do so when the letters were on controversial topics or written by leaders of political parties.

Working for a political leader, who was not in the government, was challenging for me, since bureaucrats naturally like to think and react apolitically. Vajpayee also did not want it otherwise. Writing letters, sitting in on meetings with foreign dignitaries or even Indian VVIPs, was fine. But how do you help research a topic and prepare talking points on his reactions to the budget presented? And when Vajpayee had to address the chambers of commerce or make important policy pronouncements, how was one to go about it? Without formal discussions, we came to an agreement that I was not to attend the BJP parliamentary party meetings but to sit in the small room nearby. Nor did I accompany him on his visits to the BJP office. I accompanied him on his tours all over the country, except to his constituency, Lucknow. This was the domain of Shiv Kumar, his long-term aide who had acted as his secretary and driver for decades. Kumar was getting old, and his full-time presence was not required in a more formal setting. He did come regularly, though, bearing requests, from constituents and others, that he wanted followed up.

Lacking bureaucratic paraphernalia and constant intellectual support, I had to learn how to research and write speeches. R.V. Pandit, an East Indian Catholic from Mumbai and the former publisher of the magazine *Imprint*, was close to both Vajpayee and Advani. He was always full of ideas. Both Sudheendra Kulkarni and Kanchan Gupta were occasionally drafted to write speeches, sometimes the same speech—which I would then have to reconcile. At times, Arun Shourie would be called upon to discuss and prepare a speech (this was when Vajpayee was prime minister, 1998 onwards). It meant that for some speeches, we had a number of ideas, some contradictory, and each with very different syntax. Blending them was a nightmare.

It was much easier when I had to do it on my own, but Vajpayee was a difficult man to satisfy in this respect. This was because, contrary to popular impression, he used to work hard at his important speeches. His able ally in these exercises was the Parliament House library. We used to ask them for information on any topic. They would compile a short factual note and attach photocopies of relevant newspaper and magazine articles. If Parliament had ever discussed that particular issue, the package had it. Vajpayee would devour all the material, then start writing notes in longhand. These notes were not in the form of a speech or even an essay; they were neither methodical nor comprehensive. They ran into pages, which he carried with himself when he had to speak in Parliament, but he never referred to them while speaking. Obviously, he had worked out the structure of speech in his head, had mulled over the arguments, yet left himself open enough to react to what would be said before he spoke.

The only time he looked at his notes was when he was quoting somebody else. In fact, in the Indian parliamentary tradition, other than formal statements, members cannot read out their speeches. Members have been pulled up for doing so, but when Sonia Gandhi entered Parliament as a member in 1999, she read out her speeches without any objection. I guess Vajpayee and his team felt they would look petty and impolite if they raised objections.

The first really important formal speech I had to prepare for him was when he accepted an invitation from the environmentalist Anil Agarwal to release a report on water prepared by the Centre for Science and Environment. This was a field I was a bit aware of, and I was very excited. I wrote what I thought was a well-argued piece. Vajpayee went over it very carefully. He said that it read like an essay instead of a speech. So I went back to the drawing board, determined to do better. It must have been the fourth or fifth draft that finally satisfied him. I wonder if he was just tired.

The one speech I really loved working upon, one which Vajpayee used, was delivered after Finance Minister P. Chidambaram presented what was called a 'dream' budget in 1997. When Vajpayee asked for my instinctive reactions to the budget, I told him I was not very impressed. Though he was distinctly uncomfortable with the nitty-gritty of economic policy, he listened very carefully and then said that he would like to speak on the budget. This was unusual, so I went to work on the speech and managed to put one together. He cut out some of the jargon, added his substantive points, like the need for transparency in the budget process, and presented the speech in Parliament. I could only watch it on television, as I had fallen sick. The hard work had paid off. The speech was much appreciated, though it went against the grain, as everybody was in awe of the Chidambaram budget. But by year end it was clear that the 1997 budget was a lost opportunity. Ultimately, it helped the BJP come to power in the 1998 elections.

VAJPAYEE, AS THE LEADER OF opposition, could show Parliament
how the nation must come together on security issues. Mulayam
Singh, as defence minister, made a statement in the Lok Sabha
about the successful conclusion of the Sukhoi deal in November
1996. Vajpayee got up immediately, broke parliamentary tradition
and praised the UF government for concluding the deal, which
was in the national interest. This praise took not just the members
but also the minister by surprise. I remember a senior BJP
parliamentarian expressing surprise, even bewilderment, in front
of me later, asking why Atalji had to praise Mulayam Singh's
actions. The answer, I guess, was that some things were above
party politics.

The full picture, as reported by Shekhar Gupta in the *Indian
Express* in 2005, was that initially, there had been doubts about
the deal, since the Narasimha Rao government, then in caretaker
capacity, had given the Russians an advance of $350 million, even
though the price negotiations were yet to be finalized. The *Indian
Express* had broken the story, and Vajpayee wanted to know more
about the story from Gupta. The circumstances were as usual, and
it looked like a much bigger scam than Bofors. At the same time,
Vajpayee made it clear to Gupta that in case it was not a scam,
he would not like a controversy like this to scuttle an important
defence purchase. Though too many details were not known
at the time, Vajpayee did not use this point about the unusual
advance in his election campaign, for fear of compromising
India's security needs.

Later, Mulayam Singh as defence minister organized a
detailed briefing for Vajpayee and Jaswant Singh quietly. What
emerged was that Boris Yeltsin, the Russian president, was facing
difficult times and wanted the advance to prevent the Sukhoi
manufacturing unit from going under. Narasimha Rao, conscious
of the need to keep Russia on the right side and to keep the Sukhoi
plant going, sanctioned the advance, presumably knowing that it

could compromise him during the elections. According to Lok Sabha rules, when a minister makes what is called a suo-moto statement, no questions can be asked. If members want, they can request for a discussion. This is unlike the Rajya Sabha, where such statements lead to full-flowing debates. Though his intervention went beyond the rules, Vajpayee was allowed to compliment the government on that day in Parliament because of his four decades as an outstanding parliamentarian. The message he sent was not just to Mulayam, Deve Gowda, the Congress and the nation but also to Russia, India's dependant supplier of arms and ammunitions and its biggest political supporter internationally at that moment. The message was that on national security issues, there can be no politics.

Deve Gowda, or 'the humble farmer' as he liked to refer to himself, lost office when the Congress (I), led by Sitaram Kesri, withdrew support in March 1997. When I questioned a close associate of Kesri, he told me that Kesri was convinced that the CBI, at Deve Gowda's behest, was going to arrest him. Kesri's personal physician had been found dead mysteriously some time back. No satisfactory explanation for his unnatural death was available despite extensive investigations. With Kesri's move, Deve Gowda had to go. However, his speech in Parliament during the confidence vote was a feisty one. He was defiant, showed no sign of remorse or any sense of loss. Instead, he called Kesri an old man in a hurry, and he warned his putative successor, I.K. Gujral, that the Congress would also play a trick on him. This was prescient, but then this was also the Congress being true to form, pulling down the government it had propped up.

In private, Vajpayee was quite appreciative of various aspects of Deve Gowda's personality, especially his stubbornness and defiance. The UF government had increased fertilizer prices in 1996. There was an uproar in Parliament, with the BJP, the Congress and even constituents of the ruling UF demanding a rollback. But Deve Gowda held firm. He would not buckle under pressure. One, because he was stubborn; he had come to a decision after a deliberate process and understood the rural issues better than the others. Two, he saw this as a challenge to his authority as prime minister and to the credibility of his government. His government depended on the Congress for support, his party had only forty-four MPs in the Lok Sabha, of which only sixteen at best would rally behind him. Yet, he held firm.

Kesri's withdrawal of support from the UF government suddenly brought life back into national politics. There had been no pressure building up. No doubt the transition in the Congress (I) leadership, from Narasimha Rao to Kesri, affected the Congress–UF relations. Kesri was simply not in the same league as Narasimha Rao in terms of strategic planning and as someone who commanded respect within the party.

I was at Delhi's Sarojini Nagar market with my family when I got a call informing that Kesri had pulled the plug. Another holiday gone, I thought and rushed to 7 Safdarjung Road. There was excitement all around. The BJP leadership, the parliamentary party and allies met often. By this time, a formal political grouping, the National Democratic Alliance (NDA), which now included the Akalis in addition to the Samata Party, had come up. George Fernandes became its convenor. Since then, the NDA has been the platform on which the BJP has worked with other parties, whose numbers have gone up substantially, though the alliance has also seen many of the BJP's old partners leave.

The NDA did not see the fall of the Deve Gowda government as an opportunity to try and form its own government, though the vulnerabilities in the anti-BJP platform were becoming obvious. In fact, before the trust vote, which brought down the Deve Gowda government, C.M. Ibrahim, the civil aviation minister who was also Deve Gowda's man Friday, sent a message to Vajpayee through a third party, asking the BJP not to go along with the

Congress (I) in deposing the government. Though nobody asked for my advice, I found the idea intriguing. However, Vajpayee and the BJP leadership had their own ideas. Deve Gowda soon joined the ranks of Charan Singh and Chandra Shekhar as PMs who had to quit when the Congress pulled the rug from under their feet for undefined reasons.

The Congress found it easier to dislodge a prime minister than to find a replacement. G.K. Moopanar was a senior Congress politician from the Thanjavur delta in Tamil Nadu. He had quit the party just before the 1996 elections in protest against Narasimha Rao's decision on forming an alliance with Jayalalithaa and set up his own Tamil Maanila Congress (TMC). The resultant DMK–TMC blitzkrieg swept through Tamil Nadu, leaving no seats for the AIADMK. Moopanar was keen to become the prime minister once the vacancy arose. While he spoke English, it was difficult to decipher what he said. TV channels actually used subtitles with his sound bites so that viewers could understand what he was saying. It was not just his language skills that prevented him from becoming PM. There were many claimants besides Moopanar, like S.R. Bommai, I.K. Gujral, Ram Vilas Paswan and Sharad Yadav from the Janata Dal, and Mulayam Singh Yadav of the Samajwadi Party. The DMK did not want Moopanar but didn't say so in public. The Congress was happy with him but did not agree on the others. Finally, Gujral made it, though the decision had taken almost three weeks. The TMC stayed out for some time, so India had no finance minister. The nation ran on autopilot, it seemed.

India faced serious external challenges in the 1996–98 UF government period. Some of it was because it was not seen as an important player in the global governance architecture. The most important development insofar as India was concerned was that the negotiations over the Comprehensive Nuclear-Test-Ban Treaty (CTBT) were being concluded. India was the lone outlier, with Ambassador Arundhati Ghosh singlehandedly having to defend the country's interests before the international community. India's stand was clear: it was for universal disarmament but would never accept nuclear apartheid. The parliamentary standing committee on external affairs discussed the issue many times. Once, when Arundhati Ghosh was briefing the committee, Vajpayee, in mock-seriousness, expressed his fears about her safety in Geneva as the whole world was ranged against her. This intervention brought a welcome relief to the grimness of the meeting. Throughout this period, Vajpayee very effectively stood shoulder-to-shoulder with the government. Never for a moment did it seem like he was the leader of the Opposition who felt that he had been deprived of power by a nexus of parties, whose only raison d'être for working together was to keep him out.

MANY FOREIGN VISITORS MET VAJPAYEE, for he was a potential prime minister, the leader of Opposition in the Lok Sabha and chairman of the parliamentary standing committee on external affairs. These visits were all routed through the Ministry of External Affairs. The standard drill was that the concerned joint secretary (JS) would walk Vajpayee through the background of the visit and the visitor, the issues that the visitor was expected to raise and the position of the government. At the meeting itself, the JS would be present to take notes but not to participate in the discussions. Vajpayee's standard line to each visitor was that in India, there was broad consensus on foreign policy. He would also explain very gently how politics was practised in India by saying, 'The opposition must have its say, but the government must have its way.' When he said this to the then Commonwealth secretary-general, a gentleman from Nigeria, the latter was very moved and explained that in many African languages the word for 'opposition' and for 'enemy' was the same.

The Chinese President Jiang Zemin visited India in 1996, the first high-level visit from China in decades. The time fixed for

Vajpayee's call was not convenient, since he was travelling. But the Chinese refused to adjust the timings. I thought this reflected their inability to appreciate a democracy where the Opposition is very much a legitimate part of the state, even if not in the government. Vajpayee did go for the dinner at Rashtrapati Bhavan. A few BJP members in Parliament told him that the BJP should boycott Jiang's visit, as the Chinese were squatting on 50,000 square kilometres of Indian soil, referring to Aksai Chin in Ladakh. Vajpayee had to remind them that he had visited China as foreign minister, the first ministerial visit to that country in almost two decades, and that the way ahead in India–China bilateral relations lay in negotiations.

During Nelson Mandela's visit to India in 1997, Vajpayee called on him at Rashtrapati Bhavan. The conversation between the two leaders was convivial. But Vajpayee's next meeting with Mandela was quite the opposite. This was at the Durban Non-Aligned Movement (NAM) meeting in September 1998, by when Vajpayee was the prime minister. Mandela, as chair, in his inaugural speech referred to everyone's concern about the situation in Jammu and Kashmir and the need for its peaceful resolution. This was against the backdrop of India's nuclear tests and the fact that the Gandhian L.C. Jain, India's high commissioner to South Africa, and the new government hadn't hit it off.

Jain was a political appointee of the previous government and not a professional diplomat, and many in the current government believed that a Gandhian would not, or could not, defend India's nuclear tests effectively. There was considerable discussion on this in the Ministry of External Affairs. I knew Jain slightly. I had visited him in his Barakhamba Road consultancy office sometime before and had a high regard for him, but I could not figure out why he did not quit on his own since it was clear that he was not on the same page as the Vajpayee government, differences aggravated by the conduct of the nuclear tests.

At the NAM meeting, Vajpayee was livid at the Kashmir reference and expressed himself to Mandela very bluntly at the banquet hosted by the latter that same evening. The next day, Thabo Mbeki, then South Africa's vice president, called on Vajpayee at his hotel and sought to reduce the temperature.

As foreign minister, Gujral had negotiated the India–Bangladesh Ganges River Treaty quite satisfactorily, ending a longstanding grievance of Bangladesh. No treaty is perfect, since it entails give and take, but at no stage did I see Vajpayee try to find fault with the treaty or try and make political capital by criticizing the government for allegedly 'selling out India's interests'. In fact, I accompanied him to the Gulf in late 1997, when he led a delegation of the parliamentary standing committee. There were members of Parliament from different political parties, both from the Rajya Sabha and Lok Sabha. The Ministry of External Affairs had prepared detailed country 'briefs', which, ironically, ran into hundreds of pages. I was still amazed to see that Vajpayee had devoured these documents.

Consequently, when Indian ambassadors met him to brief him and his delegations, the meetings were friendly but business-like. The easy camaraderie among the members and the uniform sense of respect they showed to Vajpayee was remarkable. One member, adhering to an ideology totally different from the BJP's, confided in me that he hoped to see Vajpayee as the prime minister. We visited Bahrain, Oman and Kuwait, but before the visit was over, Vajpayee had to rush back to India due to political crisis in UP. All these countries have parliaments with varying degrees of functional autonomy. Meetings with their speakers, committee members, ministers and rulers went very well. Vajpayee requested the Sultan of Oman for a piece of land for a Hindu temple, the second in Muscat. In Kuwait, he wanted land for a crematorium. Both requests were accepted.

THE ASSEMBLY ELECTIONS IN UP in October 1996 were inconclusive. The BJP won the most seats but were still forty short of a majority. Mulayam Singh's Samajwadi Party had 110 seats. The BSP–Congress alliance won a hundred seats, with Congress gaining an extra five seats but the BSP at sixty-seven, the same as in the previous assembly. Romesh Bhandari, the controversial diplomat-turned-politician, decided against inviting Kalyan Singh to take the first shot at proving his majority, a reversal of what President Shankar Dayal Sharma had done just months ago. Instead, UP saw President's rule, which ended only in March 1997, when the BJP and BSP were able to stitch together an alliance. As per the agreement, Mayawati would be chief minister for six months, to be followed by Kalyan Singh.

This was the second time that Mayawati had become the chief minister of UP, both times with the help of the BJP. After six months, when Mayawati had to step down, she raised different issues that made life difficult for Kalyan Singh. She said that since BJP was holding the post of chief minister, the speaker should be from her party. This was despite the fact that the agreement was clear—the speaker would be from the BJP, the larger party. With the enactment of the anti-defection legislation, the speaker of the legislature had suddenly become important and was given the power of adjudicating on the disqualification of legislators held to be defectors.

With Kalyan Singh holding firm, Mayawati pulled the rug from under his feet, or so she thought. In retaliation, Singh engineered a split in the Congress and a new group was formed—the Akhil Bharatiya Loktantrik Congress party, led by Naresh Agarwal, which supported the BJP government. The BSP, too, lost members of the legislature, with seventeen of them joining Kalyan Singh. Earlier, Mayawati had forcibly kept all BSP legislators at one place, but unlike in the past, cell phones allowed people to plan their escape from confinement and their route to power. When the assembly met to take up the vote of confidence, the BSP and Congress legislators resorted to violence, which led the BJP and its supporters to respond in kind. Ultimately, the Opposition walked out, and the BJP government proved its majority convincingly. Romesh Bhandari, at this stage, sent his report to the union government, recommending President's rule on the grounds that the constitutional majority had broken down.

The delegation in Kuwait was attending a dinner hosted by the Indian ambassador at his house when the news of impending President's rule in UP reached us. Vajpayee decided to fly back to India immediately, dropping out of the United Arab Emirates stage of the visit. We flew to Mumbai and spent half the night in the VVIP lounge of the airport, where a bed had been hastily arranged. In the meantime, President K.R. Narayanan returned the cabinet's recommendation for imposing President's rule for reconsideration, saying that the government had established its majority in the legislature. If the cabinet were to send it back to him, the President would have had no option but to sign the order. The state parties in the UF (DMK, TDP and AGP), with a better appreciation of the federal balance of powers, having been subject to its whims, now forced the issue and killed the proposal. As it later emerged, the whole exercise had been a Kesri–Kanshi Ram bid to come to power, with Mulayam a late but aggressive participant. They were backed in this by the CPI (M), who wanted to see the BJP out of office in UP. Sadly, Gujral came out of this looking diminished—not because the President had returned the recommendation but for going along with the plan to impose President's rule in the first place. Arguably, the President saved the day for Gujral and the UF.

The result of this sordid episode was that Kalyan Singh had to accommodate all the defectors and some of his own party's men as ministers. The size of the council of ministers went up from twenty-three to ninety-three. Kalyan Singh's desperation and compromise meant that he lost his reputation of being a straightforward disciplinarian. His relationship with Vajpayee deteriorated slowly, becoming almost non-existent by the time of the 1999 elections. Meanwhile Romesh Bhandari was not going to fade away quietly.

The Gujral government's and the Congress's loss of credibility arguably helped the BJP, negating the effect of the compromises Kalyan Singh had to make to retain power. Gujral himself was unable to run his government, as he lacked any popular political base. Analysts appreciated his opposition to the Emergency, which had led Indira Gandhi to move him out of her council of ministers and make him India's ambassador to the Soviet Union. Post-Emergency, the Morarji government allowed him to continue in office, itself an acknowledgement of his mistreatment by Indira Gandhi and of his capable handling of India–Soviet relations.

However, Gujral was a political lightweight and his ministers knew it. As prime minister, he once called an all-party meeting to develop a common approach to dealing with a Supreme Court decision that made all discretionary allotment of government housing illegal. Sheila Kaul had been the urban development minister in the Narasimha Rao government; and Narasimha Rao's style of governance was that so long as he was not challenged, he let people work independently. For years in the urban development ministry, no regular allotment of government housing was made. There was only discretionary allotment by the minister of state (P.K. Thungon) up to a certain level and by the urban development minister for the higher categories.

I was pitchforked into the job as Sheila Kaul's private secretary, though I did not know her personally. Ultimately, the scandal was exposed in the papers, and a public interest litigation case came up before the Supreme Court. Later, the Central Bureau of Investigation (CBI) filed a case against Sheila Kaul and some junior officials in her staff. The Supreme Court quashed all these discretionary allotments. If carried out, this would have meant thousands of families thrown out of their government housing. The affected went around knocking on the doors of all political parties. Though elections were not imminent, thousands of disaffected government servants and their families translated to a sizeable number of votes that couldn't be ignored. No political party could allow this to happen, even accepting that the allotments themselves were wrongly done.

At the all-party meeting, as the conversation moved into Hindi, two ministers, Kinjarapu Yerran Naidu (TDP) and another one from the DMK, sharply told Gujral to speak in English. Gujral remained polite, but the message was clear—the PM counted for little in their eyes. There were limits to Gujral's patience, and at one point, Gujral told Naidu that he was quitting. Naidu rushed to Delhi and apologized to Gujral.

What made Gujral's position even more difficult was the split in the Janata Dal, to which he belonged. Lalu Yadav had lost his job as party president to Sharad Yadav. Facing increasing pressure to quit as the chief minister of Bihar, on account of the criminal charges against him, Lalu split the Janata Dal. He became the president of the newly formed Rashtriya Janata Dal (RJD), whose numbers included the two Janata Dal ministers in the Gujral government. Reluctantly, Lalu Yadav quit as the chief minister of Bihar after an arrest warrant was issued against him in the fodder scam, installing his wife, Rabri Devi, in his place. Interestingly, while the RJD angrily left the United Front, its ministers continued in the UF government.

Gujral's government lasted until the end of November 1997, when the Congress (I), after paralysing the winter session of Parliament on the issue of the continuation of DMK ministers in the UF government, withdrew support. In its interim report, the Jain Commission of Inquiry, probing into the assassination of Rajiv Gandhi, had indicted the DMK and its chief minister,

Karunanidhi, for colluding with the LTTE and allowing them to work unchecked in Tamil Nadu. Once the report came, the Congress (I) demanded the dismissal of the DMK ministers, with Mamata Banerjee leading the charge in the Lok Sabha. Once the government fell, quite unexpectedly—as until then there had been no serious disagreements between the UF and the Congress and no alternative government could be formed—Parliament was dissolved and new elections were announced, with the Gujral government continuing in a caretaker capacity.

The weak bench strength of the United Front meant that the government lacked the credibility needed to push decision-making. In addition to lightweight politicians, from small, often single-member parties, holding important portfolios, the UF tried to induct people based on either their professional skills or for representational purposes. Yogendra K. Alagh, an outstanding economist, became the minister of state for planning. Reportedly, he was also used for his grasp of public policy. Balwant Singh Ramoowalia, a minor Akali figure, became a cabinet minister because otherwise there would have been no Sikh representation.

What made the position of the government even weaker was that the economy was tanking. Chidambaram's 1997 'dream budget' had run its course. India was now linked much more closely with the global economy and could not insulate itself from the aftershocks of the Asian crisis. That year, 1997–98, India's GDP growth fell to 5 per cent, from 7.5 per cent the previous year. The economic legacy that the UF government was leaving to its successor could not have been worse. The last thing a slowing economy needed was a massive outflow on account of salary hike of government employees.

The fifth pay commission had made generous recommendations for the revision of government pay scales, with the provision that staff numbers be reduced by 30 per cent. The government not only accepted the first part, it actually went beyond the recommendations and completely ignored the second part regarding the reduction in numbers. When the cabinet committee met to decide on this, Finance Minister Chidambaram, most unusually, absented himself. This was an issue with very major fiscal consequences. Possibly, he knew that the other two ministers in the cabinet committee, Indrajit Gupta and Ram Vilas Paswan, wanted to be extra generous, and he could not stop them. This hike in pay and pensions, and the need to pay arrears, knocked the bottom out of India's fiscal position. Soon, the states were forced to follow. The end result was that the economy took 3–4 years to recover from this extravaganza.

Towards the end of 1997, when the Congress plenary session was being held in Kolkata, Mamata Banerjee quit the Congress (I) and set up the All India Trinamool Congress. She had never got along with the party establishment, specifically Pranab Mukherjee and his supporters like Somen Mitra. When the Pradesh Congress Committee was reconstituted, Mamata found herself totally sidelined. Kesri went along with the state party establishment. In protest, she organized a massive public meeting, which drew lakhs of people, to show her strength. But the party leadership was not impressed, leaving Mamata with no choice but to leave the party. Her feisty personality and street-fighting abilities made her a force to reckon with. Fortunately for the BJP, she tied up with them for the parliamentary elections.

West Bengal was not the only state where new political parties were being born or new alignments emerging. In Odisha, Naveen Patnaik had entered politics after his father Biju Patnaik's death and had been made a minister in the UF government. He was not only an unknown entity but also considered apolitical. When Vajpayee went to Delhi's Apollo Hospital to pay his last respects to Biju Babu, it was Naveen's businessman brother, Prem Patnaik, who was receiving guests. Naveen Patnaik, with the help of businessman-politician Dilip Ray, left the Janata Dal and formed the Biju Janata Dal (BJD). It, too, entered into an alliance with the BJP. The assumption was that Naveen Patnaik would be a figurehead, for in addition to his social and literary interests, he did not speak Odia comfortably.

To quote Pramod Mahajan, it was unlikely that the BJD would last too long and quite likely that it would land up inside the BJP. Ironically, then, Patnaik has not only won four successive terms in Odisha but has been far more successful electorally than his father. What is even more creditable is that in each instance, his numbers actually went up. Two of his victories have been in alliance with the BJP and two without. In 1997–98, nobody could have predicted that the Congress would lose Odisha. It was assumed that at best, the BJD–BJP alliance would put up a good fight, competing with JD for the second position.

Alliance with the AIADMK cost the Congress (I) dearly in 1996, leading to the establishment of the Tamil Maanila Congress and the sweep by the DMK–AIADMK. So political alignments changed in Tamil Nadu. The AIADMK and its junior partners— the MDMK, led by Vaiko, and the PMK, led by S. Ramadoss— became allies of the BJP. The DMK–TMC alliance continued while the Congress (I) was left to fend for itself.

Even as these political developments were taking place all over the country, there was no shortage of drama and farce during the three months of the Gujral caretaker government. UP, with its eighty-five seats, was, as always, the key state for the BJP, as it was for the others. Vajpayee had been an MP from Lucknow since 1991. In fact, there has been a long-standing connect between Vajpayee and India's largest state. Vajpayee had first contested for Parliament from Lucknow in a bye-election in 1953, which he lost. He lost again from Lucknow, this time narrowly, in 1957, but finally made his debut into the Parliament from Balrampur that same year. He lost from Balrampur in 1962 and won the seat back in 1967.

In the 1996 elections, the BJP won fifty-four seats in UP
alone, out of its total of 161 MPs. As related earlier, they formed,
and retained, their government in the state with great difficulty,
with a considerable loss of credibility. The Congress was losing its
touch, down to five seats only in the 1996 parliamentary elections,
but it had seen a little bounce in the previous assembly elections,
thanks to its alliance with the BSP. Mulayam Singh, shedding
the baggage of being a member of a national party, was the one to
watch, with twenty Lok Sabha MPs and 110 legislators. Romesh
Bhandari was there to trip the BJP whenever the opportunity
presented itself or seemed to present itself.

Three rounds of voting were scheduled in the 1998 elections.
Every politician was out campaigning. On 21 February, just a day
before the second round of voting, there was drama in Lucknow.
Some legislators belonging to the newly formed Loktantrik
Congress party announced that they had withdrawn from the
Kalyan Singh government and were staking a claim to form one
of their own under the leadership of Jagdambika Pal, the transport
minister. Pal was supported by Mayawati, Congress (I), Samajwadi
Party and other smaller parties. It seemed Mayawati had had her
revenge; the Samajwadi Party and Congress were back in power.
Kalyan Singh dropped his campaign and rushed to Lucknow and
asked to prove his majority on the floor of the legislature. But
Romesh Bhandari dismissed Kalyan Singh's request and swore in
Jagdambika Pal instead, in complete violation of constitutional
propriety and settled law.

The next day, polling was peaceful, including in Sambhal,
where Mulayam was contesting from. The Allahabad High Court
set aside the governor's action in dismissing the Kalyan Singh
government in total, as if it had not happened. Vajpayee cancelled
his campaigning and sat on a hunger strike outside his home in
Delhi. With the High Court restoring Kalyan Singh, Vajpayee
broke his fast on the second day by accepting lime juice from

Niharika, his granddaughter, in the presence of former President R. Venkataraman. But the drama was not over yet.

Pal went to the Supreme Court, which, without staying the High Court decision, ordered a 'composite floor test'. In other words, the legislators could choose one or the other. This was an innovation because in the constitutional scheme of things, only an elected government can convene a meeting of the legislature. Legally speaking, there can be only one chief/prime minister at a time, not two. It is the government which calls for a meeting of the legislature. In other words, when the legislature meets, a person must be the chief minister. If neither was the chief minister at that moment, the legislature could not meet.

There has not been a repeat of this judicial innovation. Fortunately for the BJP, it increased its presence from UP in that parliamentary election. The Samajwadi Party's numbers remained constant at twenty, and the Congress was wiped out, losing even Amethi and Raebareli. Ironically, Jagdambika Pal, who had rebelled because the BJP refused to give both his wife and son tickets for the parliamentary elections, ended up years later as a BJP member of Parliament, and Naresh Agarwal has been an important leader of the Samajwadi Party.

The drama now shifted to Delhi.

3

The Incomplete Mandate

The March 1998 election results started coming in. Though the NDA was much ahead of its rivals, it did not look at getting a majority on its own. In the pre-EVM days, counting was a tedious and time-consuming task, spread over days. Initially, when it looked as if the BJP would form the government, the stock market rallied behind the party, but as the situation turned uncertain, it lost its gains.

Once Parliament was dissolved, the office of the leader of Opposition had been wound up in a month. Accordingly, I was sent to work with the Delhi government, where I was posted with the Delhi Vidyut Board. The local government felt that since it was only a matter of time before I was called back home to the Government of India, there was no point in making me the head of a department. Even as part of this new job, I would drop in regularly to 7 Safdarjung Road but did not undertake any formal work, not that there was much work to do. Even though I was following the election campaign mostly through newspapers, I was present during some crucial moments. I was there, for example, when Vajpayee broke his fast after the Allahabad High Court quashed Romesh Bhandari's orders. The presence of former President R. Venkataraman, sitting with Vajpayee, was a sign of how serious this attack on democracy was.

Later, at 7 Safdarjung Road, we watched the election results on the television. It was exciting but tiring, stretching on for hours and days. Since the initial returns were from areas that the BJP was not strong in—but there was every indication that it would do well there—on one of the channels, Jairam Ramesh rebuked other panellists on their acceptance of the inevitability of the NDA coming in first.

The NDA campaign's focus was on providing the nation with a stable government under Vajpayee's leadership. It was, therefore, probably the first 'presidential-style' election campaign in the history of Indian politics. Their slogan was catchy: '*Ab Ki Bari*, Atal Bihari, Atal Bihari' (this time, it will be Atal Bihari, which rhymes beautifully in Hindi). In fact, Vajpayee's chances of winning were so evident that during the proceedings of a parliamentary debate, when the UF was in power, Nitish Kumar (Samata Party) mockingly assured his arch-rival and fellow native of Bihar, Lalu Yadav, that the next prime minister would be a Bihari, and then, with utmost confidence, added teasingly, 'It would be Atal Bihari.'

This confidence was probably because up until mid-January, there had been no rival candidate from any other party or front. But by early February, Sonia Gandhi entered active politics as the main campaigner of the Congress (I) to mobilize the party state units, which had been unwilling to rally behind Sitaram Kesri, the party president. As the Congress found its star campaigner, media reports started pouring in, declaring the Congress campaign a success and anticipating the party to be drawing wider gains by rapidly closing in the gap with the BJP.

But when the final results were declared, the mandate remained indecisive. No pre-election alliance got an absolute majority. The NDA alone came closest to the 272 mark, having won 250 seats. Since none of the other parties could stake a claim to form the government, it was assumed that some of them would soon fall in line with the NDA, whose numbers would eventually increase. Hence, in everyone's calculation, it was just a matter of time before Vajpayee formed the government. However, no one could anticipate the difficulty of this task. The long day had just begun . . .

THE BJP'S PERFORMANCE IN THOSE elections was exceptional. It remained unparalleled for the next sixteen years, until the Modi wave emerged in the 2014 and, subsequently, 2019 elections. The party did exceedingly well in UP, where it picked up fifty-nine seats, marking an increase of five seats over the 1996 figures, and its total vote share went up to 36 per cent, again remaining unmatched for the next sixteen years. Vajpayee, too, won his seat comfortably. One of the only UF constituents to have performed better in the 1996 elections was the Samajwadi Party, which in UP witnessed an increase in its vote share from 20 per cent to 28 per cent, but the number of seats that it won increased by just four seats. The BSP, on the other hand, lost both votes and seats.

But what really took everyone by surprise was that despite Sonia Gandhi's extensive campaigning, the Congress (I) hit rock bottom in UP, with a performance worse than 1977. This time, seventy-seven of the eighty-five Congress (I) candidates lost their security deposits, i.e., polled less than one-sixth of the votes in their constituencies. Like in 1977, it won no seats and lost both Raebareli and Amethi, the Nehru–Gandhi family's bailiwick. The party has not performed worse since then in these two seats. Incidentally, four of the BJP winners in UP were ochre-wearing sanyasis, including a first-timer named Yogi Adityanath, who succeeded his guru, Mahant Avaidyanath, in Gorakhpur and was just twenty-six years old at the time.

Bihar saw the NDA surge to twenty-nine seats, with BJP's tally remaining unchanged at eighteen wins out of the thirty-two seats contested. Samata Party won ten seats out of the twenty-two contested, up by four seats. The Lalu–Congress alliance also did well, winning twenty-two seats, with the Congress going up from two to five seats. The Janata Dal, post the RJD split, was decimated.

The NDA performed miserably in Maharashtra, where Sharad Pawar stitched up a powerful anti-NDA alliance. The consolidation of the vote banks of the Congress (I), various factions of the Republican Party of India (RPI) and the Samajwadi Party was formidable. I remember Pramod Mahajan telling Vajpayee that his own seat was in doubt—prophetic words as he lost the election. The NDA in Maharashtra was formed by the BJP and the Shiv Sena, and was already in power, having won thirty-three seats (BJP: eighteen; SS: fifteen) in the 1996 elections. This tally fell to ten seats in 1998, with the BJP's share falling to merely four seats. There was much handwringing and the chief minister of Maharashtra, Manohar Joshi from Shiv Sena, was publicly pulled up by his party chief, Bal Thackeray.[1]

In fact, the idiosyncrasies of the first-past-the-post system that India follows were very visibly reflected in the Maharashtra results. The NDA's vote share had actually gone up, but the consolidation of the votes of the non-NDA parties and the collapse of the 'wasted' votes proved fatal for them. The BJP polled a total of 84 lakh votes as against 61 lakh in 1996 but saw its seats tumble. The independents polled only 5 per cent votes, considerably less than the 20 per cent polled by them the previous time around.

---

[1] The family name was Thakre, but Bal Thackeray's father, the social reformer Prabodhankar Thackeray, was inspired by the India-born English writer William Makepeace Thackeray into changing the surname.

In Tamil Nadu, the NDA received a massive boost, winning twenty-nine seats, with the AIADMK in the lead with eighteen wins. The BJP made its debut in the state, winning three seats, while the other NDA partners won eight seats. Besides other factors that led to the collapse of the DMK–TMC combine, one was the series of bomb blasts at the BJP rally in Coimbatore which was to be addressed by L.K. Advani; the attack killed sixty-one persons and shook the entire state. The local government was seen to have failed, due to its tardiness and lethargy, these being the most generous explanations. The resultant revulsion and anger worked in favour of the AIADMK–BJP alliance.

In Rajasthan, where the BJP was already in power, the party suffered a debacle. This loss was, however, compensated with the strong comeback it made in Gujarat, where it had suffered internal spilt and was later prevented from forming the government. As in UP, where the BJP had won five more seats, in Madhya Pradesh too, and despite Sonia Gandhi's campaign, the party won three more seats to end up with thirty. The NDA also swept the elections in Odisha, winning sixteen out of the twenty-one seats, with the BJD, having won twelve of these, dominating the tally.

The other states worth noting for the impact they made on government formation (and its efficient working) at the Centre were West Bengal and Andhra Pradesh. Though the Left Front retained West Bengal comfortably, Mamata demonstrated that the Trinamool was seen as the real Congress. It won seven seats to the Congress's one win. The BJP made its debut in the state as well, winning the Dum Dum seat. In Andhra Pradesh, the TDP under Chandrababu Naidu, the convenor of the UF, lost four seats and ended up with just twelve. The Congress (I) remained unchanged at twenty-two seats, while surprisingly, the BJP won four seats and around 18 per cent of the vote. While the BJP was supposed to be relatively stronger in the Telangana region, it won only one seat here.

The NDA's numbers went up even before the final results were in. The Haryana Lok Dal (B) of Om Prakash Chautala, which had won four seats in Haryana, pledged support. This was despite the fact that Haryana's government was a coalition between Bansi Lal's Haryana Vikas Party (HVP) and the BJP. However, the alliance partners won just one seat each, so Chautala's unconditional support was a shot in the arm for the NDA. Others like Maneka Gandhi, who won as an independent from Pilibhit (UP), and Buta Singh, again an independent from Jalore (Rajasthan), also came on board. Three of the six members of the Janata Party announced that they would not support a Congress-led government. This would marginally reduce the numbers that the NDA was going to require to form a government.

As Vajpayee and the NDA leadership were still assessing the results coming in, a section of the Congress (I), led by Sharad Pawar, fresh from his triumph in Maharashtra, started a 'Stop BJP' campaign. Newspapers reported that the campaigners were hopeful of being successful in their agenda of preventing the NDA from crossing the 240-seat mark. It seemed as if different people had read the Romesh Bhandari–Jagdambika Pal episode in different ways!

Reports from the Congress and the UF were mixed and confusing. There were three reasons for that. One, Sharad Pawar had mended fences with Sonia Gandhi and, having delivered Maharashtra, expected political support for his bid to form the government. Two, Delhi was full of rumours that Sonia Gandhi was apprehensive of a BJP-led government that would not only pursue Bofors but also re-open controversial deals of the Indira Gandhi and Rajiv Gandhi regimes. These included the famous pipeline laying and fertilizer import cases, through which the Italian energy major Snamprogetti and its India representative, Quattrocchi, first made their appearance in the country. Unexpectedly, Sonia Gandhi had called Vajpayee a 'liar' during the campaign, marking one of the first breaches of the tradition of no name-calling. Three, all political journalists who dropped in to 7 Safdarjung Road were unanimous that Sonia Gandhi would never allow Sharad Pawar to become prime minister, come what may. He was simply too independent, with a strong base of his own; but for Maharashtra, the Congress (I) would have actually cut a sorry figure in the parliamentary elections.

Unexpectedly, the Chandrababu Naidu-led TDP turned out to be the joker in the pack. This was despite the fact that the TDP saw its numbers in the Lok Sabha reduce from sixteen to twelve. Ironically, Naidu was the convenor of the United Front and considered to be the fulcrum which leveraged support for the grouping that enabled the UF to keep going. The BJP reached out to Naidu, but he was coy. Newspaper reports and local gossip was that the TDP MPs wanted to be a part of the government. But would Naidu bite? That question kept Vajpayee and the BJP leadership on tenterhooks. The only public message that Naidu sent out was that the TDP would not support a Congress government. This was in the context of Mulayam Singh's position that, since the UF did not have a mandate, they were open to supporting a Congress government. Political jockeying in Delhi was gaining speed, with rumours travelling faster than the negotiating ability of political leaders, but the developments in Himachal Pradesh went relatively unnoticed.

Even though the BJP won two out of the three Lok Sabha seats in Himachal Pradesh for which elections had been completed, the state assembly elections held at the same time produced a deadlock. The Congress had won thirty-one seats out of the sixty-five for which elections had been held; voting would take place in three snow-bound constituencies later on. The BJP won twenty-nine seats, but one of the winners died almost immediately after. The Himachal Vikas Party of the former Union communications minister Sukh Ram, disgraced after the telecom scandal of 1996, won four seats, with one independent, to complete the numbers.

Post-elections, the BJP sent its party *prabhari* (in-charge) for Himachal, Narendra Modi, to Shimla to try and form the government. This choice was driven by the fact that Modi had played a major role in reviving the faction-ridden BJP in Himachal and had also contributed to the party's spectacular performance in Gujarat. The media did not notice him much at the time, but in party circles, he was marked out for the future. Vajpayee had very close links with Himachal and visited Manali often; that gave me an opportunity to notice Modi's command of the situation and detailed knowledge of the state.

Even before the TDP revealed its hand, there was a near-unanimous understanding that the new prime minister would be Vajpayee, a bit prematurely since the numbers had not stacked up. The issue under discussion instead was who the next finance minister would be. Jaswant Singh's loss at Chittorgarh was a more severe shock to Vajpayee than Pramod Mahajan's loss. Jaswant Singh's counsel was always valued, and even though he was seen as pro-America, his basic inclination towards freeing up the economy was evident. Having seen them from up close many times, I knew that Vajpayee and Jaswant shared a high comfort level. Neither of them was given to too much chatter and both were comfortable in each other's silence.

For many, Murli Manohar Joshi was a natural choice for finance minister, since he had expressed himself often on economic nationalism. It was expected that the Swadeshi lobby would back this choice. But the newspapers speculated that the governor of Andhra Pradesh, the economist C. Rangarajan, could also be inducted as the finance minister. A former governor of the Reserve Bank of India, he was said to be close to Naidu, and with the BJP cosying up to the latter, his nomination seemed probable. There was Ramakrishna Hegde, who was seen to be very close to

Vajpayee and the BJP, and though his party had won only three seats, the alliance had delivered Karnataka to the NDA.

Vajpayee was duly elected the BJP Parliamentary Party leader after the results, in a meeting held at the Central Hall of Parliament. Normally, Parliamentary Party meetings were held in the Parliament Annexe, but I guess this meeting was special. A sense of drama was necessary since the BJP wanted to signal that it had arrived. Vajpayee's speech was much appreciated. I had noticed that he had a great sense of the moment. His speeches were thought through and not off the cuff. At this moment, there was a need to calm fears about any hidden agenda and to allow the TDP and other potential allies to justify coming over to his side.

Among the many things that he said on this occasion, two stood out. The first was that the Opposition in politics is not necessarily an antagonist, but just someone holding different perceptions. This was to negate the messages being sent out by the Congress (I) and the left about the BJP being 'beyond the pale', so to say. Secondly, Vajpayee also addressed the fears among the minorities that BJP rule would create difficulties for them. He said that 'we should not consider different religions as obstacles but as symbols of our cultural richness which represent unity in diversity'.

Even while the assumption that Vajpayee would be prime minister was broadly accepted, the terms of engagement were yet to be discussed. Jayalalithaa was due to come to Delhi and meet Vajpayee on 9 March. Her arrival was awaited with bated breath, rather trepidation, at 7 Safdarjung Road.

'Does she drink tea?'

'No, she should be offered coconut water.'

R.K. Kumar, her Delhi representative, had started life as a stenographer in Delhi before rising to become a chartered accountant. He was a Rajya Sabha MP, spoke Hindi well and knew how Delhi functioned. Our conversations with Kumar made clear that Jayalalithaa would be a difficult person to handle.

From all accounts, she was a deeply insecure person who trusted no one. Her difficult childhood, the insults and harassment which she had to face, could explain some of her personality traits. Apparently, she had retained every piece of clothing and pair of shoes that she had ever worn since she became the sole breadwinner of her family at the age of six. These were kept in different bungalows in Chennai. The thought was chilling.

Before leaving Chennai for Delhi, 'Amma', as she was referred to, spoke to the media. She predicted that the Vajpayee government would last its full term of five years. After all, she had campaigned vigorously for this to happen. Almost in passing, she mentioned that the AIADMK would support the government from outside. Little did anyone know that the storm was yet to begin . . .

EVEN AS VAJPAYEE AND HIS colleagues were in constant conversation on how to balance the various strands of the NDA, the Congress (I) was creating a sideshow of its own. 'Chacha' Kesri was under pressure to quit, but his self-respect would not allow him to do that. Even before he could spell out his terms, senior Congress leaders asked him to resign immediately. Kesri wanted to call a meeting of the All India Congress Committee (AICC), where he could resign and ask the AICC to elect a new president. A year ago, the then prime minister, Deve Gowda, had called him 'an old man in a hurry', but for now he did not exhibit any urgency to quit. Therefore, he was literally turfed out of office at a meeting of the Congress Working Committee (CWC). Then, completely unmindful of the rules, the CWC asked Sonia Gandhi to become the president of the Congress (I). Besides the usual Nehru–Gandhi family loyalists, the person pushing the most to throw out Kesri and install Sonia Gandhi was Sharad Pawar. 'Barkis was clearly willing', but where were the numbers? And would Pawar's own party and leadership allow him to become the prime minister?

Amma came calling finally. I was most impressed when I first saw her. The humongous SUV stopped, a security man rushed to the front door and placed a stool next to the door. She got down regally, her broad frame crowned by the cape she wore around her neck. As she walked into the house, she perfunctorily acknowledged the presence of her greeters, with an almost imperceptible nod. I have no idea what she and Vajpayee talked about, but she did thank her hosts for the consideration shown in offering her tender coconut water. Later, she publicly announced her support to Vajpayee and denounced Sonia Gandhi in fairly strong language. Soon, a broader NDA meeting was held, and it was decided that an overarching agenda that the NDA government would pursue be drafted.

I had a minor role to play in the choice of the name: the National Agenda for Governance (NAG). The initial idea was to call it 'Common Minimum Programme', or CMP, along the lines of what the UF government had. I felt that CMP was an inefficient nomenclature for any common programme. Was it a common programme, or was it a minimum programme? Since it was a case of different parties and ideologies coming together, one would assume that it was a common programme. Why would disparate elements come together otherwise? Its correct nomenclature should have been the Minimum Common Programme, with a stress on the commonality of the points agreed upon.

The UF government had decided that since many companies were trying to escape the tax net, a certain minimum tax should be collected from them. This was done with the introduction of the Minimum Alternative Tax (MAT). Instead, it should have been the Alternative Minimum Tax, the stress being on the minimum amount of tax payable through an alternative process, i.e. no processing of returns, etc. The names CMP and MAT point to a common author, presumably P. Chidambaram, who wrote the CMP and brought in the MAT. But I have no proof of it!

My NAG suggestion was accepted by Jaswant Singh in Vajpayee's presence. However, in retrospect I realize that I clearly slipped, since NAG makes for a horrible acronym. My role in NAG was not over yet. When a few days later, it was finally written, I was the scribe as Vajpayee dictated the entire document at his dining table. My not-so-perfect Hindi was a challenge, but I managed. Fortunately, I sat next to the typist when he got to work at the computer, and he knew the correct words that I had misspelt. The Agenda was a classic coalition document, reflecting the reality that since the BJP did not have the numbers, it would have to put on the back burner key issues like the abolition of Article 370, the legislation of uniform civil code and the reconstruction of a temple at the Ram Janmabhoomi. But that is jumping the gun, as the draft was not finalized until after Vajpayee finally received the call from Rashtrapati Bhavan.

With support of the parties from the north-east and Naidu's open position that he would not support a Congress government and was inclined to be neutral in a confidence vote that a Vajpayee government would move, the stage seemed clear for an NDA government to take office. President K.R. Narayanan wrote to Vajpayee, but it was not the letter that was expected. Departing from past practice, Narayanan did not invite Vajpayee to form the government; instead, he asked whether Vajpayee 'was willing and able to form a stable government'. The wording was most unusual, since nobody had staked a claim to form a government, not even Vajpayee, after the 1996 experience. Unlike in states where the temporary alternative is President's rule, at the Union level, there always has to be a government, so that Parliament can be convened within a constitutionally mandated period.

The President's letter conceded that not only was the BJP the largest single party in the Lok Sabha but also that the political formation it headed was the largest combination of pre-poll allies. The same day (10 March), the *Times of India* carried an edit-page article by retired jurist and peace activist Rajindar Sachar, arguing that pre-poll alliance had a meaning only when it had adequate numbers, which, admittedly, the NDA did not have. He did, however, point out that India had had a minority government at the Centre in the past.

Even as Vajpayee met the President and staked his claim, some of the NDA parties implicitly started negotiations over their place in the sun. George Fernandes said that while the Samata Party would be in the government, he would remain outside it. Jayalalithaa and Vaiko, the MDMK leader, said that their parties would not join the government. The general assumption was that Vajpayee would be sworn in shortly, so there was not much time for jockeying. The NDA's count was now around 267 seats, and with Naidu's stated position, the assumption seemed natural.

But then President Narayanan bowled his googly. He asked Vajpayee for written letters of support from all those backing his government, inclusive of the pre-poll alliance partners. The reason cited for this demand was that the President was keen on a stable government and was against horse-trading. No doubt a fine sentiment, but neither history nor the subsequent developments would support this requirement. In 1990, President R. Venkataraman had required Rajiv Gandhi to give him written commitment that he would support Chandra Shekhar's government for the term of the Lok Sabha; Rajiv Gandhi would renege on his assurance within four months. Narayanan's letter, on the other hand, would trigger feverish negotiations, with Jayalalithaa claiming her pound of flesh, fatally weakening Vajpayee's government and leading to its fall in thirteen months.

To me, then and now, it was clear that Narayanan's requirement was beyond his constitutional mandate. The President or governor has to be generally satisfied that the prime/

chief minister being appointed has a majority, but Rashtrapati/ Raj Bhavan cannot be the site for counting heads. Majority has to be established on the floor of the legislature. As Sachar had argued in his *TOI* piece, discretion of the President was 'bad in law'. In this case, nobody else had staked a claim, so it was logical for Vajpayee, with his near-majority, to be called upon first. It was not 1996, when the BJP and its allies were more than eighty short. When Indira Gandhi lost majority in 1969 after the Congress split, she continued in office, as nobody else staked a claim. Similarly, after the 1991 elections, the Congress was fifty short of a majority, but with no one else staking a claim, Narasimha Rao was sworn in.

Narayanan's letter hurt Vajpayee's position and weakened his ability to form a government in a straightforward manner. By now, it was not a secret that Jayalalithaa had been rebuffed by Vajpayee and the BJP. Her main demands were that Subramanian Swamy should be finance minister; that the revenue department be separated from the finance ministry and be given to her candidate; but most importantly, that Article 356 be used to dismiss the DMK state government in Tamil Nadu. Back in Chennai, she claimed that she was given no respect in Delhi. She indirectly blamed Vajpayee and Advani for these leaks, saying that she had only met these two in Delhi. According to her, her demands were actually Tamil Nadu-specific—acceptance of interim arbitral award of the Cauvery Tribunal; nationalization of inter-state rivers; constitutional amendment to allow states to fix their own limit of reservations; Tamil and other regional tongues as official languages; raising the height of the Periyar dam—and not about dismissing the TN government or saving her from the many cases against her. Not only did she refuse to give Vajpayee a written letter of support, but Vaiko, who had already given his letter, was also forced to retract.

The Congress, which had been floundering, suddenly got active. Newspapers reported that Congress leaders were contacting Jayalalithaa and expressing hope that she would walk over to their side. With Vajpayee's failure to produce sufficient letters of support, the President gave him time till 14 March, that is, another two days. This, too, was unusual, because then, without waiting for the fourteenth, the President started meeting leaders of other political parties. To say the least, Vajpayee seemed to have lost the bounce in his personality and, to quote a news report, he looked 'jaded'. But he was very stern and refused to compromise any more than what the BJP had already done to accommodate its partners. The joy of victory had not been replaced by depression yet. In fact, he looked and felt almost stoic, which in retrospect was most helpful in moving forward.

Jayalalithaa eventually relented and sent her letter of support, as did her local partners. She campaigned on the slogan of a stable government under the able leadership of Vajpayee and realized that she could not push any more. Her pique was obvious when she said that she would support the government but not participate in it. With her letter, the NDA had obtained the formal support of 267 MPs, just four short of an absolute majority. The President did not immediately send out his letter of invitation to Vajpayee but continued with the consultations that he had scheduled.

Once Jayalalithaa's letter of support had been received, Vajpayee, for his part, sent Jaswant Singh to talk to Jayalalithaa and finalize the terms of her participation in the government. He also spoke to her on phone. She came round and also agreed to fly down to Delhi for not just the swearing-in but also for the NDA meeting to finalize the National Agenda of Governance. She revealed to the press that the AIADMK and its allies would be part of the government. Later, a number of stories appeared saying that she relented when she received a fax from the

President—'Are you in the government or not?'—demanding a reply by return fax.

The fact was that while her allies like the PMK and Vazhappady K. Ramamurthy were keen on joining the government, she herself was not a reluctant participant. She extracted considerable concessions because she had delivered thirty seats. Her representative would be the minister of state in charge of revenue, but he would not be independent of the finance minister. A one-person party (Tamizhaga Rajiv Congress) and the three-person PMK got cabinet berths. Her representative would be law minister, a portfolio which included company affairs. R.K. Laxman had a cartoon in the *Times of India* which showed Vajpayee nervously sitting on a chair, with the rug under his chair held aloft by Jayalalithaa. Laxman was spot on!

ONLY WHEN SONIA GANDHI MET the President, and said that she did not have the numbers, was Vajpayee invited to form the government. The pace suddenly picked up at 7 Safdarjung Road. The composition of the government and portfolio distribution had to be finalized, both with allies and within the government. The NDA had also to finalize the NAG. While the NAG, once released, was criticized for being a 'motherhood and apple pie' statement, a closer look at it revealed what the Vajpayee government would exactly be like, or at least what it would try to be. Unfortunately, analysts frequently ignore political manifestos for their lack of specifics or for being unrealistic. This is generally when election manifestos becoming irrelevant, but NAG was different—it was a post-election negotiated compact between parties having quite disparate world views and geographical priorities.

Indeed, the National Agenda for Governance did have its share of promises and goals that were unrealistic. The NDA had very rightly realized that it was not just the inability of the UF to deliver on political stability that was responsible for the 1998 election results. The UF's failure on the economic front was possibly a more relevant contributing factor in the NDA's march to power.

Echoing the almost similar points being raised by many economic commentators in the media at the time of writing this chapter (February 2019), the NAG talked about the phenomenon of 'jobless growth'. The NAG very aptly recognized that agriculture, forestry and food processing could be game changers, but in pledging to allocate 60 per cent of development (plan) funds to them, it was unrealistic. The BJP, facing the pressure of 'Swadeshi' economics, while recognizing the need for foreign direct investment to kick-start the economy, sought to balance between empowering domestic industries and not putting up hurdles for foreign investors. Well before governments started assessing and improving the 'ease-of-doing-business indices', the NAG talked about freeing industries from bureaucratic control and encouraging voluntary compliance of tax laws. No economic agenda of India is complete without the mandatory references to investments in infrastructure and self-employment, and the NAG stayed true to form.

What made the NAG different from run-of-the-mill documents were those portions of it that were dear to Vajpayee and which he painstakingly dictated to me. The NAG mentioned setting up 'a commission to review the constitution in light of the country's experience over the past 50 years'. This idea, which drew a lot of flak when suggested in the NAG and implemented by the next Vajpayee government, stemmed from the special session of Parliament convened in August 1997, on the occasion of fifty years of India's independence. This special session was the brainchild of the then speaker, Purno Sangma, and saw a fair amount of introspection by Indian parliamentarians.

It is also true that the BJP, particularly Vajpayee and Advani, had expressed themselves in favour of decisive governance which they felt India was deficient in. Critics alleged that Vajpayee and Advani meant a presidential form of government when they talked about the pitfalls of political instability and expressed a desire for decisive governance. And the critics were probably right.

Vajpayee was often referred to as the right man in the wrong party, which meant that his approach was broader than that of his party's. This was also taken to mean that Vajpayee's personal popularity was far greater than that of the BJP, and that in a direct contest for power, he would come out on top. The argument was simplistic but had acceptance. The BJP, in turn, argued that if the constitution could be amended so often and so easily—a hundred times in sixty-nine years at the time of writing—setting up a commission to look at it systemically should not raise hackles. This was an equally valid argument.

The other set of Agenda items related to national security. Vajpayee was an old advocate of India exercising the nuclear option, which is why he welcomed the 1974 tests. Nuclearization was necessary as an act of deterrence against China and Pakistan, as a means to prevent adventurism. Most importantly, it was necessary for this country to be recognized as a great power, which according to him, was India's destiny. It was galling to him that China was a legitimate nuclear power courtesy of the Nuclear Non-Proliferation Treaty, a status India could not aspire to since it had missed the bus by not testing before NPT came into force. This nuclear apartheid was unacceptable, which is why he strongly backed the UF government on the Comprehensive Nuclear-Test-Ban Treaty negotiations.

Thus the NAG clearly stated that the NDA government would re-evaluate the nuclear policy and exercise the options to induct nuclear weapons. Vajpayee meant this, but analysts assumed that such a line was mere posturing. Vajpayee had been arguing for years that the Government of India needed a national security council to analyse military, economic and political threats to the country. V.P. Singh had indeed taken some baby steps in this direction, but then the initiative lapsed.

Vajpayee, Advani and the BJP had been trying for a while to put electoral reforms on the nation's to-do list. The NAG mentioned that the government would implement the recommendations of the Goswami Committee to this end. Vajpayee had long been in favour of having an anti-corruption ombudsman (Lok Pal) that would cover the office of the prime minister. When this was discussed, senior BJP leader Murli Manohar Joshi strongly opposed the idea of including the prime minister within the ombudsman's ambit, arguing that the government's functioning would be paralysed if this was done. He explained that a minister being investigated by the Lok Pal would, in effect, cease to function as a minister; it would hence result in disaster if the prime minister were to cease to function, because nothing would prevent the Opposition from levelling one allegation after another against the prime minister. This argument made sense to me, but I was not required or expected to speak. Ultimately, Vajpayee's wish prevailed, but the NDA government was unable to make headway on this due to lack of political consensus.

The issue of appointments to the higher judiciary troubled politicians and public policy practitioners. The system had moved from politicians appointing judges to judges appointing themselves. There was consensus that the system should not be a self-perpetuating one and that the involvement of some outsiders would lend greater credibility and help improve standards. The NAG set for itself the task of bringing in legislation to set up a national judicial commission that would recommend appointments to the different high courts and the

Supreme Court. The proposed national judicial commission would also frame an ethical code of conduct for the judiciary. Vajpayee's NDA, however, could not get this legislation through in its six-year tenure. The Modi government did succeed in passing the legislation in 2014, but the Supreme Court quashed it.

The UF government had also proposed a legislation providing for 33 per cent reservation for women in state legislatures and in Parliament. Vajpayee was a big supporter of this idea, and the NAG promised to legislate on it. During the UF government, the proposal was cleared by the Rajya Sabha but was held up in the Lok Sabha. But Sharad Yadav, the president of the Janata Dal, the largest constituent of the UF government, bitterly attacked the idea, calling it a 'game' devised by women who cut their hair and wore it short.

The ostensible reason cited by this proposal's opponents was that there should be reservation for women belonging to the other backward classes (OBCs) within this 33 per cent quota. Considering that there was no reservation for OBCs in the electoral system, the reason cited was not logical. Yet the primary fear had to do with its implementation. The reservation for scheduled castes (SC) and scheduled tribes (ST) in state legislatures and in Parliament is based on identifying constituencies where there is a preponderance of SCs/STs. This principle could not apply to seats reserved for women.

So there were two systems being discussed. One, like in local bodies, the women's seats could be rotated, so that once in three election cycles each seat would mandatorily send a women representative. Two, just reserve one-third of all seats for women. The first would not work since there would be no incentive for an MP to deliver knowing that she/he may not be around the next time. While a woman MP elected from a reserved seat could try again even if the seat was no longer reserved, this would not hold for a male MP, whose seat would become reserved for women. The second option would be patently unjust.

Vajpayee had a third option, which was to increase the strength of the Lok Sabha/state assemblies by a third. He argued that if the United Kingdom, a country much smaller than India, could have over 600 MPs in their lower house, why did India have only 541 MPs. Our constituencies are simply too big for MPs to be in touch with their constituents. Vajpayee argued that the broad outlines of his system could be fleshed out to allow for incumbency and yet ensure women's representation. More than twenty years down the line, the issue remains unresolved.

The BJP, and its earlier incarnation, the Bharatiya Jana Sangh, always stood for smaller states, which they felt was better from the governance point of view. The NAG promised new states of Uttaranchal (Uttarakhand), Vananchal (Jharkhand) and Chhattisgarh, besides promising statehood for Delhi. The Jana Sangh first came to power in 1967, when it won elections to the Delhi Metropolitan Council and the Municipal Corporation of Delhi. When Delhi held its first assembly elections in 1993, the BJP won, and when the NDA came to power in 1998, Delhi had a BJP chief minister. Realizing the limitations of running the local government in Delhi and seeing Delhi as their stronghold, the BJP was keen on statehood for the city. But reality hit home a few months later, when Home Minister Advani tried to convince the cabinet to go along with the idea.

Union ministers were uncomfortable with having to live and operate in a city with a state government. Advani then offered to keep the New Delhi Municipal Council (NDMC) out of the jurisdiction of the proposed Delhi state, since most Government of India offices and all ministers' houses were within NDMC limits. Somebody pointed out that the airport would still be outside the area, where the writ of the Union government would run. The proposal had to be withdrawn. Another attempt was made years later but did not go through.

Those promising or asking for statehood for Delhi ought to look elsewhere too. Washington, D.C. was established as a city that would be the capital of the USA precisely because the government officials and legislators refused to live in a city where some other government was in charge. Similar logic applies to Paris, Canberra, London, Tokyo and Paris. As an Indian Administrative Service officer of the erstwhile Union Territories cadre, whose officers work in the Delhi government, I cannot see Delhi becoming a state of the union. So while greater delegation of powers to the elected government of Delhi makes sense, and should be pursued, statehood is a chimera that politicians can promise till eternity.

WHEN THE NATIONAL AGENDA OF Governance was launched, it was Vajpayee who did the honours. All the top leaders of the NDA were there, but it was Vajpayee alone who was the star of the occasion—a public acknowledgement that the election was fought around the theme of Vajpayee for PM. This public anointing, indicating almost a presidential style of government, masked another aspect of democracy, which is that, you need to build and sustain alliances, and that negotiations are not limited to short periods before or after elections.

If the NAG was poetry, the discussions on ministry-making were earthy prose. George Fernandes took potshots at multinational companies which were being cultivated by every government in India since Narasimha Rao became PM. Naveen Patnaik's BJD, the third-largest component of the NDA then with nine MPs, publicly demanded four ministers. Fortunately for the NDA, attention was somewhat deflected from the nitty-gritty of their efforts at government-making by the bloodletting and jockeying for positions in the Congress (I). Recriminations among losers is a common phenomenon, but this new version of India's Grand Old Party was unique in that there were brisk manoeuvres for party posts after the significant loss they suffered in the parliamentary elections. It was amusing to follow these developments from the sidelines, actually a welcome break.

In retrospect, these events must be located within the context of broader developments that were happening in the Opposition ranks. The 1998 elections delivered a very different mandate than the 1996 elections, though superficially they looked alike. The BJP saw its numbers swell from 160 to 178, though it contested fewer seats. Its own vote share went up nonetheless, from 20.3 per cent to 25.5 per cent, marking the first time when it won more votes than the Congress (I). The pre-poll NDA won 36 per cent votes, with an increase of 12 per cent over the 1996 figures. The Congress and its allies polled just over 27 per cent of the votes, a loss of over 3 per cent.

The state of the parties of the United Front has already been touched upon. Except for the Samajwadi Party, they all lost support. The emergence of new parties like the RJD, BJD and the Lok Shakti could only be partly responsible for the near collapse of the Janata Dal. The BJD, for example, won far more votes in 1998 (27.8 per cent), when it contested just twelve seats, than the JD had won in 1996 (13 per cent), even with Biju Patnaik in their ranks. This time around, the Janata Dal was reduced to 5 per cent only. Though the Lok Shakti was an offshoot of the JD, formed by Ramakrishna Hegde after he was thrown out of the JD, it contested the elections like the BJD, as part of its alliance with the BJP. The synergies of working together cannot always be treated as given in every case. Contrary to received wisdom about voter fatigue, the final polling figures in 1998 (62 per cent) were higher than in 1996 (58 per cent). There was a message in this.

The primary reason why the 1998 election was very different from the 1996 election was that this time it was virtually impossible for a third-front government to come to office, supported from outside by one of the two national parties. This time around, it was a certainty that the smaller regional parties would have a supportive role. The reality was that the pre-poll NDA had won 252 seats, and it was expected that they would form the government. With the post-poll support, it had reached a figure of 267, not counting the TDP, which had twelve seats. Since Naidu had announced that he would not support the Congress in forming the government but would remain neutral were the BJP to form a government, it was obvious that a government without the BJP was a non-starter. Unless, of course, the NDA could be broken.

The President's requirement of written letters of support provided precisely this opportunity. The 'Stop BJP' campaign, now spearheaded by CPM's Harkishan Singh Surjeet—more of a backroom dealer than a mass leader—suddenly got oxygen. Along with Mulayam Singh, the campaigners declared that since the UF lacked a mandate, they should all support a Congress-led government. Surjeet's fellow backroom boy, Sitaram Yechury, was sent to persuade Naidu to join them. It was these developments and the possibility of power that suddenly brought the Congress (I) to life. The party saw a major erosion in its voter base, which showed up in terms of the seats won, 116—a loss of twenty-four seats. Its position would have been much worse but for its ability to completely outflank the BJP in Maharashtra and in Rajasthan. In Rajasthan, the Congress was able to best the BJP, taking its tally from twelve to eighteen. The BJP saw its numbers fall from twelve to five.

Sharad Pawar was the man of the match in so far as Maharashtra was concerned. The NDA (BJP–Shiv Sena) actually won more votes, 41.6 per cent in 1998, up from 38.6 per cent in 1996, but its numbers in terms of the seats won fell calamitously. In fact, it was almost wiped out. Thanks to its alliance with the different factions of the Republican Party, the Samajwadi Party and other minor parties, the vote share of the Congress (plus allies) reached 43.5 per cent, a huge jump over the Congress's own figure of 34.9 per cent in 1996. Had Pawar not stitched its alliance, the Congress would not have been able to sweep the state; it would conceivably have won even lesser seats than in 1996. Pawar was clearly ready for higher responsibilities than he felt he deserved.

Pawar also played a major role in having Kesri replaced by Sonia Gandhi as party chief. Since she was not a member of Parliament, Pawar could envision himself as the party leader in the Lok Sabha and a potential prime minister of a non-BJP government. All this was not so obvious in March 1998, but the public manoeuvring for leadership positions seemed a combination of building castles in the air and political brinkmanship. Pawar publicly announced that he was hopeful of obtaining a letter of support from Jayalalithaa. The denouement was swift. Jayalalithaa, as noted earlier, sent her letter of support for the Vajpayee government.

The Congress (I), choosing to not reveal its hand till a BJP government became a certainty, opted for Sonia Gandhi as the chairperson of the Congress Parliamentary Party (CPP), in addition to her newly acquired position of party president. The CPP constitution had to be amended to provide for such a position. She joined Jawaharlal Nehru, Indira Gandhi and Rajiv Gandhi as only the fourth person to be both party president and the CPP chairperson. Safely ensconced, she then nominated party leaders for both houses of Parliament—Sharad Pawar for the Lok Sabha and Manmohan Singh for the Rajya Sabha. Pawar therefore retained his position as party leader in the Lok Sabha but was severely diminished since he had been completely out manoeuvred, having a separate party leader in Parliament. The only solace, if it can be called that, was that he became the official leader of the Opposition in the Lok Sabha once the Vajpayee government was sworn in.

By late evening on 18 March 1998, the contours of the government were more or less clear. The top leaders of the BJP and its allies gathered at Vajpayee's house. I too, for the first time, was called in for the gathering, but with my laptop. Kanchan

Gupta was around to assist me; in any case he typed faster than me. I had listed out the various ministries so that nothing slipped between the cracks, or worse, two persons getting the same job!

There was discussion that the NDA should rationalize ministries. For example, did the government need a separate textile ministry? Rajiv Gandhi was the last prime minister to have attempted such an exercise inasmuch as he tried to create an overarching transport ministry, bringing within its fold the railways, roads and highways, and civil aviation. He did, however, shift the scheduled castes and scheduled tribes' welfare unit out of the home ministry into a separate entity. However, on that evening of 18 March, the textile ministry survived all efforts to subsume it into the industry ministry. A year and a half later, when the DMK had to be accommodated, commerce and industry ministries were brought together, but then the industry ministry was itself cannibalized into three components. Rationalization exercises in government often end up having perverse consequences.

The meeting at 7 Safdarjung Road was fairly smooth and ended up well before dinner. Once the letter to the Rashtrapati had been sent, my entire focus changed to organizing the logistics. Advani, as the party president, took it upon himself to inform the BJP appointees. I had to have the invitations collected from Rashtrapati Bhavan and set about meeting the demands of the newly appointed ministries for additional cards for the function. That exercise did not end until after 2.30 a.m.

At some moment in the evening, we got a message that K.S. Sudarshan, the general secretary of the RSS, would be dropping in for dinner. Ranjan, Namita's husband and a professional in the hotel industry, immediately ensured that there were no tomatoes in any of the dishes as the guest was allergic to them. The dinner itself was pleasant and uneventful, so much so that I remember very little of it. There is much conjecture about the later conversation between Vajpayee and Sudarshan. The two protagonists never mentioned the conversation to the best of my knowledge, but Jaswant Singh must have figured in it.

Earlier that evening, after the list of persons to be sworn in as ministers had been sent to the Rashtrapati Bhavan and most people had dispersed, I had quietly congratulated Jaswant Singh on his impending appointment as finance minister, and we'd exchanged some words. Though no formal order or even a press note had gone out, it was common knowledge that Jaswant Singh would be sworn in as minister on the morning of 19 March. But it was not to be. Kanchan Gupta has written a detailed piece on the developments at Vajpayee's house that evening, but he got some trivia wrong.[2] He writes that I had gone home by 9 p.m. and that I had to be called back; that we rode to Rashtrapati Bhavan to deliver the letter. Actually, I did not leave until 3 a.m., and I did not go Rashtrapati Bhavan to deliver the letter. But these are quibbles. The important thing is that Jaswant Singh did not become the minister the next morning, though he did become the deputy chairman of the Planning Commission two days later. He was given the rank of a cabinet minister and was a permanent invitee to cabinet meetings.

The standard explanation for this was that the RSS was uncomfortable with his economic ideas. It was said that he would push for greater liberalization and the opening of the economy. Another point against him was that he was too pro-America. The alternative explanation, which I find more credible, was that it would have looked bad if those who'd just lost elections were made ministers. There are many reasons why the alternative explanations look credible. One, while Jaswant Singh did not became finance minister or even a minister on 19 March, he got a cabinet rank on 21 March and, as deputy chairman of the Planning Commission,

---

[2] Kanchan Gupta, 'I Too Need to Speak Up Now!', Abplive.in, 28 September 2017.

was very much a part of the Vajpayee government's economic management team. Two, after a decent interval, when both he and Pramod Mahajan became Rajya Sabha MPs, they indeed joined the government as ministers. Three, after the Pokhran tests, when Indo–USA relations had hit rock bottom, both countries entered into quiet diplomacy over many rounds that helped normalize the relations. Unsurprisingly, Jaswant Singh was the Indian interlocutor on behalf of Vajpayee, while Strobe Talbott was his American counterpart. Lastly, in another three years, Jaswant Singh was India's finance minister.

The RSS–BJP relationship is a complex one, with most BJP leaders, including Vajpayee, Advani, Pramod Mahajan, Narendra Modi and Manohar Parrikar, having had RSS backgrounds. Vajpayee publicly declared that the RSS was his soul, and in a play of words, he told a questioner in the US that he remained a *swayam sewak*'. What's often forgotten is that the RSS doesn't run the BJP, and that not everybody in these two outfits has the same view on everything. Further, with time, the RSS has evolved, and its position must be seen in context.

However, the Vajpayee–Sudarshan relationship was a tense one, so it allowed many to speculate on the RSS running the BJP government by stealth, and the Jaswant Singh episode gave credence to this point of view. In fact, Vajpayee had to publicly dispel this rumour when he replied during the confidence motion in parliament, saying that there was no remote control that was manipulating him or his government.

AFTER THE SWEARING-IN CEREMONY THE next morning, 19 March, we went to the South Block, and, later in the day, post the India–Pakistan hockey match, the last-minute glitches in portfolio distribution became our focus. Ultimately, it boiled down to the defence ministry. Hegde was to get it, but his three-member presence in the Lok Sabha was outvoted by George Fernandes's ten members;

his case was also weakened probably by the relative importance of Bihar. Hegde was generally calm, waiting outside my room, while Fernandes was inside with Vajpayee and Advani, making his own case. Though Fernandes had publicly stated that he did not want to be a minister, he bargained hard enough to land up with defence.

Hegde meanwhile made for a fine commerce minister. Because of strong rumours, rather news, about these tensions over portfolio negotiations, an official press note had to be issued to justify Hegde's appointment as the commerce minister. The note mentioned the challenges of globalization, the critical WTO negotiations pending and the need to make India a formidable export powerhouse. Somehow, it did not look like a good way to begin governing a country.

Winning the confidence vote was the next challenge facing Vajpayee. The subtext was that though the government would survive, how exactly would the mechanics play out was anybody's guess. The next few days saw mind games at their best. Someday hopefully, a game theorist would study the subtle and not-so-subtle moves which had been designed by each side to push Vajpayee into a corner.

The first obstacle to be overcome before the confidence vote itself was the election of the speaker.[3] Purno Sangma, whose election as speaker in May 1996 was an indication that the Vajpayee government did not have the numbers, was keen on being

---

[3]   This is standard parliamentary procedure. The first business of a newly elected legislature is to elect its speaker/chair, who then conducts regular business. This was, however, violated when in December 2013, the first AAP government was sworn in in Delhi, with the outside support of the Congress party. Since the numbers were close, the Delhi Assembly on the instructions of the Lt Governor, scheduled the confidence vote first. The possibility of a clash between the partners in the choice of speaker, and the need for every vote, motivated this departure from established parliamentary procedure.

re-elected to that post. It was also a move to check Vajpayee's vulnerabilities. Sangma called on Vajpayee formally a day or so after the swearing-in. They'd known each other for decades, so Sangma came to the point soon after congratulating Vajpayee and wishing him well.

Sangma's opinion was that he had been a fair presiding officer, which is why the BJP had no complaints then, and so they should not have any problems this time as well. Vajpayee was non-committal, but Sangma did not look disappointed when he left. What was left unsaid was that in the previous Parliament, the BJP did not really matter—the UF–Congress combination was much stronger. In fact, all power politics was confined to the two partners. Could a government expect to function in Parliament with the speaker being from its principal political rival? To me this was unthinkable, particularly after the critical role of the speaker in anti-defection cases.

At that time, various news stories appeared in papers, suggesting that there was wide acceptance of Sangma across the political spectrum and that the BJP would not object to his candidature. Advani was cited as saying that it was not necessary for the next speaker to be from the BJP. This was seen as the BJP signalling distress. Sangma's candidature, unlike Pawar's aborted bid for becoming prime minister, seemed to be fully backed by the Congress and the non-NDA parties. Sangma made it clear that he would like to be elected unanimously and would not take part in a contest. Vajpayee did not seem comfortable, far from confident.

But the BJP had been talking to Naidu. The prolonged period of government formation helped the BJP–Naidu dialogue evolve into a zone of familiarity. Separately, the left parties had kept the public pressure high on Naidu to not support the NDA government or even remain neutral. They said that he was supposed to coordinate with the left and the UF on the speaker's election, even though the latter was hobnobbing with the Congress.

A day before the elections, I recall Vajpayee telling Naidu on the phone that the TDP could have its candidate as deputy speaker. In the British tradition, once a person is elected as the speaker, she resigns from her party, is elected unopposed in parliamentary elections and stays in office indefinitely. In the Indian Parliament, the speaker does not quit her party but, while in office, stays away from party politics. A healthy tradition that has emerged since 1977 is that a person from the Opposition becomes the deputy speaker.

Naidu played hard to get, and succeeded in his desire to have his person elected as speaker. On the morning of the day the Speaker's election was supposed to take place, he conveyed that his choice for speaker was G.M. Balayogi, a two-term MP. Unfortunately, Balayogi was somewhere in Andhra and nominations could only be filed till twelve noon. His flight got delayed and he made it to Parliament House literally at the eleventh hour. I remember waiting with a few others at the closest gate of Parliament House, and running with him so that the nomination could be filed. He made it just about a minute or two before the deadline. Meanwhile, Sangma had apparently been informed by Madan Lal Khurana, the parliamentary affairs minister, that the BJP would have no objection to his candidature. Assured of his unanimous election, Sangma too had filed his nomination.

Sangma looked quite peeved when the Parliament convened but was polite and correct when the election took place and Balayogi was elected by voice vote. Normally, when the two sides are more or less evenly matched, a division is asked for and actual voting takes place. However, the Congress and the other Opposition parties did not ask for a vote. The fact that Sangma was upset was obvious when he lambasted Vajpayee during the confidence vote a few days later. He said that while Vajpayee's reputation had won the nation's confidence in May 1996 without winning the confidence of the house (Lok Sabha), this time around Vajpayee would eventually establish his majority in Parliament but would lose the confidence of the nation.

Vajpayee looked distinctly uncomfortable listening to Sangma, but I thought the latter was being unfair. To even expect that the Opposition candidate could be the speaker, particularly when the numbers separating the two sides were almost insignificant, was unrealistic. It is unlikely that the government could have lasted if it had extended support to Sangma, as smaller parties and individuals would have come to the conclusion that the government lacked confidence. It would have been a self-fulfilling prophecy of no confidence.

To be fair to Sangma, he had obviously been led to believe that he was going to be elected speaker. The people responsible for pushing Sangma's candidature, which had the unintended consequence of forcing Naidu to choose sides, had certainly miscalculated. Their expectation was that if Vajpayee, and the NDA, blinked, Naidu would not go along with Vajpayee, and a non-BJP government would emerge as a distinct possibility. What makes this scenario credible was that Naidu did not come out saying he was voting in favour of the government in the confidence motion, just that he was considering the option. This was because the left parties were still pursuing him.

However, once Vajpayee's position looked strong, the United Front had begun cracking up. The National Conference (NC) and the Asom Gana Parishad (AGP) decided to throw in their lot with the TDP, and half the Janta Dal had openly said that they would not go with the Congress. This implosion was not without its complications. The NC had two members in the Lok Sabha, of which Saifuddin Soz, their senior leader, objected strongly to his party supporting the Vajpayee government. A year later, he would help bring down the Vajpayee government. He has since emerged as a top leader of the Congress in Kashmir.

The AGP, the ruling party in Assam, failed to win even one seat in the parliamentary elections. However, the overall effect of these developments was positive, and Vajpayee seemed to have got back some of his old aplomb as he prepared to face the confidence vote.

A LOT WAS HAPPENING AROUND the country at that time. A cyclone had hit the Midnapore district of West Bengal and neighbouring areas of Odisha. At NDA's new ally Mamata Bannerjee's insistence, it was decided that an aerial survey of the affected areas will be organized. I had just about figured out a way to arrange for the Indian Air Force for the task. We knew Indrajit Gupta's constituency fell in Midnapore, but he refused to go along. Not only did Mamata Bannerjee go to Midnapore on that flight, though her own constituency was in Kolkata, she took along the entire contingent of Trinamool Congress MPs, with possibly no representative of the actual affected areas. All hell broke loose when Parliament convened next. The Left Front MPs were livid at having been left out even as their local rivals had all participated in the survey. Though Vajpayee apologized, what saved the day was the fact that Indrajit Gupta had been contacted.

The government got two opportunities to present its vision to the people. Once directly, on March 22, when Vajpayee spoke to the nation, with all TV and radio stations carrying the speech live. The other one was through the President's address to both houses of Parliament, when the eleventh Lok Sabha was formally constituted and its speaker elected. Till then, I did not pay much attention to such speeches, full of generalities and platitudes, other than one or two that were delivered on special occasions, like Narasimha Rao's first speech, when he talked about freeing the economy. But I soon realized that a lot of effort went into them, even into the negotiations over language. This was particularly the case with the President's speech, which the cabinet approves.

Vajpayee worked really hard at his own speech, which was the more substantive one, and which came earlier, than the President's.

While a lot of what Vajpayee told the nation came from the NAG, he went beyond it on a number of issues. He said that the productive potential of the people would be unleashed and India would abolish hunger within ten years. He spoke of doubling women's literacy in ten years, of vastly improving health care and of political reservation for women. Vajpayee announced specific delegation of powers to states in respect of foreign direct investment in the power sector. In view of the apprehensions being made public, he committed his government unequivocally to secularism and appealed to the country to 'give up the harmful path of confrontation'.

On the issue of India's relations with Pakistan, he used the phrase that contributed to enhancing the India's reputation worldwide. He said that he was prepared to go the 'extra mile' to improve relations with Islamabad. He committed his government to 'strain every nerve' to work with neighbours, and being the bigger country, India would be more sensitive to their aspirations. At the end of the day, 'our lives are intertwined'.

Not only did Vajpayee revise the draft many times, but he was also extremely patient during the recording session of his TV address to the nation. I saw this in all future recordings. He would happily submit to re-recording many times without a trace of annoyance. Like most upper-middle class, English-speaking Indians, I too tended to underrate politicians. Vajpayee's ability to work hard at his speeches, handwrite pages and pages of notes, remember contents of parliamentary debates and patiently record speeches was so different from what I'd expected. This was in addition to the hours spent in political work, attending meetings and delivering speeches on the stump. What needs to be also considered here is that in the process of conducting free and fair elections, the Election Commission has stretched the process to almost absurd lengths. While the actual campaigning period has been limited to only two weeks, the whole voting process is now spread over more than one and a half months. This makes the election a long and exhausting journey for politicians, like sprinting through a marathon. Vajpayee, the consummate politician, had mastered the art of his calling.

Parallel developments in Himachal Pradesh reflected the advantages and limitations of coalition politics. Though the Congress and the BJP (plus allies) were equal, the governor, Rama Devi, appointed Virbhadra Singh, the incumbent Congress chief minister, to form the government. However, Virbhadra Singh resigned on the day the assembly was to meet since he was short of numbers. The governor recommended President's rule, and when this item was put up before the Vajpayee government's first cabinet meeting, I thought it was a done deal. However, the cabinet returned this recommendation to the governor, who was asked to explore all possibilities. The official spin put on this decision was that the government did not want its first decision to be about using Article 356 of the Constitution to run a state government. Sukh Ram, the disgraced communications minister in the Narasimha Rao government, had formed his own party (HVC) in Himachal Pradesh, which picked up four seats in the assembly elections. Ultimately, a BJP–HVC coalition took office, with Sukh Ram as the deputy chief minister.

The debate on the confidence vote in many ways mirrors contemporary times. The Opposition accused the BJP of having a hidden agenda. The party was accused of hypocrisy, as they had pressed hard for dropping Sukh Ram as minister in the Narasimha Rao government in 1996—when currency notes worth a few crores were found in his house—and were now teaming up with him. The Vajpayee government had also got two Anglo–Indians nominated to the Lok Sabha, as allowed by the Constitution, but before the government could win the confidence of the house. Even I was surprised that President Narayanan had gone along with this step, since it effectively added two MPs to the ruling side.

The quality of the debate in parliament on the confidence vote seemed pedestrian. Somnath Chatterjee sarcastically said that the Vajpayee government had not won the hearts of the country but Jaswant Singh had won the heart of Jayalalithaa. Sangma's outburst has already been referred to.

At the end of day one of the debate, Vajpayee appeared calm, assured of winning the vote. In his reply on day two, he went out of the way to praise Nehru and rejected the insinuation that the BJP had a hidden agenda. Just before the elections, *Frontline* magazine had published a series of articles on Vajpayee's role in the 1942 Quit India Movement. To cut a long story short, the articles claimed that after he and his elder brother were arrested from their village post a Quit India meeting, Vajpayee had begged forgiveness and in fact helped the British by giving them information and testimonies against some nationalists. He rejected this allegation forcefully.

Politically, Vajpayee said that he believed in consensus, and that the National Agenda of Governance was a negotiated document. The no-confidence motion was won by a margin of thirteen votes, 274–261, with the Telugu Desam voting with the government. The NC abstained. The UF had already removed Naidu from being their convenor, and the TDP was expelled. Naidu, in turn, accused the UF and left parties for being insincere and negotiating with the Congress to support a government led by the latter behind his back. In any case, the BJP was a distant enemy, while the Congress was an enemy close by, as Naidu saw it.

There was near unanimous agreement among political commentators and even politicians that it was Vajpayee who needed Naidu more than Naidu needing Vajpayee. In fact, the situation was far more nuanced, and I was convinced that it was the BJP which paid the higher price of the partnership. In the 1998 elections, the BJP had not only won four seats on its own, of which three were in coastal Andhra, it polled over 18 per cent of the votes. By becoming the junior partner of the TDP, it sacrificed its presence in the state. The TDP won the state assembly polls of late 1999 only because of these 18 per cent votes, else the Congress would have won the elections.

The 1998 parliamentary elections showed the TDP's limitations—its seats went down from sixteen to twelve, with the Congress winning twenty-two, same as the previous elections. The TDP could reverse this in the 1999 assembly elections only because the BJP transferred its votes. Worse, the Vajpayee government could not move on Telangana because of Naidu's pressure. The demand for a new state of Telangana was revived by K. Chandrasekhar Rao in 2001, when he quit the TDP to form the Telangana Rashtra Samithi (TRS). Though the BJP was sympathetic to this demand, it held back from either endorsing it or moving ahead on it.

The TRS teamed up with the Congress in the 2004 general election and became a partner in the UPA government. The TDP was rejected by the people and lost power in the state of Andhra Pradesh, leaving the BJP as the hollow shell of a party it was in 1998. Worse, when Telangana was finally created in 2014, the BJP could not claim any credit for championing its cause, though its revived alliance with the TDP meant that it saw a contingent in the Andhra assembly, but one without an independent existence.

In the end, as the Vajpayee government demonstrated its majority in the Lok Sabha, the seeds of its limited lifespan had already been sown. Subramanian Swamy, the newly elected member of Parliament from Madurai, who had ironically emerged as Jayalalithaa's close adviser, did not attend Parliament to vote in the confidence motion. Swamy, who had filed many cases of corruption against Jayalalithaa in the past and who had lately become her candidate to be the finance minister in the Vajpayee government, was known for his targeting of Vajpayee over the years. Swamy's one vote was not missed that day, but he was only biding his time to strike.

4

The Ground Moves

'*Today at 1545 hours, India conducted three underground nuclear tests in the Pokhran range. These tests conducted today were one with a fission device, a low-yield device and a thermonuclear device. The measured yields are in line with expected values. Measurements have also confirmed that there was no release of radioactivity into the atmosphere.*'

—Atal Bihari Vajpayee, 11 May 1998

The most interesting aspect of the Pokhran II tests, conducted on 11 and 13 May 1998, was that even though intense speculations already existed that the Vajpayee government was soon to test India's capacity to go nuclear, when the tests did happen, the event took everyone by surprise. I went back to some of the newspaper reports of that period, specifically just the month or so before the tests, to refresh my memory. I was looking particularly for articles, analyses and statements of commentators and political leaders, national and international, which could have explained this paradox.

Senior journalist and peace activist Kuldip Nayar wrote in an article that the feeling in Pakistan was that the BJP would declare India a nuclear state; in short, that India would conduct a nuclear test. This was as early as 3 March, when it became clear that the BJP-led NDA was the frontrunner to form the government, but over two weeks before Vajpayee actually became the prime minister. Just a little over a week later, as Vajpayee's efforts at forming a government ran into the 'Jaya wall', Pakistan's foreign minister, Gohar Ayub, was quoted in the *Indian Express* (12 March), saying that 'South Asia was facing the growing rush of a new arms race with a BJP government about to take over'. This was in reference to Vajpayee's call for a nuclear option.

The US, with a view to understanding the thinking of the new government and to prepare the ground for a proposed visit of President Bill Clinton to India later that year, sent a delegation to New Delhi, led by Bill Richardson, the secretary for energy and the former US Ambassador to the United Nations. Richardson had been the main US negotiator in the nuclear deal with North Korea, and his department ran the US nuclear programme, including all the research laboratories. The nuclear component of the trip was clear from its composition, with Karl Inderfurth and Robert Einhorn completing the team. The obvious purpose was to persuade India to sign the Comprehensive Nuclear-Test-Ban Treaty (CTBT), with the threat that if it did not, aid would be cut off. It was also to make it clear to India that it simply could not afford these nuclear tests, since such a move would definitely lead to global opprobrium. Their reasoning was that as an aspiring member of the UN Security Council, India could not run the risk of going nuclear, despite the fact that all the existing UNSC members were nuclear states.

During the President's address in the Rajya Sabha, senior Congress leader Pranab Mukherjee, citing the BJP manifesto and the National Agenda of Governance, criticized the government's intention to review the nuclear option. President Clinton, while asking the US Congress to ratify the CTBT, also publicly asked India to sign the treaty and keep the thought of exercising the nuclear option at bay. The *Washington Post* carried an article on 5 April, pointedly referring to the US law that mandated sanctions in case of nuclear tests. To further bring the point home, it told its readers that international banks, public and private, were bound to penalize any country that was using its resources to pursue its 'nuclear ambitions'.

Meanwhile, Pakistan muddied the waters on 6 April by announcing that it had tested the Ghauri missile. This was supposed to be an improved version of Hatf, with a range of 1500 km, capable of striking key Indian cities like Kolkata and Chennai; the announced payload was 700 kg, which made it apparent that the new missile was meant to carry a nuclear warhead. The veteran security analyst Jasjit Singh, in his piece in the *Times of India* (7 April 1998), was unequivocal in his belief that Ghauri was a product of Sino–Pakistan collaboration. In his own words, 'Obviously Pakistan is legitimising its missile programme as indigenous.'

For many reasons, there was a fair amount of scepticism about the Ghauri test. The first of these was born of an observation of Ghauri's test path, which covered some of Pakistan's most densely populated areas. This meant that the missile was clearly not being tested for its capability but was demonstrating its already proven technology. Second, doubts about Pakistan's claim of having tested Ghauri were further strengthened because Pakistan did not issue a Notice to Airmen (NOTAM), despite the missile's flight path covering a busy part of the Arabian Sea.[1] George Fernandes

---

[1]   NOTAMs are issued to warn planes and other vessels that a missile test, or other similar activity, could pose a threat to those passing over the test-path area, so that they could keep away.

openly speculated about the possibility of Chinese involvement in Pakistan's arms development and even went on to declare Ghauri as a Chinese missile.

A very interesting and challenging four-nation conundrum now emerged on the Indian subcontinent, involving India, Pakistan, China and the US. Though the Cold War was long over, it was clear, going by the reactions coming from Washington, D.C., that the US had a lingering soft corner for Pakistan. The US called upon India and Pakistan to exercise restraint, but since the latter had already carried out its provocative act, the message was effectively targeted only at India.

The US was deliberately ignoring China's key role in nuclear proliferation in the South Asian region; it continuously maintained that it could not with certainty 'assume' a Chinese role in the provision of arms components to its neighbouring countries, since there could have been a number of suppliers to the region concerned. This seemed to be a hypocritical stand on the part of the US, since by then there was enough evidence that Sino–Pak cooperation was deep, and that China had in the past supplied M-11 missiles to Pakistan. Still, the US chose to remain silent on these blatant acts of proliferation on India's borders. In fact, it accepted the Chinese commitment to follow the Missile Technology Control Regime (MTCR) and went out of its way to declare the Ghauri test a success. Pakistan maintained that Ghauri was indigenous, so there was no case for the imposition of sanctions, and the US bought this argument.

Almost every day, the 'N question' was in the news. The UK and France ratified the CTBT. However, this could not come into force till India, Pakistan and Israel signed it. On the one hand, the US administration was not making headway on ratifying the CTBT; yet, on the other hand, it was pressuring India to sign the CTBT and move even further away from the nuclear option. Bill Richardson's meeting with Vajpayee was short and full of generalities, but his message to India was clear—not only should India maintain restraint on the nuclear issue, it should rather unequivocally give up the nuclear option. India's point to the Americans in the context of the CTBT was that it faced threats not only from Pakistan but also from China. This was emphasized repeatedly, but it seemed to fall on deaf ears.

A couple of weeks later, still before Pokhran II, the US ambassador to India, Dick Celeste, advised India to 'cap, roll-back and eliminate', so that the proposed visit of President Clinton that year could be successful. Richardson and Celeste's private conversations with senior Indian officials, particularly with Jaswant Singh, became the cause of much misunderstanding and bad blood between India and the US. This was in the context of the common understanding that India would decide to test only after its National Security Council had carried out a comprehensive Strategic Defence Review, a position Defence Minister George Fernandes often took publicly. Since India was yet to establish a National Security Council, this meant in effect that there was going to be no nuclear test in a hurry.

On a completely different level, I found Richardson's visit very instructive as I picked up another aspect of the India–US relations at the time. Richardson calling on Vajpayee with his team was the first high-level international visitor engagement that I was witness to. The meeting itself was formal, but Vajpayee stressed on India's refusal to move on the CTBT and its discomfort at the impunity of its neighbours in threatening India's security.

The standard operating procedure for such meetings is that the first 4–5 minutes are devoted to photo ops.[2] Photographers, still and video, were brought in batches, so that they could

---

[2]   Standard Operating Procedure (SOP)

take their photos and move out, allowing another lot to come in. On this particular occasion, there was a large gathering of photographers, so it was taking time and there was much jostling. I went out to see what was happening and was shocked to witness that even though we were in South Block, it was the American security men who were lining up the photographers and sending them inside in batches. I lost my temper and asked the Special Protection Group (SPG) to take over the job.[3] Seeing that on an average, American security personnel were over six feet tall and four feet across (or so it seemed), our guys felt intimidated.

Years later, when US Secretary of State John Kerry visited India, I remember seeing a photograph of American security personnel with their sniffer dogs, carrying out sanitization exercises in the Palam Technical Area, used as a terminal for VIP planes. I cannot imagine the US, or even any of the middle powers, allowing security personnel of a foreign country such liberty. In fact, later in 1998, when Vajpayee went to Colombo for the SAARC summit, the Sri Lankans objected (rightly) to our plan to fly in bulletproof cars for use in road journeys during the visit.

Vajpayee was unfailingly polite and straight in his conversations with visitors in formal settings. He played by the book and never minced words, with no double-speak. At his meeting with Richardson, Vajpayee specifically mentioned India's unease with China's role, but it did not get the attention it deserved.

---

[3] Special Protection Group (SPG), a security organization responsible for the personal protection of the prime minister, ex-Prime ministers and their families. They wear safari suits in summer and business suits in winter and are not to be confused with the Black Cats, who are drawn from the National Security Guard (NSG), another security organization headquartered in Manesar (Haryana), near Delhi. The NSG are meant for various specialized duties, including counter-terrorism operations, etc.

I imagine Richardson's ire had more to do with the fact that he completely misunderstood the Indian position and carried in his mind a picture which reinforced what they thought India ought to do and not what it was going to do. The resultant loss of face when India tested had to be blamed on the Indians, and not on their own incompetence. They refused to acknowledge that American thinking was still stuck in the old groove, given their adherence to the old hyphenated approach to the subcontinent, clearly visible from the fact that Richardson went to Pakistan after his Delhi visit. Further, the US turning a blind eye to Pakistani proliferation efforts and support to terrorism was public knowledge throughout this period.

Pakistan kept up its tirade against India, and sabre-rattling became their way to attract attention. The loudest and shrillest voice belonged to hard-line foreign minister Gohar Ayub Khan, who seemed to be picking from where his father Ayub Khan had left off in 1965.[4] Not to be outdone, was the Bhopal-born metallurgist Abdul Qadeer Khan, the father of Pakistan's nuclear programme. He said that Pakistan was ready to conduct a nuclear test any time. If this was not enough, he said that Pakistan was developing a long-range (2000 km) Ghaznavi missile.

ANOTHER INTERESTING EARLY VISITOR TO Delhi during Vajpayee's term was, General Fu Quanyou, the head of the People's Liberation

---

[4]   The self-appointed Field Marshall Ayub Khan was the military dictator of Pakistan who launched two operations against India in 1965, setting off a fierce twenty-two-day war after Operation Gibraltar, which was premised on Pakistani infiltrators engineering a banner of armed revolt in the Kashmir Valley. Instead, some shepherds, who'd seen the infiltrators, promptly informed the Indian armed forces, who nipped their designs in the bud. The resultant war was fierce, with both sides making some gains at different sectors, but which ended in a ceasefire that sent both armies back to their original positions.

Army of China. A word about the PLA: it is not the army of the People's Republic of China but the army of the Communist Party of China. Consequently, the party is deeply embedded in the PLA. Also, the PLA is an integrated military with the PLA Navy and PLA Air Force forming a part of it. These aspects make the head of the PLA a very important person.

My only impression of the meeting was that General Fu looked distinctly uncomfortable throughout the meeting, as if expecting a dressing down. Vajpayee followed the script of the meeting as suggested, which unfortunately did not make for anything beyond a formal conversation, with both sides agreeing to take into account the concerns of the other side. The briefing was that in meetings with the defence minister, India's specific concerns about the Sino–Pak nuclear and missile cooperation would be raised.

With President Clinton elevating the US–China relationship to one that defined the new world, there were misgivings not just in Delhi but also in Washington, D.C. A news item appeared that said Congressional sources did not think that either North Korea or Pakistan was the main culprit in so far as proliferation was concerned; they directly blamed China. Unfortunately, US sanctions on China, for transfer of technology and equipment, were no more than a slap on the wrist, which did nothing to deter China from pursuing its policy of support for the North Korean and Pakistani programmes. These Congressional sources were also convinced that the North Korean missile Nodong was actually made using a Chinese platform, which meant Ghauri, a derivation of the Nodong, was also a Chinese missile after all. George Fernandes had effectively said the same thing but was not taken seriously. Later, he would be pilloried for attempting to project China as an enemy.

Not unexpectedly, Clinton lifted the ban on dual-use items (which can be used for civilian as well as military purposes) available for sale to China. That Clinton was determined to make his China trip, scheduled for end-June, a success could not have been clearer, since this step was taken disregarding all evidence about the latter's undermining of the non-proliferation regime. The step was taken regardless of the alarm bells that rang loudly in countries that shared borders with China. India definitely felt its security was compromised, something that the US and the West refused to notice time and again.

Such fears were most vividly expressed by George Fernandes with increasing regularity, as it was becoming clearer with each passing day that India's security was being compromised because of China's violation of non-proliferation. What was discussed between the prime minister and his defence minister stayed between them, so it is best to not make conjectures or controversial statements that cannot be either substantiated or refuted. It would rather be more suitable to present the relevant statements and actions, and let readers form their own opinions.

For over a period of one week in early May, either while delivering formal speeches—like the V.K. Krishna Menon Memorial Lecture—or speaking to journalists who wanted to probe him further, Fernandes only had one story to tell: that potentially, India faced the greatest threat from China. What he did not say, but which critics nonetheless denounced him for, was that China was the *immediate* threat or that India needed to engage China more thoroughly. Far from it. But in a controversy, facts often become the first casualty.

The reason for Fernandes's assertion was obvious to all of us— China wanted the transfer of nuclear and missile technology to Pakistan and the activation of airfields in Tibet. That he was not alone in his assessment seemed implicit from his announcement that in response to these developments, the stalled Agni missile programme was being resuscitated and would be developed further. He was prescient in his warning that though the PLA

Navy was weak at the time, it would eventually be strengthened enough to operate in the India Ocean. Interestingly, he said one thing that seemed to have escaped the attention of analysts. The *Hindustan Times* of 4 May 1998 quotes him as saying, 'Earlier, nuclear weapons were not ruled out, now they are ruled in.' In the heat of the controversy, nobody was listening to what was being said fairly explicitly.

The Chinese backlash was expected; what wasn't expected was the domestic opposition. In hindsight, this too should not have been a surprise, but those were early days, and we were not aware of how much anger the emergence of a BJP-led government had generated in many people, not just in the political opposition but also in the media.

The Chinese lashed out at Fernandes, calling his statements 'absolutely ridiculous and not worthy of refutation'. Then, with an irony that was too obvious to ignore, they promptly went on to refute his assertions. On the specific allegation of its nuclear and missile assistance to Pakistan, China termed it 'utterly fictitious and entirely baseless'. On Fernandes's understanding of China as 'potentially' the biggest security threat to India, China's reply was that 'his comments had seriously sabotaged the atmosphere of improving relations between the two countries'.

Fernandes's clarifications—that what he had said were not his personal views but were based on what the defence ministry had been publicly saying in its annual report for years—did not get any serious attention. Instead, former prime minister I.K. Gujral said that Fernandes was 'temperamentally an adventurist', and that this proclivity in 'his present incarnation could very dangerously affect India's security'. The left parties went even further—they wanted Fernandes to be sacked for upsetting China. Editorial writers and analysts were almost universally critical of Fernandes, advising him to avoid commenting on strategic matters. A number of them reminded Vajpayee that

India could only have one foreign minister and that Fernandes should be reined in.

The resultant pressure had to be defused. The Ministry of External Affairs went into damage-control mode, stressing that only 'minor differences' with China existed. The ministry's spokesperson said that the Government of India had resolved to improve its ties with China, specifically committing 'to develop a friendly, cooperative, good neighbourly and mutually beneficial relationship'. It reminded the media that it was when Vajpayee was foreign minister that 'the first understanding regarding maintenance of peace and tranquillity along the India–China border was reached'. Fernandes himself explained that his intention was to promote dialogue and understanding. But far from being pulled up, Fernandes went on to confirm that troop deployment levels on the border with China would 'not be lessened'.

A few days before the tests, the chiefs of army, navy and airforce were briefed, followed by another briefing for the key members of the government, who constituted the cabinet committee on security. The morning of the test, 11 May, was pregnant with possibilities. Vajpayee had just shifted to 3 Race Course Road from 7 Safdarjung Road. Army units had installed special, direct lines from the Pokhran site, to avoid tapping, delays in communications or the non-availability of lines. The wind direction was adverse, and it delayed the tests. Books, by Raj Chengappa (*Weapons of Peace: The Secret Story of India's Quest to Be a Nuclear Power*) and Jaswant Singh (*A Call to Honour: In Service of Emergent India*), carry graphic details of what happened that day, so it is best not to repeat those details.

The control room was set up at 5 Race Course Road, which was a bungalow between the office (7 RCR) and the residence (3 RCR), and was mostly used as a guest house (though prime ministers have occasionally stayed in this bungalow, preferring to use No. 3 as the guest house).[5] Besides Vajpayee, other key figures present during those crucial hours were L.K. Advani, George Fernandes, Jaswant Singh and Yashwant Sinha. The team of officials was led by Brajesh Mishra, supported by Prabhat Kumar (cabinet secretary), K. Raghunath (foreign secretary) and me.

All of them sat at the dining table. They were very quiet. It was a long wait. Nobody said anything to each other. Maybe because of the old Indian habit that you don't talk about something until it happens for fear of jinxing it. When the news finally came, the effect was electric. The atmosphere was completely surreal, full of joy, yet there was no jumping or backslapping. Instead, there was a visible sense of relief, almost as if the unreal had become real. There were a lot of tears in that room that day—all of us felt the rush of the 'we have done it' confidence.

But Vajpayee's face reflected a feeling of sombre responsibility. The pressure of taking such a momentous decision, and the realization that the consequences would have to be met, had taken a toll on him. He had done well to hide the fear of the unknown, though the mask occasionally slipped when people questioned his lack of assertion of prime ministerial responsibility, of his being strangely silent and inarticulate. Now he allowed himself to smile, even laugh.

He had been arguing for India to conduct a nuclear test for the past forty-five years, since China had first tested. This arose from two lines of thinking. Hiroshima and Nagasaki had deeply affected him. He wrote a poem, 'Hiroshima Ki Peeda', where he talked of waking up in the middle of the night and wondering how the scientists who had made those powerful atomic weapons slept after hearing about the destruction caused by their creations. Did they not for a moment regret what they had done? If they had

---

[5] Interestingly, Namita's daughter, Niharika, all of nine years old, suspected something was happening when she saw army personnel installing telecommunications equipment.

a sense of remorse, then time would not judge them. But if they did not, then history would never forgive them. Vajpayee's poem and his decision to go ahead with the test are not contradictory. He came to the conclusion that if India had to live in peace in its neighbourhood, credible nuclear deterrence was essential. Nuclear weapons prevent wars, was his constant refrain.

The second, seemingly contradictory, line of thinking behind the tests was his deeply held view that India was destined to be a great power. Possession of nuclear weapons, in the world we inhabited, was the minimum entry criterion for that club. Japan and Germany, whose recent economic successes did not guarantee them the status of a great power, underscored this idea. Vajpayee's belief in India was immeasurable, and while he did not say it, his body language that day seemed to indicate that he was happy to be an important instrument in that quest. An insecure nation could not be a great power—this was the powerful motivation that drove this decision to test. In all his discussions and speeches afterwards, Vajpayee highlighted that there was a price to be paid for becoming a nuclear power, and the country must be ready to pay it.

Coming back to 11 May, immediately after the test, I got down to typing the statement dictated by Jaswant Singh and Brajesh Mishra. Vajpayee was clear that it should be a short and factual one, which it was. This was to be read out to the press. But how to go about it? Pramod Mahajan, who had joined us by then, ever the master of the dramatic, suggested that the press briefing be held on the lawns of 7 RCR. Only a single podium was placed, with the national flag next to it. Vajpayee, Mahajan and I walked out of the side door of 7 RCR and on to the lawns (actual footage of those moments can be seen in the movie *Parmanu* at the very end). The rest of us stopped well short, and Vajpayee walked alone to the podium.

He read out the brief statement in Hindi and English. We stood away from the podium, so that all the frontal shots captured only Vajpayee in the frame. However, some photographers were standing on the sides and a few papers carried the shot that had Mahajan and me standing in the corner of the frame, laughing. None of the ministers were present there. Vajpayee left as abruptly as he came; there were no questions and no chit-chat. The full weight of what had happened had not sunk in, not for me and not for the others I imagine.

The same day, 11 May, which happens to be my birthday, India also tested the Trishul, a short-range (50 km) missile. Later that evening, Brajesh Mishra met the press and gave a detailed briefing. What he said could be described as a mixture of hope, bravado and naivety. Basically, he said that we hoped there would be no sanctions and that the government had taken the effect of sanctions into consideration. The last was difficult to believe, since nobody in the know could have carried out an econometric analysis using scenario planning to assess the effect of sanctions on the economy. Not that such an analysis is infallible, or was possible to resort to, given the compulsions of maintaining secrecy. While some sanctions could be predicted, it was impossible to know how different countries would actually react, as the following narrative would explain.

The initial American reactions seemed too understated, but not for long. Suddenly, the appreciation for India—based on the idea that it had conducted the tests because of a threat perception from China, its own security concerns and the feeling that the NPT was discriminatory—was gone. Clinton reacted angrily in public. He said that India's action 'not only threatens the stability of the region, it directly challenges the firm international consensus to stop proliferation of weapons of mass destruction'.

Clinton drew attention to US laws that mandated tough sanctions, which he said he would implement in full measure. These did not amount to much on their own. The US would withhold aid and there would be no defence sales. Further, there would be no guarantees issued by the US Export–Import Bank or its overseas investment protection agency (OPIC). The US Congress also criticized the tests, while US analysts were quick to point out that US companies would probably suffer more than India. On a lighter note, we heard that Clinton's first reaction was of dismay because he would no longer be able to visit the Taj Mahal.

The Japanese reaction was expected, as it was the only country to have been at the receiving end of nuclear weapons. It froze all aid, which, unlike in the case of the US, was a substantial amount, in excess of US$1 billion. Their subsequent statements and efforts, under Prime Minister Ryutaro Hashimoto, were less appreciated. It was only with his removal from office that Indo–Japanese relations began to move forward again.

The Germans also announced a moratorium on aid, which, at US$300 million, was far above American levels. China's initial reaction was subdued, probably because they were aware of Indian ire at the Sino–Pak cooperation. In fact, to our surprise, Russia's language was stronger; Boris Yeltsin said that he was disappointed and felt let down.

The Canadian statement was a mixture of hypocrisy, racism and realism. They condemned the tests in strong language, but more interestingly, their foreign minister, Lloyd Axworthy, was quoted as saying they would 'have to take the tough nationalism represented by the Hindu party much more seriously because they are clearly up to what they would do'. I remember there was genuine puzzlement at Canada's reaction. The Canadians had lived under the American nuclear umbrella, so it was hypocritical to talk down to India. Their reference to the BJP as a Hindu party was condescension of the lowest level, even though the Canadian opinion in the international scenario did not really matter.

Denmark also got into the act and announced the holding up of its US$28 million aid programme. An Australian Labor Party spokesperson, mistaking the real world for a cricket match, used language more appropriate to the locker room. She called India's tests 'an outrageous act of nuclear bastardy'. Australia was to go further when it offered to divert its minuscule aid programme to Pakistan, so that the latter was persuaded not to test! It all seemed quite unreal.

After the initial domestic euphoria, which forced the Opposition to keep mum, domestic criticism gained force. The left parties criticized the Vajpayee government for deciding to change national policies unilaterally. They felt that the other political parties should have been consulted. The Congress was confused as to how they ought to react. Should the tests be celebrated as a programme begun by Indira Gandhi, which received a major fillip during Rajiv Gandhi's regime? Or would such a stand make Vajpayee look good, hinting at the Congress's implicit acceptance that this was the right thing to do? Their initial reaction was, 'Why now?'

Essentially, the Opposition did not know how to react, as was soon illustrated by I.K. Gujral.[6] His remedy was that India should sign the CTBT, like France and China did after conducting tests. This ignored the fact that both these countries were recognized nuclear weapons states under the NPT, and the CTBT allowed them to test if they felt that their national security was imperilled, a luxury denied to India. Another Opposition leader, Mulayam Singh Yadav, had a simpler criticism—that the tests should have been kept a secret.

Even as reactions to the initial tests, conducted on 13 May, were coming in, two days later, India conducted two more tests. These 'were required to demonstrate our capacity to miniaturise, at sub-kilo yields, and with that India concluded its planned series of tests', as the media was informed by the government. The next step taken was possibly the best thing to have been done as a follow-up to the tests, though it received a lot of flak at that time. This was to write to world leaders explaining the circumstances

---

[6] I.K. Gujral was elected from Jalandhar as an Akali Dal-supported candidate. The Akalis and the BJP had an alliance in Punjab and were very much a part of the Vajpayee-led NDA government.

which had made testing a compulsion for India. Unlike normal diplomatic correspondence, which is all sweet and cloying, this one was direct but polite. A great deal of effort went into the writing of these letters.

No sooner had Vajpayee's letter reached the White House than it appeared in the *New York Times*. This caused considerable embarrassment for us, since we had pointed to the 'China factor' as the primary reason for our decision to test. It was said that the compulsion to go nuclear was driven by, to quote from the letter, '. . . overt nuclear tests on our borders, [conducted by] a state which committed armed aggression against India in 1962, [and] although relations had improved in the last decade or so, an atmosphere of distrust prevails mainly due to unresolved border problem. That country has materially helped another neighbour of ours to become a covert nuclear weapons state, [due to which, we] have suffered aggression from that neighbour, [making us] victim of relentless terrorism and militancy.'

Factually, the statement was correct, but all hell broke loose. The Chinese were livid and made their outrage known. Domestically, too, a lot of people criticized the government for having spoilt relations with China; Chinese perfidy in supplying nuclear and missile technology to Pakistan which undermined India's security was conveniently ignored.

The international reaction to Vajpayee's letter was subdued, almost bordering on disbelief. The American analysts only picked up the 1962 part, ignoring the rather nuanced reference to India–China relations in the letter. I remember reading an American comment that India could not expect to be taken seriously if it used the 1962 war as justification for the tests. Clearly, the commentator either did not read the statement, or if he did, its meaning escaped him.[7]

---

[7] He also did not seem to know that the US policy towards Cuba was frozen because of the Cuban revolution of 1959, led by Fidel Castro,

In the letter, Vajpayee had conceded that despite the lingering border dispute, relations with China had been improving. It was the Chinese nuclear and missile assistance to Pakistan that had resulted in India facing two nuclear-armed neighbours. What made it worse was that such Sino–Pak cooperation allowed Pakistan to use jihad as an instrument of state policy to destabilize its neighbours. But this was three years too early. In any case, it seems doubtful that Vajpayee's prescient reference in this letter to the use of jihadi terrorism was taken seriously. Nor did anyone pay much mind to his speech before the UN General Assembly in 2000, where he specifically pointed out the dangers of jihadi terrorism.

The international reaction after the second series of tests and the letters was several degrees 'hotter' than what had followed the initial tests of 11 May. And yet, there were some realistic voices who singly agreed with India's need to move ahead but in group-speak went along with condemnatory statements. Clinton said that India had made a terrible mistake. He even moved on removing the hurdle of the Pressler Amendment so that arms sanctions on Pakistan could be lifted.[8] Nelson Mandela condemned the tests. The United Nations Security Council expressed its dismay.

On the other hand, France said that sanctions made no sense. They were joined by the UK and Russia, who also said that they would not impose sanctions. Within the US itself, different voices

---

which overthrew the pro-US dictator Fulgencio Batista. It was not till 2014 that the US, under President Obama, reopened its embassy and allowed individuals to travel between the two countries, though much of that was reversed under President Trump.

[8] The Pressler Amendment, named after Sen. Larry Pressler, who moved the statute, was enacted in 1990. It required the US president 'to certify that Pakistan does not possess a nuclear explosive device and that the proposed United States assistance programme will reduce significantly the risk that Pakistan will possess a nuclear explosive device'. On President Bush's refusal to issue any such certificate, US had to limit its economic and military assistance to Pakistan as required by the Pressler Amendment.

now started speaking up. House Speaker Newt Gingrich said
that Clinton was being one-sided, blind to China's doings, and
was in fact selling nuclear technology to them, which was adding
to India's security concerns and making the latter more worried
about China than about Pakistan. Congressman Frank Pallone,
co-founder of the India Caucus (a group within Congress,
sympathetic towards India), opposed the tests but asked Clinton
to consider the situation India was in and put it in perspective.

India had a long and contested border with China and faced
a large PLA presence on its border. The Chinese presence in
Burma was of concern to India as well, and there was Chinese
support for hostile groups operating against the Indian state.
Pallone's recommendation was that the US should take the threat
India faces from China more seriously and consequently work
in closer coordination with India. A few years later, as India's
position as a rising but responsible power was being recognized,
Henry Kissinger backed the tests. Despite his long ties with the
Chinese regime and an old history of rubbing India the wrong
way, he conceded that India had a case for a deterrent against
China. Like many others, he felt that the American sanctions
were probably a mistake.

The Dalai Lama sent a personal letter to Vajpayee, in effect
supporting the decision to test by alluding to the point that the
possession of nuclear weapons would deter any offensive actions
and would therefore ensure peace. Vajpayee was very touched when
he read the letter. Later, the Dalai Lama went on record saying
that India should not be pressured into giving up nuclear weapons;
it should have the same rights as developed countries. His basic
point was that he thought 'nuclear weapons are too dangerous.
Therefore we should make every effort for the elimination of
nuclear weapons.' However, he disagreed with the assumption
that it was all right for a few nations to possess nuclear weapons
when the rest of the world did not; it was undemocratic.

Western news reports also indirectly supported our stand by pointing out that Ghauri was derived from a North Korean missile and was in fact closer to Nodong-I than to Hatf. There were also reports that the CIA was probing its intelligence failure in detecting India's test preparations. Vajpayee's reactions to these developments were manifold. Within a day or so of the tests, he invited Sonia Gandhi for a briefing, where he told her that what he had done was in continuation of what Indira Gandhi and Rajiv Gandhi had started. He specifically told her that weaponization was initiated by Rajiv Gandhi in 1988, and that what was needed now was to validate the designs of nuclear devices, based as they were on the results of the 1974 test. He later told us that her reply was that the 1988 decision had been kept a secret. Later on, before the Parliament session, a number of briefing meetings were held with representatives of various political parties. As a concession to the Congress, a separate briefing was kept only for the two leaders of Opposition in both houses, Sharad Pawar and Manmohan Singh.

For the rest of the month, as the pressure built up internationally, and domestically, Vajpayee gave interviews to a number of foreign journalists. His basic message was that though India was now a nuclear weapons state (NWS), 'ours will not be weapons of aggression'. He said that India would not be cowed down by sanctions, and that it was prepared to sign the CTBT but only as an NWS. We had announced a moratorium on testing, so we had agreed substantially to adhere to the conditions of the CTBT. Significantly, we also announced a 'no-first-use' policy to demonstrate that India's interest was deterrence, not using nuclear weapons as instruments of offence or coercion. China's allegations against India were also dismissed. As Vajpayee made clear, 'After all, the Chinese themselves went for nuclear weapons, claiming that these were necessary for their security.' China had conducted its last, and forty-fifth test, as late as 1996, just before the finalization of the CTBT, but was not willing to extend the same logic to India. Vajpayee hoped that the US would develop a 'better understanding of India's security interests'.

Far from abating, the pressure on India actually started increasing. In hindsight, it seems that there were two mutually reinforcing factors driving the US. One, for fear that Pakistan would follow suit and conduct its own nuclear tests, the US was pressurizing India to deter Pakistani ambitions. Two, the ire caused by the fact that India had managed to test without being stopped had to be taken out on somebody. Narasimha Rao had given the go-ahead to the tests in late 1995, but the Americans had found out about this and had warned India of the consequences. How did they fail this time?

Since the Americans could never be wrong, the fault obviously lay with the Indians. Karl Inderfurth, who had come to India with Bill Richardson, said that the latter and Bruce Riedel had been told by senior Indian officials that 'India would continue to show restraint in the non-proliferation field, and would do nothing to surprise us'. But then they went further. In his testimony to a senate committee, Inderfurth said, 'We were assured privately and publicly, that India would continue to show restraint in the non-proliferation field, and would do nothing to surprise us.' No such assurance was asked for, nor was it given, at the meeting that Vajpayee had with Richardson and his delegation.

Jaswant Singh, in his book *A Call to Honour*, gives an entirely different, and more plausible, explanation. There had been talks about India conducting a Strategic Defence Review before deciding on whether to go ahead and test or not. When asked about this specifically, Jaswant Singh writes that he told the American delegation that 'India's overall security concerns would be central to any decision that the Government would take'.[9] This,

---

[9]   Jaswant Singh, *A Call to Honour* (Rupa: New Delhi, 2006), p. 124.

he says, the Americans took to mean that India would not test till it first conducted the Review. Later on, US Ambassador Dick Celeste, who was going home for a holiday, told Jaswant Singh that he hoped India would not surprise him as he wanted to enjoy his time at home.

Since Pakistan had just tested the Ghauri, Jaswant Singh assumed that he was being asked whether India would basically go ahead with a tit-for-tat test, which he sincerely denied. These meetings were held in mid-April, days after Vajpayee had given the go-ahead to Dr R. Chidambaram and Dr A.P.J. Abdul Kalam, and it is most probable that Jaswant Singh was not aware of this momentous decision. A few years after, when living in the US, I had it on good authority that the US State Department had done detailed discussions about whether Vajpayee really meant it when he said that India would test, and in a clear error of judgement, their conclusion was that he would not go ahead.

What would have been much more galling was that the US satellites had not detected the preparations in the Pokhran range. Again, I have it on good authority that the satellites had captured these images, but in the pre-artificial intelligence days, manual examination was necessary to detect and analyse changes shown in satellite images. Remember that this was 1998, and even the cell phone was in its earliest, primitive 1G days, with internet speeds measured in kilobytes.

The Indians had to be officially painted as perfidious villains, even though the US diplomats conceded in private that the situation was quite different. The US State Department's official spokesperson, James Rubin, told the media that India could say bye-bye to its UN Security Council ambitions. The G8, a group comprising eight of the leading economic powers of the world, met in Birmingham and condemned the tests. The US also strongly condemned Advani's statement that Pakistan must stop its interference in India and specifically its use of jihadi terrorism, else it should be prepared for a proactive response from India, something that would actually have to wait for almost two decades. The US saw Advani's statement as provocative.

Even though Pakistan had publicly rejected America's plea to not test, they gave their word that they 'would not act in haste'. The US was more or less convinced that it had managed to get officials in Pakistan to postpone their tests. This was despite the public Sino–Pakistan consultations being held in Beijing, after which came Pakistan's foreign secretary Shamshad Ahmad's statement highlighting China's promise not to retaliate with sanctions on Pakistan should they go ahead with their test. He added to good effect that, 'China will not ask us to do anything which is not in our national interests.' During his visit to Beijing, Ahmad had met the Chinese foreign minister, Tang Jiaxuan.

The spin that the US gave to it was—or maybe they actually believed in the idea—that they had asked China to pressurize Pakistan. This led to fears that if Pakistan was not going ahead with the tests, it could mean that China had given Pakistan a nuclear umbrella. The US was quick to dispel this notion, with James Rubin stating, 'We are not aware that China is about to extend a nuclear umbrella to any country, *nor would it.*'[10] If this certificate to China was not enough, he added that China had played a very restrained and helpful role in this situation.

Such statements added to the pressure on Vajpayee. I remember that on 17 May, less than one week after the tests, while Vajpayee was at the dais inaugurating the Amrita Institute of Medical Sciences (AIMS) near Kozhikode, Kerala, I received a message, false as it turned out, that Pakistan had tested. I passed on a slip to Vajpayee, and he turned grim, for even though such a move had been expected, it meant that our worst fears about Pakistan's nuclear programme were true.

---

[10] Italics added

The one-day visit to Kerala proved to a blessing, a welcome change from the tensions of Delhi's politics and pressures. On the flight to Kochi from Delhi, Vajpayee was told that the Kerala chief minister, E.K. Nayanar, had made scathing remarks against the Vajpayee government. Vajpayee wondered about the reception he would get in Kerala. I pointed out that Nayanar's criticism was in the form of an article in a CPM party paper, not a public statement, and hence should be seen differently. Nayanar received Vajpayee warmly and they got along very well. When in Delhi, he would often drop in and have long conversations with Vajpayee, despite the language hurdle.

Besides AIMS, Vajpayee also inaugurated Kerala government's Kudumbashree scheme at Malappuram, later the same day. Kudumbashree sought to abolish poverty by empowering women through neighbourhood associations under the larger umbrella of local governments (panchayats). Though NABARD, a Government of India body, was also involved in the scheme, it was nonetheless unusual that a CPM-led state government had invited a BJP prime minister to inaugurate a project in a district carved out to ensure Muslim majority. Nayanar had obviously not heard of political untouchability, or if he had, he did not believe in it!

The drive through Malappuram was an eye-opener, with thousands of Moplah women lining the roads and waving to Vajpayee. This was a spontaneous gesture and an insight into the fact that these women were sending a message of hope and expectation. Two people, besides Nayanar, who played a part in ensuring that there was goodwill generated through the visit, were the Muslim League leader (and later Union minister of state) E. Ahamed, and the journalist T.V.R. Shenoy, both sadly not around any more. I still treasure the gold-bordered *mundu* that E. Ahamed gifted me at the Kozhikode Circuit House, where we spent the night.

Amid the turmoil, the visit to Pokhran took place. We left Delhi on the evening of 19 May and landed a little while later in the furnace that Jaisalmer becomes at that time of the year. In addition to George Fernandes and Jaswant Singh, the other political figure with us was Farooq Abdullah, the chief minister of Jammu and Kashmir, whose presence would unsettle Pakistan. Rajasthan's chief minister, Bhairon Singh Shekhawat, joined us in Jaisalmer, along with Col Sonaram Choudhary, the then Congress MP who, in the 2014 elections, contested as a BJP candidate, defeating Jaswant Singh, who had himself rebelled and fought as an independent. One person Vajpayee wanted to take along, but somehow we'd slipped and could not coordinate, was K.C. Pant. He was then head of the taskforce on national security and as the minister of state (defence) had accompanied Indira Gandhi to Pokhran in 1974 after the first tests. It was an unforgivable lapse on my part.

I had been to Jaisalmer before, but that was in December 1996, when the city's climate is salubrious and inviting. My son and I had hired cycles and went all over. Little did I realize at the time that within a year and a half, I would be back in totally different circumstances. Now, Jaisalmer was sizzling and almost completely unbearable. After the boss settled in, Jaswant Singh very graciously invited Brajesh Mishra and myself to the hotel built by his son on the outskirts of the city. A quiet drink or two, wine for the host and whisky for us, sitting on the veranda overlooking the central courtyard—it was almost ethereal. The hotel was unoccupied, except for a few attendants and us, and was very quiet. Back at the defence mess, I thought, rashly, of having a shower before going to sleep. The tap water was hot enough to boil eggs in or make tea with. I escaped being scalded, so I did the next best thing, which was to fill up two buckets and to have my bath in the morning. The air conditioning tried its best but at 45 degrees, it was no match for the Thar winds.

Despite the name, the actual testing range is not near Pokhran; the nearest village is actually Khetolai, which suffered some cracks in its walls as a result of Operation Shakti. The scene at the testing range was jubilant and chaotic, more like a Sunday school picnic of a bunch of unruly schoolchildren than the solemn visit of the prime minister. This was excusable since the tests were to become a momentous event in Indian history. In 1974, Pokhran-I had caught the world, and India, by surprise, but we had to fudge it by calling it a 'peaceful nuclear explosion'. The world did not believe us and promptly took steps to isolate us from the nuclear supply network. Fuel supplies stopped and the Nuclear Suppliers Group was set up to block India's, and other potential nuclear aspirants', access to necessary supplies.

It was amusing to see the heroes, Dr Chidambaram, Dr A.P.J. Abdul Kalam, Dr K. Santhanam and Dr Anil Kakodkar, in army uniforms, though none of them resembled a *fauji*, especially not Dr Kalam, with his long hair. The men of the Engineer's Regiment mobbed the PM and his team at the site, and the photos show their enthusiasm and camaraderie. Farooq Abdullah led the cheering brigade, whose 'josh' made all of us forget the unbearable heat.

Meanwhile, back in Delhi, reality hit us. The kid-glove treatment of Pakistan continued. US Secretary of State Madeline Albright declared that Pakistan, by not testing, had avoided sanctions. She then certified that Pakistan had 'shown a level of maturity and responsibility India's current leaders have not'. Her advice to Pakistan was that it would 'earn [the] international respect that India yearns for, [its] people deserve but which its leaders have thrown away'. India, according to her, had been 'reckless, rash, unjustified, wrong-headed, unwise', and had committed 'a great historical error'. The torrent of adjectives was simply amazing.

In an article a few days later, the *New York Times* called it an intelligence failure on the part of the USA, which it partly blamed for what it called 'India's sophisticated misinformation'.

As we saw a few years later, in 2003, at the time of the Iraq War, this paper generally buys the US administration's point of view uncritically and then tries to sell it to the world. Vajpayee's letter appeared in the *NYT*. The article drew attention to Bill Richardson's meetings in Delhi, referred to earlier, where he heard what he wanted to hear, not what was being said to him. It also referred to Foreign Secretary K. Raghunath's visit to Washington, D.C. and his meeting with Clinton's national security adviser, Sandy Berger. To be fair, the article also mentioned that India was expected to respond to Pakistan's Ghauri test.

The Vajpayee government tried to defuse the tension while maintaining its priorities. Advani called upon Pakistan to roll back its anti-India policies and stop sponsoring terrorism in Kashmir. Pakistan was advised to join India in the common pursuit of peace and development. The warning attached to this message was that anything else would be costly. This message apparently did not land, neither with Pakistan nor with the USA. This was clear a few days later when President Clinton called Nawaz Sharif for the third time. The latter asked Clinton to pressure India to not provoke Pakistan. Clinton assured him that the US was monitoring the situation and 'would ensure that the peace and stability of South Asia was not disturbed'. Further, the US said that it recognized that 'the Indian tests had not only dealt a severe blow to the non-proliferation regime, but more importantly, they had created a serious security threat to Pakistan'. Just before Pakistan actually conducted the test, Gohar Ayub attacked India for indulging in what he called 'brinkmanship'. He then went on to directly threaten India, saying that it would not be able to absorb the strike of Ghauri.

Building on what we said was India's responsible behaviour, especially our lack of interest in taking an aggressive pose, we announced a moratorium on tests, and said that we were ready to convert the announcement into a legal obligation, which would be possible if the CTBT was opened and renegotiated. Our spokesperson quietly chided the US for James Rubin's use of intemperate language against Advani's statement.

In the US itself, there began a re-evaluation of the efficacy of their policies. A leaked White House assessment was that the sanctions hurt the US more than anybody else. It said that in the execution of such policies, the US was 'shooting ourselves in the foot'. The White House also expressed frustration that Congressional sanctions impeded foreign policy. This was as much a salve to Pakistan, which stood to face sanctions in case it tested, and its economy was in a far worse condition than India's. Contrary to the hopes of the White House, which wanted an extremely successful summit with China, the US Congress voted to block satellite sales to China, on the grounds that Clinton's decision to allow the sale was not in national interest. This, as we in Delhi hoped, would somewhat dampen Clinton's attempt to form a G2 with China.

Even as Pakistani preparations at ground zero were progressing, we were trying to figure out how the US sanctions would impact the US$11 billion India–US bilateral trade. In present-day terms, this does not look like a big enough amount, but in 1998 this was a significant figure. As the Pokhran '*hawa*' was subsiding, the political temperature in Delhi was rising in direct proportion to the proximity of the first full-fledged budget session of Parliament since the Vajpayee government took office. Veteran parliamentarian Purno Sangma, apparently still smarting from having lost the speaker's election, attacked the government. He mentioned that both the BJP manifesto and the National Agenda on Governance had talked about exercising the nuclear option, but that this did not find a place in the President's address. His conclusion was that the omission was due to pressure from the US. This was just the beginning.

The new Congress (I) president, Sonia Gandhi, said there were no credible reasons for the government to have carried out the tests. Like many others, she shared the fear that India's relations with Pakistan and China would worsen as a consequence. Then, she mentioned the secrecy with which this decision had been taken and executed, and concluded that there was lack of transparency. Carrying on, she said that there was no evidence that the tests were conducted for security reasons; instead, she felt that the nuclear issue had been thrust upon India. Her logic was that India had acquired nuclear-weapons capability in 1974 itself, and not after the 1998 tests. Why was no Strategic Defence Review carried out? How had the security environment deteriorated? How had our security been enhanced by carrying out the tests?

As Parliament met for its regular session, Vajpayee read out a detailed statement in the Lok Sabha on 27 May 1998. This statement had been prepared with great care, and a lot of research, done by officers of the MEA and PMO, went into it. Vajpayee's own memory of earlier events, including those of the parliamentary debates, was very useful, particularly when deciding what to prise out from where.

Essentially, Vajpayee traced India's nuclear journey to the decisions taken by India's leaders in 1947 and in the years that followed. They, he recalled, chose self-reliance and freedom of thought and of action, refusing to take sides in the Cold War and adopting the difficult but correct path of non-alignment. India, Vajpayee explained, realized that a nuclear-free world would not only enhance its own security but also the security of all nations. Remembering Nehru, whose death anniversary fell on that day, Vajpayee said that disarmament had always been a major plank of India's foreign policy. But India's many attempts to push for disarmament over the decades did not result in anything tangible; instead, the current situation was a nuclear apartheid, where five countries had a legal monopoly over possessing nuclear weapons. Hence India did not, very consciously, sign the Non-Proliferation Treaty (1967) nor the Comprehensive Nuclear-Test-Ban Treaty (1996).

India had demonstrated its nuclear capability in 1974, and Vajpayee reminded the members of Parliament that Indira Gandhi, speaking on the nuclear issue, had told Parliament in 1968 that 'we shall be guided entirely by self-enlightenment and considerations of our national security'. He complimented all governments since 1974 for safeguarding India's nuclear option by not signing the CTBT, despite the mounting international pressure. Having established a continuity in policy, running from Nehru to Indira Gandhi to her successors, Vajpayee was being true to the facts, even if it meant underplaying the huge courage that he'd exhibited in deciding to carry out the tests. Despite demonstrating its capability in 1974, India had exercised restraint for twenty-four years, since it believed in a nuclear-free world. But India's different proposals to that effect did not get any positive response. Vajpayee alluded to Rajiv Gandhi's 1988 grand proposal for nuclear disarmament. Restraint, Vajpayee said, can only come from strength, not from indecision or doubt.

He situated his decision to test in the context of the India's deteriorating security environment due to missile and nuclear proliferation in its neighbourhood. The increase in the number of nuclear weapons and the deployment of sophisticated delivery systems could not be ignored. Worse, India faced terrorism, militancy and clandestine war. In the absence of any movement towards disarmament, and keeping in mind the needs of national security, the difficult decision to test had to be taken. Again, implicitly linking it to Nehru, Vajpayee said that with this decision, India's policy of self-reliance could be continued.

Taking his argument further, Vajpayee made it clear that India did not seek the status of a Nuclear Weapons State from anybody because it was already one. This was a reality, and with this added strength came added responsibilities. India's nuclear weapons were not to be used for aggression or for mounting threats to other countries. Rather, Vajpayee explained, they were weapons of self-defence, which would prevent India from being subject to nuclear threats or coercion in the future. India did not intend to engage in an arms race. Vajpayee announced that India had declared a voluntary moratorium on underground nuclear testing and was taking steps to convert this into a de jure obligation.

As if he was anticipating the 2019 Balakot attack, Vajpayee drew attention to the requirement of 'focused leadership which attends to security needs' and pledged that he would do so 'as a sacred duty'. He ended by again emphasizing the continuity of policies of the previous five decades and speaking about the sense of responsibility and obligations that came with being an ancient civilization.

Sitting in the officers' gallery, barely ten feet away from Vajpayee, I thought the performance was masterful. It was neither triumphal nor self-congratulatory. Rather, it was understated, conciliatory, factual and appreciative of Nehru, Indira Gandhi and all past governments. Even an impartial observer would have concluded that it answered all the domestic doubts raised about the rationale behind the tests. But the vintage Vajpayee, so much missed in the present times by those who opposed him politically then, failed to convince his critics in May 1998, not because of what he'd said, but for who he was and what he stood for.

Speaking for the Congress (I), veteran diplomat, sometime minister and author Natwar Singh sought to pick holes in Vajpayee's arguments. Singh said that while there was consensus in keeping the nuclear option open, there was no consensus on exercising that option. Singh added that Vajpayee had 'taken the profound step of reorienting our foreign policy without taking us into confidence'. It did not occur to those who supported this line of reasoning that an option that is never supposed to be exercised is not an option at all. Or, that in the international climate that had increasingly delegitimized nuclear weapons for all except the P5—the five permanent members of UNSC—it wasn't feasible to have an open debate on whether India should test.

The common theme of the Opposition, first articulated by Natwar Singh and then by members of the left parties among others, was that the BJP government was essentially guided by its political compulsions, rather than by the reasons cited, in reversing the nuclear policy followed since 1974. They probably failed to notice that internal cohesion within the NDA, or the lack of it, was not affected by the Pokhran tests. In fact, while this debate was on, Mamata Banerjee announced that her Trinamool Congress would boycott the Parliament session in protest against Vajpayee government's 'indifferent attitude' towards West Bengal.

Advani's statement asking Pakistan to join India in the common struggle for poverty abolition and warning it to desist from sponsoring terrorism in India, failing which India would be forced to take proactive measures—a statement which had so upset the Americans—was also questioned. What did 'proactive' mean? Singh specifically asked if it involved hot pursuit. In his reply, a day or so later, Advani clarified that he never said 'hot pursuit'. Would a country wanting to carry out hot-pursuit campaigns into areas administered by another country first publicly debate or even announce it?

Even as the Indian parliament was debating the nuclear tests, Pakistan's preparations for carrying out their own tests were almost complete. In a last-minute effort to dissuade Pakistan from proceeding, Clinton called Nawaz Sharif for their fourth conversation in just over two weeks. His argument was simple—if Pakistan tests, it would walk into the trap that India had set for it. Clinton tried to persuade Sharif that India would welcome Pakistan's tests, as it would defuse the pressure on them. But Clinton's expectations were unrealistic, and as Sharif informed him, the decision was out of his hands. The Americans record Sharif telling them, 'I don't think that I will last in office for more than 2–3 days if I don't test.'

More and more reports emerged, establishing that Pakistan actually did not need to test at all and that its nuclear programme had been built clandestinely, in violation of international law, in collaboration with China. According to the respected defence journal *Jane's Defence Weekly*, the Pakistani nuclear arsenal was basically of Chinese design. China had been 'extraordinarily' generous because Pakistani nuclear scientists had shared with them secrets about the process to enrich uranium to weapons-grade using high-speed centrifuges. In turn, China shared nuclear bomb designs from its 1966 Lop Nor test. Pakistan had to modify these so that the missiles could be carried by the American-built F-16s.

China had, in fact, test-fired the Pakistani-modified designs, so there was no need for Pakistan to test. The Pakistani delay in testing (May 1998) was on account of problems with the trigger. The *Jane's* report also confirmed that Ghauri's range was only 600 km, and not 1500 km as it was claimed. The report said that, on the other hand, India's nuclear and missile programme was largely home-grown and far more advanced. Critically, India had a command structure, so that while it was producing nuclear warheads, political clearance was needed to fit them on to missiles.

It was on the second day of the debate on the nuclear issue that we got confirmed news that Pakistan had tested. Many Opposition members pilloried the government for napping; this was despite the fact that the tests were widely expected. Pakistan claimed that it had carried out five tests, even though the signals only picked up one. Pakistan also announced it had mated the nuclear warhead to the Ghauri missile, taking China into confidence. Sharif thanked China for appreciating Pakistan's concerns. Later that evening, as Vajpayee left Parliament House, the media accosted him.

He strongly denied that Pakistan's tests were in reaction to ours; instead, he said that we pre-empted their preparations. One could detect a hint of anger in his reply.

To go back a bit, earlier in the day, during the parliamentary debate, representatives of the Congress had blamed the Indian government for Pakistan's tests and for initiating a nuclear arms race. Somebody reminded the Congress that their 1991 manifesto mentioned the need for carrying out a nuclear test. What was left unsaid was the fact that this manifesto was prepared when Rajiv Gandhi was the Congress president and contender for prime ministership. Replying to the debate in the Lok Sabha, Vajpayee again made the point that unless Pakistan had already been ready, it could not have organized everything and carried out the tests within sixteen days. He said that Pakistan was using the design of China's old medium-range ballistic missile, tested in 1961. He was clear that Pakistan's back-to-back tests showed the limitations of the United States' non-proliferation policy, which had special provisions targeted against Pakistan. Unfortunately, the US did not agree with India that China's support of Pakistan placed India in a disadvantaged position.

The international reaction to Pakistan's test was rather interesting. The US imposed sanctions on Pakistan, which was expected, since they were legally bound to do so, but its statements were quite soft on the latter. The White House spokesperson, Mike McCurry, almost justified the tests. He said, 'It would be accurate to say that the Prime Minister clearly struggled with what was, for him, a very difficult decision . . . He sounded, in short, like someone who is very pained by a very difficult decision.' McCurry pointed out that the Glenn Amendment sanctions to be imposed on Pakistan were automatic. However, he added, 'there was a qualitative difference to India's disadvantage'. According to him, Nawaz Sharif was straightforward, while India was manifestly not. These statements sidestepped years of US apprehension about

China–Pak nuclear cooperation, which had led to the adoption of the Pressler Amendment.

The European Union was caught by surprise, having just condemned India and praised Pakistan for its restraint. The British foreign secretary, Robin Cook, who had been admonished by Prime Minister Gujral less than a year ago, expressed his dismay.[11] Japan imposed sanctions on Pakistan again, as expected. The Australians, who had dangled a bait of US$6 million, by diverting the moneys intended for India, withdrew their offer (did Pakistan even notice?). China, who was on board with the tests, as revealed by the Pakistani prime minister, expressed deep regret initially but was quick to balance this mild statement by blaming India instead. It further rescued Pakistan at the UN Security Council, whose statement of condemnation included not just Pakistan but also India.

Even as Pakistan said that it had conducted another test, the focus remained on India. As if nothing had happened and as if an Indian prime minister's statement in Parliament had no meaning, the US State Department's spokesperson, James Rubin, rejected Vajpayee's statement on a moratorium and his offer on no-first-use. Instead, India was told to sign the CTBT, to not nuclearize and to join the negotiations on the Fissile Material Cut-Off Treaty (FMCT). The US was not done. Rubin linked the nuclear test to Kashmir and therefore expressed the need 'to take steps to reduce the possibility of escalation, to reduce the possibilities of conflict in Kashmir, and to deal with the underlying dispute in Kashmir'. Clearly, Rubin was reflecting the views of his boss, Secretary of

---

[11] Cook, in a visit to Pakistan, reportedly made loose comments about Kashmir and offered to mediate between India and Pakistan. Gujral, then on a visit to Egypt, lambasted the British for Partition, which was the cause of the problem, and called Britain a 'third-rate power' that should mind its own business. Of course, both sides denied these statements but they were widely believed to be true.

State Madeline Albright, whose links, and disappointment, with the Indian case on Kashmir were said to go back to the time of her father, Josef Korbel, who, in his heyday, was the chairman of the United Nations Commission on India and Pakistan.

The beauty of US democracy, and this is something that must be appreciated, was on full view in this debate on the tests. CIA director, James Woolsey, publicly said that China had a 'major hand' in Pakistan's nuclear and missile programme. US media reports said that in relaxing export controls in respect of China, the US further allowed China to help Pakistan. In fact, the state department had acknowledged in 1996 that the 'the entire Pakistan strategic weapons programme should be styled "made in China"'. Such assistance and collaboration covered a whole gamut of issues. For example, nuclear-weapons design, ring magnets, M-11 short-range missiles, special furnaces, nuclear material, etc. In effect, the CIA had also said the same thing. The much-respected Stockholm International Peace Research Institute (SIPRI) confirmed that China had given short-range missiles to Pakistan, which the latter did not deny.

In passing, we noticed that after conducting its tests, Pakistan rejected the idea of a moratorium on future testing but said that it was amenable to dialogue with India. There was much scepticism about the actual number of tests that Pakistan had carried out. Reliable reports state that the first series comprised only four tests, not five, of which three failed. There was a single test on 30 May. Which is possibly why there was so little international attention given to Pakistan, while Vajpayee had his hands full in this regard.

Clinton's determined bonhomie did not help. The US and China were coordinating their stands on the nuclear tests. Spokesperson Rubin, 'We all have to bear in mind the evolution that has occurred in China's policies, including a commitment that we believe they are honouring not to assist unsafeguarded nuclear facilities, especially those in Pakistan.' As history bears out, this statement was as far from the truth as possible, but it is important to mention it as an illustration of the kind of pressures being exerted on Vajpayee, since his actions had upset the geopolitical calculations of the US and China.

It was with these two countries that India faced the most challenges, and it was fascinating to see how Vajpayee coped with them. The results were visible within the year, when the subcontinent faced a crisis that threatened power dynamics the world over. There was a clear difference between the attitudes of India and Pakistan. Our meticulous preparations, sensible decision-making and some luck averted disaster, but at the end of May 1998, all this seemed unlikely, with no sign of any light at the end of the tunnel. Domestically and internationally, the Vajpayee government appeared wobbly, but it was only our faith in India's manifest destiny, and our belief that the decision to test was in the national interest, that kept us going.

THE SRI LANKAN FOREIGN MINISTER, Lakshman Kadirgamar, visited Beijing a few days after our tests and said words to the effect that his country felt threatened by the situation in the subcontinent and wanted to help rescue Sino–Indian relations, as he argued Sri Lanka had done after the 1962 war. This was in reply to the Chinese foreign minister Tang Jiaxuan's request for Sri Lankan help in smoothening 'ruffled feathers'. About ten days after his Beijing visit, Kadirgamar visited Delhi and a meeting was fixed with Vajpayee, who was also the foreign minister at the time. Kadirgamar's statements in Beijing had been noted in Delhi but ignored. The general belief was that his visit was likely triggered by some rather strong statements made by a politician in Chennai on the Lankan Tamil issue. It was simply inconceivable that Sri Lanka, or anybody else, could act as a mediator to resolve tensions between India and China.

Moreover, it was not as if India and China were not talking to each other, or their tensions had degenerated into a dispute threatening peace in the region.

Unfortunately, Kadirgamar took his self-appointed task rather seriously, something he would regret doing. Vajpayee was polite but firm; his message to Kadirgamar was direct. Vajpayee did not raise his voice or use strong language; in fact, he was absolutely polite. But the message was hard and direct. Vajpayee told Kadirgamar that if he felt unease about the situation, he should have come to Delhi instead of going to Beijing and making public statements. Over the fifteen minutes or so that the meeting lasted, the message that India had never favoured third-party mediation was hammered home, as was the point that Sri Lanka, as a friend, should frankly share its fears with India. It was a lesson in diplomacy that is not taught in diplomatic academies. It was also a lesson in management—how to pull up somebody, effectively and without any drama.

The only other time, I saw this aspect of Vajpayee was just before the break with Jayalalithaa that brought down his government in April 1999. This must have been a few weeks before the final collapse. AIADMK's K.R. Janarthanan, a minister of state in Vajpayee's government, with important responsibilities in finance and personnel, made some public statements that challenged Vajpayee's authority as PM. Janarthanan was summoned and Vajpayee expressed his displeasure. Inside the soft exterior, Vajpayee was far more a person of steel than was apparent.

But China was not going away anytime soon. Vajpayee reacted strongly against the statement of the UN Security Council on the Pakistan test, which had unnecessarily included India. He advised the permanent members, the P5, to work on disarmament, and rejected all references to third-party mediation. It was at this moment that the new Chinese ambassador formally presented his credentials to the Indian President.[12] In his speech, President Narayanan extended an olive branch and tried to de-hyphenate Pakistan from the India–China equation. He said, 'The bonds that united India and China did not impinge upon the interests of any other country in Asia or in the world . . . the common bonds between the two countries actually contributed to friendship and co-operation and peace and security in the region and in the world.'

The message did not resonate in Beijing, which, a few days later, blamed India for initiating an 'arms race' and threatened to resume testing, as allowed under special circumstances by the CTBT. The hypocrisy of the CTBT as a deterrent policy has already been highlighted in Chapter 2, 'A Hung Parliament'. President Jiang Zemin himself accused India of 'targeting China since it aspired for a long period of time to be the main power in South Asia'. However, he ruled out testing. The Chinese spokesperson, echoing the earlier statement of Canada, said that the bomb would not get 'you into the Security Council'. According to the Chinese, this time echoing a number of statements of the Indian Opposition parties, the Indian test was a case of a coalition government trying to win public support by acting tough. It added that these tests had been 'condemned by far-sighted peace-loving Indians'.

The Sino–American efforts led to the Security Council calling upon both India and Pakistan to refrain from further tests and suggested that the two countries should instead hold talks on the 'root causes of tensions, including Kashmir'. This was strong language and could not be ignored. Vajpayee publicly stated that India was ready to talk to Pakistan on all issues, including Kashmir.

---

[12] This is a diplomatic ceremony where a newly appointed ambassador appears before her/his host country's head of state and presents her/his appointment order as ambassador, only after which she/he can function as ambassador.

However, he was upset with the language of the UNSC resolution and called it 'unhelpful'. The Ministry of External Affairs went further and called the resolution grotesque for asking India to end testing, which the government had already announced.

Realizing that India had to make its case heard, Vajpayee sent Brajesh Mishra, the principal secretary to the PM, as his special envoy to Russia, France and Britain. In France, whose reaction to the test was the most realistic, Mishra met Jacques Chirac and his foreign minister, Hubert Védrine. In Britain, he met Tony Blair and Robin Cook. The Russian establishment was generally with India, but Yeltsin was not very inclined to go against the American line.

Sending a special envoy was necessary, as in the absence of a full-time foreign minister, the government was constrained in its ability to engage foreign governments at high levels, often outside the purely formal diplomatic frameworks. Essentially, a special envoy must have political clout, the ability to bypass normal bureaucratic channels, enable an informal exchange of views and help narrow differences. Jaswant Singh was the natural interlocutor as far as the Americans were concerned; in fact, *they* reached out to him. However, unlike with the countries Brajesh Mishra was reaching out to, the conversation with America was going to be long and difficult. Ultimately, it would be the USA that would determine when and how India was to be brought in from the nuclear 'cold'.

However, even before the dialogue with the Americans could begin, they were already shifting the goalposts. Accordingly, they seemed ready to wipe the Chinese slate clean of all past nuclear, missile, chemical and other transgressions. To quote Rubin, '. . . reality dictates that we focus on what co-operation we can get now, and it has been significant.' On the Pentagon's report that Pakistan had mated nuclear warheads with its M-11, also obtained from China, Rubin justified American inaction by saying, 'We have not

determined that Pakistan has received M-11 missiles from China.'
Further, on proliferation, something well-established, he said that
'the Chinese government behaves in a way that would have been
unthinkable ten years ago . . . our cooperative responsibility with
them enhances the security of the United States, making it easier
for us to fight the battle against proliferation'. If this was not
enough, China's past proliferation was explained away by him as
something that happened due to the inexperience of the Chinese
in export control regime.

Keeping up the pressure on India, State Department official
Karl Inderfurth told a US congressional committee that, 'We are
only recognizing the international fact of life that Kashmir is the
fundamental dispute between the two countries . . . At the same
time, we do believe that China will be the key to addressing the
security concerns of the sub-continent. We will encourage China
to play a constructive role in South Asia.' This was a double blow
to India. First, by making Kashmir central to the nuclear tests,
the entire logic of Chinese nuclear proliferation posing a threat
to India was sought to be sidestepped. The Kashmir question was
picked up by all—the UNSC, G8, EU, etc. Second, by seeking to
make China the arbiter, the US gave India a tough pill to swallow.
The fact that Clinton was about to go to China and make his visit
a success was written all over these two propositions of Inderfurth.
Interestingly, newspapers reported that the US was keen that
the US–China joint military exercises be announced during the
Clinton visit to China, while the Chinese were still non-committal
on the timing. Later, Inderfurth somewhat toned down his stand
and clarified that though Kashmir was a bilateral issue between
India and Pakistan, it was 'an international reality that cannot be
wished away'. He tried to dispel the notion that there was a tilt in
the United States' attitude towards the tests.

The tests had thoroughly discredited the non-proliferation
regime, which was essentially unequal, since it gave a monopoly

over possession of nuclear weapons to five countries based on an arbitrary date and made it illegal for others to join the nuclear club. The whole idea of disarmament behind the NPT was distorted, and it led to a 'nuclear power apartheid'. There was widespread criticism. But Madeleine Albright, the US secretary of state, did not agree that the non-proliferation regime had failed. Clearly, the Indian tests had unnerved her. In her speech at the Stimson Centre, an institution dedicated to upholding the non-proliferation regime, she said that the 'India–Pakistan blasts do not, as some suggest, discredit the NPT regime. To the contrary, they illustrate its logic and its necessity. India's leaders predicted that the tests would make India more secure, more respected . . . the leaders are wrong.' She added that till just the previous month, India and Pakistan could look forward to better relations with the US and other powers, to push their Security Council ambitions, but for the time being those hopes had been demolished. Later, asked about China's role in the Pakistani tests, Albright diverted attention and said that India's test did not enhance its security, instead 'it lowered respect for India and its people'.

The hardball shadow negotiations that Vajpayee had entered into continued to increase in pitch. The G8 announced that they would block all fresh loans to India and Pakistan. They also set up a task force on disarmament. In response, India said that any criticism would be short-sighted and counterproductive. To queer the pitch, Pakistan also declared a moratorium after having repeatedly ruled it out. They said that they wanted to initiate talks with India, with the issue of concluding a 'no nuclear test agreement' on the agenda. Signing such an agreement would have effectively reduced the Indian tests to being solely Pakistan focused, which they most decidedly were not. The MEA replied that such a no-nuclear-test agreement was not necessary, as a moratorium was in place already. India offered dates for talks with Pakistan, but the latter, in turn, offered a different set of dates.

It was against this backdrop that Jaswant Singh met his US counterpart, Strobe Talbott, the deputy secretary of state and an old friend of Clinton's. In fact, it was said that when the two of them were Rhodes scholars in the UK in the 1960s, it was Talbott who was seen as more cerebral, whose lead others followed. A scholar who specialized in Russia and a journalist of long standing, Talbott had acquired the kind of political capital that made him an effective negotiator.

The United Nations General Assembly had convened in a special session to discuss drug trafficking. Jaswant Singh was sent to represent India, so that he could meet Talbott and begin the conversation. The meeting lasted two and a half hours over lunch and both sides described it as frank and cordial. It was agreed that the dialogue would continue. Over the next couple of months, Singh and Talbott met often at different locations, even airports! Both the interlocutors have written about it, in books that make for fascinating reading.

True to form, the US planted a story which said that it was the Indians who had asked for the meeting, which I knew to be false. I clearly remember Jaswant Singh asking Vajpayee *'Toh main unko kya jawab doon* (What reply should I give them)?' This was before Vajpayee had agreed to begin the dialogue with the US. There was considerable scepticism brewing in the internal, informal meetings about what the talks with the US would achieve. Vajpayee was clear, though he did not articulate it directly, that India must not only *engage* with the US but move away from the beaten path and forge good relations. That is why he gave his full support to the Jaswant Singh–Talbott dialogue, despite considerable scepticism. In retrospect, his decision made a lot of sense, and it became evident in less than a year, when Kargil happened.

Even though the two countries had started their dialogue at such a senior level, the Clinton administration kept building pressure on Vajpayee relentlessly through their public statements and newspaper articles. And so, we had to be on guard constantly, though occasionally one could sense the emergence of a marginal change in the United States' stance. Clinton had a certain vision of China's role in the subcontinent and what he saw as its responsibilities within South Asia and beyond, but his proposal on China's position found no takers in India. In fact, China also made it clear later that it was not keen to mediate. It preferred that India and Pakistan talk bilaterally. Clinton added that because of its history with both countries, 'China must be part of any ultimate resolution in the matter'. This was an interesting statement, delightfully ambiguous, for it could have been interpreted to mean that since China is an integral part of the problem, it had the responsibility to take an active part in the solution. The evidence for this was weak, as just a week later, while in China, Clinton said that together, they were two great nations who 'have a special responsibility to the world . . . [and therefore] appreciate your [China's] efforts at peace and stability in Korea and South Asia.'

Going back to his pre-visit remarks, Clinton added that had China been isolated and the US not worked with it, 'would China have agreed to stop assistance to Iran for its nuclear program, to terminate its assistance to unsafeguarded nuclear facilities such as those in Pakistan, to tighten its export control system?' History would prove him wrong on these points, as China itself confirmed a decade later when it first informed the Nuclear Suppliers Group (NSG) that it had 'forgotten' to list its assistance to two unsafeguarded facilities. Just when this sank in, they informed that there were two more such facilities assisted by them in Pakistan, which they had also forgotten to inform the NSG about.

'Over time, the more we bring China into the world the more the world will bring freedom to China . . . China can only reach its full potential if its people are free to reach theirs.' This touching faith that Clinton had in China would not be taken seriously at present, but back in 1998, the hubris that had resulted from post-Cold War triumphalism was not yet obvious. The expectation was that every nation would evolve into a clone of the Anglo–Saxon market-led liberal democracy. Contextually, Clinton was building up momentum to his forthcoming China visit.

Vajpayee went on a public-relations overdrive, meeting correspondents of the Western media. For example, he expressed his concerns to the French daily *Le Figaro* about the China–Pakistan nexus. He balanced it by saying that in recent years India's own relationship with China, which he called a great civilization, had improved. This nuanced messaging was absolutely necessary to establish, for the rest of the world, India's maturity and sense of responsibility. This gained greater credibility as Vajpayee's special envoy made visits to leading countries and the India–US dialogue moved forward.

Gradually, due to India's consistent efforts at bringing its security concerns in front of the international community, India's case gained support and people started speaking up. Congressman Frank Pallone told the US administration not to link Kashmir to the nuclear tests and warned against third-party mediation. He argued that India conducted nuclear tests because of the China–Pakistan nuclear and military nexus. He questioned Clinton's proposed role for China, saying that China could not mediate when it was aligned to one party. Similarly, Senator Connie Mack criticized the US administration for rewarding authoritarian China and penalizing democratic India. Reports in the international media mentioned the placement of Chinese missiles in the Qinghai province on the Tibetan plateau, targeted at India, Russia, etc.

There seemed the gentlest of shifts in the US administration's stand. Speaking to CNN in June 1998, Albright mentioned Kashmir but agreed that the issue could be settled bilaterally. Inderfurth ruled out any mediatory role for the US but emphasized their interest in seeing India and Pakistan engaged in dialogue. This was basically in response to Pakistan, which played up the risk of heightened tensions in the region and asked for third-party mediation. The result of all this was that even as positions in the US shifted, the 'K word' and the India–Pakistan hyphenation remained central to their worldview. Of course, long-held positions are not given up easily, even when the facts on the ground have changed.

As part of the effort to make India's case better understood, and to convey that Delhi did not in the least feel contrite about what it had done, George Fernandes spoke to the *New York Times* about the hypocritical attitude of the US and Clinton administration. His basic grouse was that the US trusted China but not India. He explained that India only sought deterrence against China and Pakistan. Fernandes was critical of the P5 'shutting out countries like India that believe they need nuclear weapons for their own defence'. He argued that the minimum deterrence India talked about was not equivalent to the USSR–USA arms race of the Cold War. Also, that India's decision must be contextualized by the fact that Pakistan was in receipt of nuclear and missile technology from China.

At the end of Clinton's visit, there was a US–China joint statement on South Asia, which called upon India and Pakistan to desist from carrying on more tests and asked them to sign the CTBT. 'We stand ready to assist in the implementation of confidence-building measures between them.' Both countries also agreed to not sell missiles, missile equipment, etc., to either India or Pakistan, but strangely remained silent about the sale of missile designs.

Naturally, India dismissed the statement issued, saying that the 'approach of the two countries was reflective of hegemonistic mentality of a bygone era that was completely unacceptable and out of place'. We further asked how the US and China could 'arrogate to yourself, jointly or individually, responsibility for peace, stability and security in the region'. India could not help but point out the hypocrisy of these countries who talked about proliferation when they, directly or indirectly, had contributed to unabashed proliferation of nuclear and delivery systems in India's neighbourhood. This led to the Americans toning down the temperature, and Inderfurth acknowledged that both India and Pakistan had security concerns and must talk to each other.

India was simultaneously developing its own options. While in Manali, on a week-long holiday, Vajpayee hosted the Russian minister for atomic energy, Yevgeny Adamov, who was accompanied by Dr R. Chidambaram, the chairman of the Atomic Energy Commission and one of the key players behind Operation Shakti. During Adamov's visit to India, the two countries signed a bilateral nuclear deal for a 2x1000 MW nuclear power plant at Kudankulam. This was a genuine diplomatic coup, the negotiations for which had begun during previous governments but were followed through even in the aftermath of the nuclear tests. Fortunately, the Russian establishment, despite Yeltsin, were able to assert their autonomy. The signing of this agreement showed Russia's open defiance of the US-led sanctions regime. The leader of the Russian Communist Party, Vladimir Zhirinovsky, and others openly supported India's tests.

A day or so after Vajpayee met the Russian minister at Manali, we flew to Shimla, where the chief minister of Himachal Pradesh, Prem Kumar Dhumal, wanted to demonstrate public support for the BJP regime. He had just come into office after the close, indecisive verdict, propelled by some deft manoeuvring by the then BJP prabhari for Himachal Pradesh, as described in Chapter 3, 'The Incomplete Mandate'. Besides demonstrating public support for the Vajpayee government, the fact that the BJP formed a government in Himachal for the first time had to be publicly acknowledged.

President Narayanan was also in Shimla for a summer break. After calling on the President and briefing him on the latest developments, Vajpayee addressed a very large and celebratory meeting at the Mall. He used this occasion to send a message out to the world. He called upon Nawaz Sharif for a dialogue on all bilateral issues, including Kashmir. He said that the two sides should work for a revival of the Shimla spirit, recalling the 1972 agreement between Indira Gandhi and Zulfiqar Ali Bhutto, where the two countries had agreed to settle their disputes bilaterally. He assured Pakistan that Prithvi missiles were not being deployed against them. Since there was a lot of uncertainty about the effect of the sanctions on the Indian economy, he explained that the US sanctions would have limited impact and called them counterproductive.

Later, Vajpayee would formally write to Sharif, calling for a dialogue and reiterating the points he'd raised in Shimla. This was in line with his firm belief in India's need to have a peaceful neighbourhood. He used to often tell people that one could choose one's friends but not one's neighbours. It was inconceivable that India could be seen as a global player if its own backyard was unstable, or if it was bogged down in local disputes. As a result, within the span of a fortnight, there was formal announcement that Vajpayee and Sharif would meet by the end of July in Colombo during the SAARC summit.

Soon after the Shimla speech, the second round of the Jaswant Singh–Talbott talks was fixed to be held in Frankfurt in early July 1998. The US diplomatic pressure was persistent, with James Rubin, reflecting the state department's views, basically rubbishing India's pitch for a credible minimum deterrence on the eve of these talks. Rubin said that they 'strongly believe that the deployment of nuclear weapons in South Asia would be a dangerous precedent – one that would seriously undermine the security of both India and Pakistan'. Once again, Vajpayee had to show flexibility in order to address some of the genuine fears of many well-wishers, who were alarmed at what they thought, wrongly, was a dangerous situation in South Asia. Brajesh Mishra put forward India's position that the country was willing to sign the CTBT, though with a few caveats. One, the sanctions had to be lifted; two, India should have access to dual-use technology; and three, that certain reactors would be kept out of the International Atomic Energy Agency (IAEA) inspections, which meant that India retained the right to reprocess plutonium for its security needs. It took another ten years, but finally, without signing the CTBT, India all but joined the nuclear club.

RETURNING TO 1998, THE ONE-STEP-FORWARD-ONE-STEP-BACK scenario in the Indo–US relations continued. Albright told the world that it was not China or the US–China bonhomie but India's domestic politics that had led to the tests. She added that China played a 'significant and helpful role in trying to move India and Pakistan back from the brink of nuclear arms race'. These remarks were completely off the mark, and anybody with even a limited understanding of India's regional dynamics can estimate how wrong she was. Fortunately, Senator Daniel Patrick Moynihan, former US ambassador to India, criticized Albright and said that, contradictory to her assessment, it was very much China's nuclear and missile assistance to Pakistan that had forced India to test. He regretted that US policy towards South Asia was still based on the Shanghai Communiqué between Nixon and the Chinese. This document declared its support for 'the Pakistan government and people in their struggle [against India] to preserve their independence and sovereignty and the people of Jammu & Kashmir in their struggle for the right of self-determination.'

Even as the third round of the Indo–US diplomatic talks was initiated, when it was announced that Talbott was to be in Delhi from 20–21 July, India faced another extremely provocative action. Dr R. Chidambaram, who had to attend a routine meeting of crystallographers in the United States, was denied a visa by

the US Embassy, no doubt because he was the head of India's
Atomic Energy Commission. He was gracious in his response,
saying that if he knew that he would be denied a visa, he would
not have applied in the first place, to avoid unnecessary bilateral
embarrassment. When a few days later the US gave its reasons
for the rejection, it only made matters worse. The legal provision
cited were those relating to 'espionage, sabotage, illegal export of
technology'. Rationally, none of these was defensible.

The economic situation of Pakistan was making the US
nervous, though the latter did nothing to help reduce Islamabad's
belligerence towards India. Pakistan's foreign exchange reserves
were drying up, and there was widespread panic in the country.
The US State Department made an extraordinary statement on
the economic sanctions imposed by them on Pakistan, saying
that their sanctions should ideally have roughly the same effect
on India as they do on Pakistan; but this was not possible, as the
two economies were of vastly different sizes. In other words, India
was being blamed for the disproportionate effect of US sanctions
on Pakistan!

In order to deal with a situation that seemed to be getting out
of control, the US Senate gave Clinton unprecedented powers of
sanction waivers. This was soon followed by an announcement
by the US that Pakistan's structural adjustment loan with the
International Monetary Fund (IMF) would go through. The
announcement was most hypocritical, since the only exemption
to the sanctions regime was assistance and aid for humanitarian
causes, which the structural assistance loans were definitely not.
This announcement effectively meant that the sanctions had
been waived in practice, though not on paper. In effect, it freed
up Pakistan's budgetary resources, enabling a higher level of
defence expenditure, the negative repercussions of which were to
become obvious in less than a year. The generosity shown towards
Pakistan by the Clinton administration was in striking contrast

to the decision taken by the World Bank to indefinitely delay the consideration of a large loan (US$865 million) to the state of Uttar Pradesh just a month previously. The US State Department had hailed this decision.

In retrospect, when I became familiar with the work of the American political theorist and public official Joseph Nye, I realized that these decisions, by the management of the IMF and the World Bank acting under the pressure exerted by its largest shareholder, were examples of the United States' soft power at work. Contrary to popular belief that soft power emanates from the popularity of movies and cultural norms, Nye had argued in his book that the US, instead of flexing its muscles openly, ought to use its controlling powers over the IMF, World Bank, etc., to achieve its strategic objectives.[13] Correspondingly, Nye was critical in his work of President Bush's tendency to get the US directly involved in 'setting things right' internationally, instead of using these institutions to pursue the same goals and extract the desired results.

I was directly exposed to this in 2000, when I joined as an adviser to the executive director representing India, Bangladesh, Bhutan and Sri Lanka on the board of the World Bank. The senior management, in private conversations, expressed their frustration that they could not go ahead with its India lending programme due to 'instructions' from the US. Rather than put up these proposals to the board and have a vote on it, the US ensured that these proposals were kept pending within the bank bureaucracy. It was only after the mid-2000s that the spigot on the India pipeline was turned on.

The US was not yet done with its public humiliation of India. Within days of the Jaswant Singh–Talbott meeting in Delhi in July 1998, and more than two months after India's tests, it packed

---

[13] Joseph Nye, *The Paradox of American Power: Why the World's Only Superpower Can't Go It Alone*, (New York: Oxford University Press, 2002).

off seven Indian scientists who were on attachment with US government laboratories, with seventy-five more scientists on the list. Clinton now came up with a new formulation when he said that Russia and China have influence over India and Pakistan, and had been helpful in ensuring that India–Pakistan relations did not deteriorate beyond a point.

India's neighbourhood—countries in the immediate vicinity as well as those in the larger region—was also getting into the act of 'normalizing' the situation in the subcontinent. The Association of Southeast Asian Nations (ASEAN), other than Thailand and Philippines, started evolving its own stance, away from the American one. Now, it only deplored the tests and did not condemn them. This was a major shift, but I suspect if India had paid more attention to ASEAN countries and spent more energy on explaining India's strategic environment, there would have been greater appreciation for our position among them. For too long, till Narasimha Rao launched his 'Look East' initiative, successive governments since Indira Gandhi had looked upon the South-East Asian countries with suspicion, given that they were largely a part of a US-led defence alliance.

All attention now shifted to Colombo's SAARC summit. The Indian Air Force's desire to have a refuelling halt in Chennai was seen as unnecessary by us, since the Delhi–Colombo route was well within the ageing Boeing 737's range. In fact, the initial idea was for a night stopover at Chennai, in order for a much shorter hop to Colombo that would enable Vajpayee to plunge into meetings as soon as we arrived. However, the optics of a Chennai stopover en route to Colombo could be seen a message to Sri Lanka, even if unintended.

Pakistan's efforts to 'regionalize' tensions by bringing those within the ambit of SAARC had failed, because this was incompatible with the organization's charter. When the organization was set up in 1985, it was explicitly agreed upon to keep out bilateral disputes; its founders—like the President of Bangladesh, Hussain Muhammad Ershad—had felt that if this was not so, India would not join.

Lakshman Kadirgamar, the Sri Lankan foreign minister, had been wrong in rushing to Beijing to try and bridge the gap between India and China, but his unease at the political tensions arising out of the tests was not unjustified, nor was he alone in his apprehensions. The prime minister of Bangladesh, Sheikh Hasina, considered a good friend of India, had visited Delhi at short notice, apparently alarmed by what she thought was the deteriorating security situation in the subcontinent. She had, in fact, made a statement offering to mediate between India and Pakistan, but the MEA publicly repudiated the notion of third-party mediation. Still, she was the first foreign dignitary to visit India after the tests and the first head of government that Vajpayee hosted as prime minister. The visit itself passed off smoothly, with a rather pleasant round of talks at the Hyderabad House in Delhi.

In Colombo, Vajpayee had to address these misgivings of our neighbours without conceding India's position on the tests. Economically, this was done, for example, by initiating substantial movement on the South Asian Free Trade Agreement (SAFTA), with such measures as lifting import curbs on about 2000 items, besides other concessions. Politically, India initiated a bilateral meeting with Nawaz Sharif. The meeting was one-on-one and lasted ninety minutes. The two delegations waited outside, but ultimately there were no delegation-level talks. Normally, in a summit, there are both—delegation-level talks and talks without aides. The Pakistani foreign minister, Gohar Ayub, looked restless, as if he wanted to be called in.

The two leaders spent the time getting to know each other better and understanding their respective positions. Sharif was on a weaker wicket, having limited autonomy over his country's India policy. The two sides only formally agreed that the two foreign secretaries should meet. Later, the Pakistani delegation let on to the media that their line on third-party mediation had not been dropped. My own assessment at the time was that both prime ministers, with their efforts at starting the talks and hoping to achieve progress, were skating on thin ice.

Less than two months after this, in the fourth week of September 1998, Vajpayee and Sharif would meet again in New York, on the sidelines of the UN General Assembly session. First, the two leaders met privately and then with the delegations, over lunch. Sharif had to leave early, since his turn to speak at the UNGA was soon coming up. The two leaders showed that they had developed an easy camaraderie. Sharif mentioned that he had driven down to Delhi with his wife in 1982 to watch the Asian Games. As he was leaving before the lunch was over, he started saying, '*Ijazat hai?*' but spontaneously switched to Hindi and asked, '*Aagya hai?*' and Vajpayee, equally quickly, said, 'Ijazat hai.'

The light banter could be misleading as, within half an hour, Sharif was bashing India in his speech at the UN, but to expect otherwise, as some in our delegation did, was unrealistic since the bilateral meetings had not resulted in any real progress. And Sharif had to be wary of an important domestic constituency that would not look kindly on his attempted rapprochement with India, as the Kargil war was to demonstrate in mid-1999.

The New York visit was an important one, but more relevant to this chapter is Vajpayee's speech at Asia Society, for it was here that he called India and the US 'natural allies' for the first time. In fifty years since Independence, the word 'ally' had not featured in the vocabulary of India's foreign policy. It is still a term that is not used, obsessed as we are with retaining 'strategic autonomy'. Even though his speech was otherwise preachy, with Vajpayee listing a litany of disappointments that India felt, the coinage firmly indicated that as the world order was poised to change, India and the US had more interests than disagreements in common, which must motivate the two countries to try and work together.

Even as Vajpayee worked hard to defend India's strategic interest globally, domestically he had to weather many storms that made international politics look simple.

5

The Stumble

'Jayalalitha daily; Mamata Banerjee weekly; the Akalis and the Samata Party occasionally: the BJP-led alliance resembles a government less and a confederation of sulks more.'

—Editorial, *India Today*, 24 August 1998

If we thought that crossing the hurdle of the confidence vote or the speaker's election would allow normal functioning of the government to kick in, we were sadly mistaken. Vajpayee, the moderate, was expected to be someone who would perennially allow people to ride roughshod over him. Even a relatively non-partisan analyst like Kuldip Nayar expected Vajpayee to function with his hands tied, when he wrote in a column (*Indian Express*, 1 April 1998) that if 'the BJP was sincere about cooperation, it would have allowed Sangma to become the Speaker.'

Had Vajpayee and the NDA allowed the Opposition to have its candidate get elected as the speaker, the government would have become a lame duck at the very start of its innings. No doubt

Sangma had been an outstanding speaker of the previous Parliament, but India does not share the British tradition where a speaker resigns his party membership in complete measure, which is why speakers in India fight elections as candidates of their parties, go on to become ministers, and so on.

WHILE INTELLECTUAL ARGUMENTS LIKE THESE were creating a climate of non-confidence in Vajpayee's government, more debilitating for the government, however, was the political pressure within the ruling alliance. Jayalalithaa reached Delhi on 2 April and met Vajpayee the next day with a long list of her demands, the sum and substance of which was the dismissal of the DMK government in Tamil Nadu. But there was little that Vajpayee could do in this regard, besides asking her to have faith in him.

That was when I began, for the first time, to appreciate the value of the second chamber in Parliament, in our case the Rajya Sabha. A government elected on a popular mandate does feel frustrated, often rightly, when their legislative agenda is held up in the Rajya Sabha, where they often lack a majority.[1] Assuming that the NDA *had* a majority in the Rajya Sabha, one can only imagine how impossible it would have been for Vajpayee to put off Jayalalithaa's demand that the DMK ministry in Tamil Nadu be dismissed. In fact, as it was to be seen in the coming months, it was not just Jayalalithaa, but almost all NDA constituents who wanted the governments in the states to be dismissed, since it was run by their political opponents.

Meanwhile, Pramod Mahajan was at a loose end, as he was neither a minister nor a parliamentarian. Once the process of

---

[1] Rajya Sabha members are elected for six-year terms by state assemblies, other than the twelve members nominated by the President. One-third of the members retire every two years. As a result, Union governments often lack majority support in the Rajya Sabha.

government formation was over, his key role in mediating and negotiating with allies was over. Vajpayee needed help with retail political management, so he appointed Mahajan as 'political adviser to the prime minister', with the rank of cabinet minister. This set off a major controversy, since the move was unprecedented. Was Mahajan a minister or a civil servant? Would he attend cabinet meetings? To settle these issues, Mahajan was sworn into office by Vajpayee himself, as is done for the deputy chairman and members of the Planning Commission.

Mahajan's appointment, and the fact that he started sitting in a room at 7 RCR, was a source of comfort for me. He took care of most political visitors; in turn, I could find out information about different cases/complaints, etc., from the bureaucracy at my level. It generally worked out but could also cause some embarrassment at times. I remember a specific case when I rang up the joint secretary concerned in the industries ministry to check when the minutes of a meeting of the Foreign Investment Promotion Board would be issued. The matter was reported to Sikander Bakht, the minister who, in turn, reported the matter to Vajpayee, saying that I was interfering in his ministry. Vajpayee was quick to understand the context and did not tick me off. Meanwhile, the poor investor wanting to put his money into the Indian economy kept waiting.

Vajpayee's efforts to strengthen his ministry by getting the Telugu Desam Party (TDP) to join in were going nowhere, since Naidu refused to budge. Oddly, he instead suggested jointly contesting the assembly elections that Andhra Pradesh would face in 1999 but was not prepared to be seen as part of the BJP-led government. Obviously, secularism was not the issue. I held then, and stand by it today as well, that this reluctance arose from a fear of seeing the rise of alternative power centres in his party. Naidu's experience with his nominees led him to adopt this policy, wrongly I would argue.

Renuka Chowdhury from the TDP was the health minister in the United Front governments of Deve Gowda and I.K. Gujral. Unlike the other TDP representative in the UF government who remained low-profile, Chowdhury was quite visible in the media and became the most known face of the TDP after Naidu. Politically, she was not a threat to Naidu, but since most regional parties have become closely held private limited companies, even this was not acceptable. Chowdhury expected to fight the 1998 parliamentary elections, but the TDP did not give her a ticket. Some assumed that since her Rajya Sabha term was about to end, she would be re-nominated, but even that did not materialize. Much later, a repeat would be seen in Mamata Banerjee refusing Vajpayee's offer of a second cabinet slot for her party, preferring to make senior leader Ajit Panja, a former cabinet minister, a minister of state.

Even as the government was slowly getting down to work, the Opposition was getting more active. Sonia Gandhi was asserting her control over the Congress party. She declared a 'war on communal forces'. She was duly anointed as Congress president, with the disgraced Sitaram Kesri formally proposing her name, a tradition the Congress adopted post its 1969 split, when it discarded the elective principle for nomination by the 'High Command'. Sonia Gandhi's extremely aggressive statements betrayed the Congress's nervousness that parties at the Centre, avowedly secular, were prepared to engage with the BJP, which no longer was 'untouchable'. Vajpayee as leader of the government and the National Agenda of Governance—which showed the BJP's acceptance that its core agenda, of Ram Mandir, the removal of Article 370 and uniform civil code, would have to be put on the back burner—allowed other parties to work with it.

This fear about BJP becoming the central feature of Indian politics, which would prevent Congress (I) from staging a comeback, was clear from Sonia Gandhi's speech on becoming party president. She said that before the elections, the Congress party should have connected better with leaders of different communities and taken them on board. There was constant harping by her and by other leaders of her party that the government must be kept under watch and that it was the RSS that was actually running the show; they cited as proof the proposed Constitution Review Committee, whose purpose was to turn India into a 'Hindu Rashtra'. The All India Congress Committee's political resolution declared that the party would do anything to ensure that 'the BJP government does not tamper with the basic secular, democratic and egalitarian fabric of the nation', and that the party would challenge 'all communal, divisive and authoritarian forces'.

Putting Vajpayee further on the back foot, Sonia Gandhi sent him a detailed letter criticizing certain changes in the security setup at her residence, 10 Janpath, made by the SPG. She basically conveyed that her and her children's security was being compromised. There was a sketch accompanying the letter, showing the location of the fixed-point deployment, before and after the changes. The letter was obviously written by someone from within the SPG, or someone who'd had a long association with it. The letter upset Vajpayee, and the SPG was told to roll back the rationalization done by them. M.R. Reddy, who was the director of the SPG, was clear that his changes would have improved Sonia Gandhi's security, since individuals deployed would have their guard duty hours shortened and hence would be more alert. But Vajpayee's concern for Sonia Gandhi's security was to be expected.

Bharat Vir Wanchoo had been involved in security arrangements for the Nehru–Gandhi family. In 2004, the Manmohan Singh government made Wanchoo the director of the SPG, superseding dozens of his seniors. After Wanchoo's retirement, the same government also made him governor of Goa.

Things were not much better on the NDA front either. On some day, it would be the law minister, M. Thambidurai of the AIADMK, expressing his annoyance that the Central government was most hesitant to sack the DMK government in Tamil Nadu to avoid misuse of Article 356; and on another day, it would be Jaswant Singh telling a TV channel that almost all of Vajpayee's energies were consumed by 'coalition compulsions'. Singh also added that unlike Nehru, Indira Gandhi or Rajiv Gandhi, Vajpayee 'cannot cast India in his vision'. The Punjab chief minister, Parkash Singh Badal, expected Vajpayee to give his state a fair deal by hiking procurement prices of wheat and paddy, while the petroleum minister, V. Ramamurthy, declared war on the DMK on another day.

Not to be left behind, even the finance minister, Yashwant Sinha, got into the act and asked for the dismissal of the Rabri Devi government in Bihar, citing gross violation of constitutional norms and provisions. This was a demand that the Samata Party would come back to quite often. And later, even the Janata Dal leader, Ram Vilas Paswan, then in the Opposition, joined the demand. This issue of using Article 356 to dismiss Rabri Devi was going to hound the Vajpayee government later at a critical time. The Akalis also let it be known that they would like a candidate of their choice as the commissioner of police of Delhi but, to be fair, did not press the point.

Even as the media was raising serious doubts on Vajpayee's capacity to be firm on important matters, he had to handle a crisis in his cabinet. A court in Chennai framed criminal charges against S.R. Muthiah of the AIADMK, the shipping and transport minister in Vajpayee's government. The case was related to the period when he was speaker of the Tamil Nadu state legislative assembly. Muthiah was defiant that he would not go, though, traditionally, if a person was charge-sheeted by a court, it meant resignation from the government. Vajpayee, however, was firm that Muthiah would have to resign and he had his way, though the latter publicly lashed out at his perceived victimization.

Lost in all this din was the final report submitted, on 3 April, by the Jain Commission of Inquiry about the assassination of Rajiv Gandhi. Unlike the preliminary report, which pointed a finger of suspicion at the DMK and Karunanidhi, the final report exonerated them completely. Interestingly, the Congress (I) had used the pretext of the preliminary report to ask for the removal of DMK ministers from the UF government of I.K. Gujral, thereby precipitating its fall. After the final report came out, there was no sense of contrition anywhere, and of course, Vajpayee became its beneficiary, because it was the fall of the Gujral government that led to the mid-term polls that brought the former to power.

On 7 April, a few days after the release of this report, Karunanidhi came to Delhi and met Vajpayee. Compared to Vajpayee's meetings with Jayalalithaa, this one could not have been more different. The relaxed body language and the comfort level of the two was so obvious. This was despite the limitations of not having a common language to converse in, with Murasoli Maran acting as translator. The memories of having jointly opposed the Congress and of the high-handedness they'd faced during the Emergency were evidently quite strong.

But this period was not just about the compulsions of running a coalition government with a narrow majority. Vajpayee received a very warm letter from the Japanese prime minister, Ryutaro Hashimoto. It made three specific points, which are worth mentioning in the present context of India–Japan relations led by the two prime ministers, Narendra Modi and Shinzo Abe. One, that Japan wanted India to play a greater role in 'international management' of power, 'given its pre-eminence in Asia'. Two, bilateral relations should not just be about business and economics but strategic as well, since both countries shared strategic goals. Third, Japan felt encouraged by the National Agenda of Governance and looked forward to greater economic liberalization.

Clearly, Japan had already developed misgivings about the rise of China, which it had liberally financed at the prompting of the US. And it saw that this rise threatened India's strategic space too, something which Indian analysts seemed unwilling to articulate and Indian policymakers refused to countenance. That understanding and articulation would have to wait for some time in the future. At that moment, Vajpayee did not let on that his decision to go ahead with Pokhran-II would severely test India–Japan relations despite the emerging strategic convergence.

It was assumed that a BJP government, particularly one headed by Vajpayee, would pay attention to national security issues, especially to structural issues, like setting up a National Security Council. Vajpayee's first important intervention in Parliament was in September 1957, when he spoke on foreign policy. Over the years, he developed considerable interest, and expertise, in strategic issues. A former foreign minister in India's first non-Congress government (March 1977–August 1979), he attempted to change India's strategic positioning.

Despite all the domestic tensions, Vajpayee found time to appoint a task force on national security, to be headed by K.C. Pant, a former minister of state of defence in the Indira Gandhi government. Not unexpectedly, Jaswant Singh was named as a member, with Air Commodore Jasjit Singh as the convenor.

Meanwhile, Vajpayee made persistent efforts to get Mamata to join the government, but despite all the pressure, she still refused. I guess Vajpayee's understanding was that for the sake of stability, a Mamata or a Naidu was better inside the room than outside. In Mamata's case, she had the offer of being personally present inside the room, and not through representatives. Yet for the moment, she wasn't interested.

At this stage, no one was paying attention to the Bahujan Samaj Party (BSP), which, after all, had only five members in the 542-member Lok Sabha. Their leader, Kanshi Ram, one of most underrated persons in Indian politics of his generation, was presciently telling his party, in early April 1998, to prepare for the Lok Sabha elections in 1999. Having gone through general elections in 1996, followed by mid-term polls in early 1998, more than three years in advance, was anybody else betting on a third election so soon?

As if to give credence to the Kanshi Ram school of thought, Jayalalithaa decided to hit out at the Vajpayee government publicly. She demanded that Vajpayee drop all tainted ministers. As she told the media, there 'cannot be one set of rules for the AIADMK and Mr Muthiah and a different one for other parties or other leaders in the ministry'. In case there were doubts about whom she had targeted, Subramanian Swamy informed everybody that L.K. Advani had been charge-sheeted in the Ayodhya case. It also seemed like her immediate target was Buta Singh, a Congressman turned independent who was telecom minister in Vajpayee's government. Buta Singh, along with Narasimha Rao, Bhajan Lal, Satish Sharma and others, had been charge-sheeted in the Jharkhand Mukti Morcha bribery case, but they had filed an appeal in the Supreme Court, where the case was pending at that time. Yet, it didn't take a genius to understand that Jayalalithaa's real target was neither Advani nor Buta Singh but the DMK ministry, which she wanted sacked.

Responding to Jayalalithaa's charge that the DMK government in Tamil Nadu was soft on terrorists, the home ministry sent a team to Tamil Nadu, led by Special Secretary Ashok Kumar, former chief secretary of Jammu and Kashmir. This decision was administratively correct but politically a disaster for Vajpayee. At the conclusion of his visit, Ashok Kumar informed the media that the law-and-order situation in Tamil Nadu was 'satisfactory'.

In fact, he added that the 'law-and-order situation has improved considerably and it would continue to improve due to effective steps taken by the administration'.

Even as Ashok Kumar was giving, rightly but unnecessarily, a clean chit to the DMK government of Tamil Nadu, two Union ministers, Ramakrishna Hegde and Ram Jethmalani, severely criticized Jayalalithaa for putting unnecessary pressure on Vajpayee. In turn, the petroleum minister, V. Ramamurthy, a Jayalalithaa ally, attacked the Hegde–Jethmalani duo. Adding to the confusion, Buta Singh declared that he would not resign. However, the Supreme Court had delivered its judgment, which held that Buta Singh and the others could be prosecuted. Even though Buta Singh tried to hang on by claiming that there was no need for him to resign as the court had only clarified on the jurisdiction and not, in essence, on the case, his days as minister were numbered.

The Supreme Court judgment and the home ministry's clean chit to the Tamil Nadu government gave Jayalalithaa enough ammunition to start firing her salvos. She assailed the home ministry team, calling it a joke, as it had only spent a few hours in Chennai meeting state government officials. Her representatives in the Vajpayee government took on Jethmalani for his adverse comments on Jayalalithaa, advising him to refrain from making remarks that could endanger the coalition government. The irony of their advice on how to save the Vajpayee government was obviously lost on them.

In any case, the internecine war of words between Hegde and Jethmalani on one side and the Jayalalithaa combine on the other would only pick up in momentum, and nastiness. It was hard to believe that technically they were all on the same side. Though, to be fair, Hegde maintained his dignity throughout, even he felt exasperated enough to advise Vajpayee that rather than face daily humiliation, it would be better to go in for a fresh mandate. That it would happen so soon was not what most people had expected.

Facing the Jayalalithaa heat, Advani conveyed his 'extreme displeasure' to the central team for talking to the press. In fact, he said that the team was sent to assess the growth of militancy that had resulted in the pre-election blasts in Coimbatore and not the general law-and-order situation in the state. But the damage had been done. A few days later, Ashok Kumar, who had led the team, was posted out of the home ministry and sent to the Planning Commission. Advani's clarification was not enough to mollify Jayalalithaa, who now stepped on the pressure by sending Vajpayee a six-page letter asking him to either drop Buta Singh, Jethmalani and Hegde, or to reinstate Muthiah.

Buta Singh meanwhile was trying all sorts of tricks to escape having to resign. Initially, he said that the entire exercise was a conspiracy to replace Vajpayee with Advani. When this did not get him Vajpayee's sympathy, he stopped taking calls, and even challenged the authority of the former to sack him. According to Buta Singh, Vajpayee could not pick and choose, overplaying the government's dependence on one-person parties like his. Vajpayee sent Pramod Mahajan to try and persuade Buta Singh to resign, but even that failed. Ultimately, he had to be sacked. Buta Singh's public position was that he had been 'betrayed'. About Vajpayee, Buta Singh was quoted as saying, 'When he should have stood by me, he chose to surrender meekly to a woman [Jayalalithaa] who has as many cases slapped against her as the number of hairs on her head.'

Again, the irony—a 'charge-sheeted' politician feeling that injustice was being done to him—was completely lost on Buta Singh, who took his revenge seven years later, in 2005, when after the Bihar legislative assembly elections, as governor, he refused to allow the largest combination of the Nitish Kumar-led JD(U) and BJP to form the government. The Supreme Court again proved to be Buta Singh's nemesis, but that is another story.

As Vajpayee was handling Jayalalithaa's new offensive by sending Bhairon Singh Shekhawat to talk to her, trouble was brewing elsewhere. Mamata and West Bengal BJP got into a brawl over the upcoming panchayat elections in the state. Unlike most states, where panchayat elections are held on a non-party basis, in Bengal, to this day, these elections are fiercely contested by political parties, with very high levels of intimidation and violence. It would have made eminent sense for the two parties to jointly take on the CPI(M)-led Left Front, but Mamata and Tapan Sikdar, the state BJP leader and newly elected MP from Barrackpore, could not stand each other and were trading charges. The colourful language employed by one about the other would make even a hardcore politico blush. At the same time, Mamata lashed out at Jayalalithaa for her 'blackmail' tactics that were weakening the Vajpayee government. Fortunately, before the actual panchayat elections, the two sides came together. This was not enough to depose the Left Front, but they did put up a spirited fight at the village panchayat level. But that was still some time away.

Vajpayee then decided, after consultation with some allies, to hold the NDA coordination meeting on 9 May, so that some alignment of views could be brought about. The first issue to be sorted out was its composition. There were so many one-person parties that it would have been impossible to achieve the right balance in terms of representation. Having tried Pramod Mahajan, Yashwant Sinha and Bhairon Singh Shekhawat, it was to Jaswant Singh, the veteran negotiator and conciliator, that Vajpayee turned again to sort out the composition of the Tamil Nadu delegation for the coordination committee meeting. Singh flew to Chennai and after two long sessions and arrived at the decision he was sent to achieve. Subramanian Swamy would not be invited to the meeting.

Swamy had been demanding the sacking of both Hegde and Jethmalani on the grounds that inquiries were pending against them. Faced with exclusion, Swamy announced that he would now oppose the government and support the Opposition but continue to be in the AIADMK-led front in Tamil Nadu, which in turn continued to be part of Vajpayee's government. If it had not affected the government's functioning, one could have afforded to laugh at the farcical state of affairs.

Now came the turn of the Samata Party to demand its pound of flesh. The NDA government had appointed some governors, including senior BJP leader Sunder Singh Bhandari, who went to Bihar. The Samata Party said that it was not consulted about his appointment. This was a valid point, since Home Minister Advani had consulted the West Bengal chief minister before shifting Bihar's governor, A.R. Kidwai, to Bengal for the remainder of his five-year term. Similarly, in Maharashtra where the Shiv Sena–BJP alliance was in power, Governor P.C. Alexander was re-appointed because the Shiv Sena wanted it. Apprehensive that if Jharkhand was hived off as a state, then Bihar would suffer a perennial financial loss, the Samata party demanded a special package for Bihar in the event of such division of the state. Finally, it wanted the Rabri Devi government to be sacked.

The issue of tainted ministers was simply not going away. The BJP had formed its first government with the help of Sukh Ram's Himachal Vikas Congress. Many of BJP's well-wishers were uncomfortable with this fact, as the BJP had paralysed the Parliament's functioning in the Narasimha Rao government. Sukh Ram was now PWD minister in the BJP-led state government. BJP's general secretary and the person behind this alliance, Narendra Modi, justified this by drawing a parallel with Vibhishan in the Ramayana.

The President then gave the CBI prosecution sanction in cases involving Sukh Ram and two other former Congress ministers, Sheila Kaul and P.K. Thungon. Vajpayee was clear that charge-sheeted ministers had to go. Earlier, it had been Muthiah and Buta; now it was Sukh Ram. Since Swamy had raised complaints against Hegde and Jethmalani, Vajpayee said that he would seek legal opinion on them, since their cases were different. Sukh Ram resigned, but he was persuaded by Modi to continue the alliance so that the Himachal ministry was safe.

VAJPAYEE'S TROUBLES WERE NOT ONLY domestic. Despite the change in government and Vajpayee's open support for the Tibetan cause in the past, the Indian system still found it difficult to handle the Tibet question. Before the chief of China's People's Liberation Army (PLA) was to visit India in end-April 1998, a few Tibetan demonstrators sat on a peaceful dharna near Jantar Mantar, far away from where the Chinese general would stay or travel to. However, the Delhi Police forcibly evicted these Tibetan protestors, of whom one, Thupten Ngodup attempted self-immolation and died in the hospital later. This touching concern on the part of the Indian authorities for Chinese sensibilities, purely one-sided, represented to me the pervasive inferiority complex that the Indian system suffers from. It did not strike me that the trauma of 1962 has been so internalized that despite Vajpayee's ascension to office, there was no difference in how things were handled.

The Vajpayee government had inherited a weak economy, with plummeting growth rates, despite the hype of P. Chidambaram's dream budget of 1997. Just to check that my memory was not playing tricks or that my personal bias did not lead me to make this comment on the economy, I decided to look at independent assessments made at that time. I ran into this edit-page article by Prem Shankar Jha, the noted economic commentator and no friend of the BJP, in the *Hindustan Times* of 7 May 1998. According to him, the United Front left the economy in a mess; the fiscal deficit was understated by 1.5 per cent; it was not 4.6 per cent of the GDP but 6.1 per cent. This was achieved by keeping borrowings out of public sector undertakings (PSUs), which had sovereign backing. There was a considerable shortfall in customs duty, since imports had been falling since July 1997. Industrial growth rate, which was 7.1 per cent in 1996–97, had fallen to 4.5 per cent in 1997–98. Similarly, the growth rate of exports, which had been 20 per cent in 1993–96, fell to 4 per cent in 1996–97 and to 3 per cent in 1997–98.

I had done a similar exercise in May 2014, which was published in the *Dainik Jagran* on 15 May 2014—that is, before the counting of votes. I estimated that the interim budget for 2014–15, presented by Chidambaram just before the elections, had plugged the fiscal deficit more than 1 per cent below its actual level by rather unusual executive action. The profitable PSUs were asked to declare interim dividend before the end of the financial year, and in many cases the amounts exceeded the previous year's dividend. The government collected a further amount as dividend tax and also stopped paying food and fertilizer subsidies in the last quarter. In simple terms, dodgy steps were taken to dress up the government accounts for the financial year, ending on 31 March 2014, to look good by pre-empting next year's revenue while passing on expenditures to it.

The power sector was crying for reforms, so this was attempted by Vajpayee, but using the ordinance route. It was accepted wisdom that private investment would flow into the sector if tariff setting was de-politicized and power generation made profitable. Accordingly, the power reform ordinance, piloted by Rangarajan Kumaramangalam, proposed the setting up of a Central Electricity Regulatory Commission (CERC) and state commissions along similar lines (SERCs). Substantially, the ordinance was based on a draft bill on the power sector that the UF government had drawn up after getting it endorsed by state power ministers. However, due to its contentious nature, the draft bill never made it to Parliament.

The ordinance moved tariff setting from state governments to autonomous regulators. It also shifted to a more robust system of tariff determination, away from the cost-plus methodology in use, which pushed up the cost of power. It laid down the rule that the minimum tariff could not be below fifty per cent of the costs of generation. Understanding that any immediate shift to this modest tariff level could be destabilizing, it allowed a transition period of three years in the case of the farm sector. If state governments wanted to subsidize the supply of electricity, they would have to give cash compensation to state generation utilities. State electricity boards that were in default would be denied power supply till they cleared their dues. Lastly, that there would have to be a transparent bidding process for mega projects. This would enable the best offers to go through, so that the country wasn't saddled with high-cost power.

Initially, nobody reacted negatively to these sensible changes being made. In fact, they were generally welcomed as a much-needed corrective. Vajpayee then went to address the annual session of the Confederation of Indian Industries (CII). It was a powerful speech, with a lot of announcements and many of these had extremely ambitious timelines. There was a need to send out a strong message that the government was working, and that it was focused on solving problems and developing a long-term vision.

Some of the ideas he articulated reflected his long-held views on the economy. These included the beliefs that (i) citizens should pay for what they use 'and must also get what they pay for'; (ii) the government would be less and less of an active player in the economy, and more and more of a legislator, facilitator and regulator; (iii) 'My government's relationship with industry will be based on trust, not marred by mistrust.' He added for good measure the he came 'from a political tradition that does not look upon commerce and industry with distrust. When it was conventional political expediency to decry entrepreneurship, we championed their cause.' He tried to allay fears about swadeshi by explaining that it meant 'that the bulk of the resources needed for our development must be mobilised by ourselves'.

The aim was for the economy to grow at 7–8 per cent; the government would substantially increase its investment in infrastructure; there would be a new housing policy; a task force would develop a new informatics policy; there would be new and unconventional sources of funding to facilitate investment in infrastructure; the Foreign Investment Promotion Board would have to follow strict timelines to facilitate FDI; the inordinately high non-performing assets (NPAs) of the banks would be brought down; the Foreign Exchange Regulation Act (FERA) would be reformed; disputes between industry and government (revenue/telecommunications) would be sorted out; and the prime minister's office would actively monitor the implementation of large projects.

Vajpayee was in his element and words flew with the full force of his sincerity and conviction. Each announcement was greeted with thunderous applause, and the 'feel-good' mood pervaded every nook and cranny of Vigyan Bhavan. All the tensions of managing what was a ramshackle coalition seemed far away. Later, a journalist friend reminded me that if an economy could be talked up on to a higher plane, this was the way to do it. Vajpayee was an instinctive reformer, almost a libertarian, but the road ahead was not going to be easy. Ultimately, Vajpayee would be judged not by his words but by what he achieved.

The mood in the government became better when it emerged that two of the Tamil Nadu parties—the PMK, led by S. Ramadoss, and the MDMK, led by Vaiko—were moving away from Jayalalithaa and were not willing to endorse her brinkmanship. Vajpayee, reacting to Hegde's advice to seek a fresh mandate, said that it was not necessary to do so. Meanwhile, trouble was brewing in the east. The Biju Janata Dal (BJD) wanted a special package for Odisha and an assurance that Naveen Patnaik would

be the CM face in the next assembly elections. Mamata wanted
a fact-finding mission to be sent to West Bengal, to assess the
law-and-order situation; she also wanted the state government
dismissed and the public investment in West Bengal to be
stepped up. Moving on to Bihar, the Samata Party wanted the
dismissal of the RJD government, more ministries in Delhi and a
special package of Rs 50,000 crore on account of Jharkhand being
separated.

AMID ALL THE POLITICAL UNCERTAINTIES, there was one
inauguration that I particularly remember—of the Konkan
Railway in Ratnagiri on 1 May 1998. The agreement to set up the
Konkan Railway was finalized on Good Friday in 1990. George
Fernandes, railway minister in V.P. Singh's government, had come
to Panaji, Goa, where I was posted. Being a holiday and a day
of sorrow and introspection, the official dinner hosted by Goa's
first Catholic chief minister, Luis Proto Barbosa, was a quiet one.
Fernandes, who was from Mangalore and had cut his political
teeth in Mumbai, knew how important this line was for the tens
of millions who lived on the west coast. He was determined to
push this project and was supported by the then finance minister,
Madhu Dandavate, whose parliamentary constituency, Rajapur
(now Sindhudurg), Maharashtra, lay just north of Goa, and who
understood how this region's development had been held back by
lack of connectivity.

Instead of taking the usual route and doing it through the
Indian Railways, the Konkan Rail Corporation (KRC) was formed
as a company, whose shareholders were the Indian Railways, the
three States (Maharashtra, Karnataka, Goa) through which the
railway line would pass, and Kerala, which would benefit by it.
Based on the equity paid for by its shareholders, the KRC floated
long-term bonds and built the 740-kilometre line, India's biggest
rail project in over a century. Incidentally, India's metro man,

E. Sreedharan, headed the KRC and established his reputation as an outstanding project manager.

Though it was warm by late morning, when the inaugural function began, the mood was celebratory. There was a feeling that this was a non-Congress project that had been successfully implemented. Besides Vajpayee, Nitish Kumar (rail minister) and his minister of state (Ram Naik), the chief ministers of Maharashtra (Manohar Joshi), Karnataka (J.H. Patel) and Goa (Pratap Singh Rane) were also present, to demonstrate the federal nature of the project. Since the function was in Maharashtra, the state's governor (P.C. Alexander) was present. It was only fitting that George Fernandes, without whose initiative the project would have remained on the drawing board, was in attendance as well. There was a stamp to be released, so the communications minister, Sushma Swaraj, was also there.

With so many speakers, the function was a long-drawn one. I remember the clamour demanding that Chief Minister Rane should speak not in Marathi but in Konkani, which he did. I also remember having to juggle so many VVIPs and arranging for them to fly back to Mumbai in helicopters, so that none felt deprived. Vajpayee added a touch of Marathi to his speech, a language he was familiar with, having spent his childhood and youth in Gwalior. He also remembered that Ratnagiri was among the four seats that the Jana Sangh won in 1957, the year Vajpayee was first elected to Parliament. In hindsight, one wonders if his trips to Ratnagiri—considered a backwaters despite having produced such stalwarts as Lokmanya Tilak—had a role to play, in stressing for him the importance of connectivity, when Vajpayee came up with the game-changing idea of linking India through excellent highways, the Golden Quadrilateral.

After spending the night in Mumbai, we proceeded to Gandhinagar for the BJP's national council meeting (3–4 May), which was preceded by a meeting of its national executive. Much before Mamata Banerjee talked about *poriborton* (change), the complex where this meeting was held was called Parivartan Nagar. With Advani now a minister, the party presidentship passed from him to Kushabhau Thakre, a low-key organizational person who had moved to the party from the RSS. Not all ministers, or holders of high office, were enthusiastic about attending the national council meeting.

Before leaving for Gandhinagar, I had put it to Jaswant Singh that we would be seeing him at the meeting. He shook his head rather firmly, indicating that this was not a forum where he was comfortable! I did not have to sit through either of the meetings, spending my time in my office-cum-bedroom in the Raj Bhavan, which turned into an oven every afternoon. Till I experienced the Jaisalmer summer about two weeks later, on our way to Pokhran, this was the hottest climate I had ever experienced. You could have fried an egg on the roof without any fire. This was despite the fact that I'd spent a summer in Jodhpur in 1979, when I first started working for the State Bank of India. And yet, Vajpayee, Advani and other leaders were sitting down and finalizing the nitty-gritty of party and governance in such weather.

Thakre's message to the BJP was clear. He expected the party to provide oversight, and feedback, to the government. He cautioned against an ostentatious style of living consequent to acquiring political power. He was strong on national security, asking the government not to give in to Western pressure on India's missile programme. In his speech, Advani described the previous six weeks—it was difficult to believe that the government had been in power for so short a time—as the 'birth pangs' of the new order emerging from the womb. Though he did not say it, there was a sense of disappointment in what he was saying, that the Vajpayee government did not get the benefit of a honeymoon period.

This feeling pervaded the entire assembly of thousands who had come from all over the country. The mood was more sombre than joyful. Vajpayee, during his interventions in the party forum, and later at the public meeting at the conclusion, made one very powerful point. Coming to power in the Centre at the head of a coalition government 'was a milestone, not our destination'. This was necessary to state for two reasons. One, there were murmurs that the party had given up its core agenda of Ayodhya, Article 370, and uniform civil code, which did not figure in the National Agenda of Governance. Not till the BJP was able to come to power on its own and win a majority could these be taken up. Two, Vajpayee maintained that there should be no complacency, something which could have easily crept in with the perks of office and influence.

That the government can function and take important decisions even when the prime minister and home minister were not in Delhi was brought home to me around the same time. I got a call from Union Home Secretary B.P. Singh that the Delhi Police commissioner had to be replaced. He had spoken to his minister, the relevant file was being sent. So could I get the PM's approval, after the home minister had given his nod to the proposal? This was done. In fact, wherever the prime minister goes, his office is present there. We always had with us a small staff contingent and a direct line to PMO's phone exchange, so that whenever we picked up the receiver, the operator in Delhi came on line and immediately connected us to whosoever we wanted to speak to. This meant that important decision-making or conversations and discussions did not have to wait for the PM to get back to Delhi. Even though cell phones were slowly permeating our lives, their effectiveness was limited—they worked only in big cities, local sim cards had to be used and the rates were astronomical. This made our patchwork communications system extremely critical.

Before moving on, I must refer to Advani's speech at Gandhinagar, where he said that the proposed Constitutional Review Panel could look at a presidential system. He, and many others, had long been votaries of the idea of having a directly elected chief executive who could act decisively. Leaving aside my personal preference, I knew that while his statement reflected his frustrations with the running of coalition governments as such, it would not go unchallenged. A few days later, Mulayam Singh Yadav referred to it and said that the BJP's hidden agenda was now emerging. As proof of his contention, he pointed to the fact that no BJP leader at Gandhinagar spoke on their three core agendas of Ayodhya, Article 370 and uniform civil code, which for him meant that those commitments had not been dropped. Veteran Congress leader Arjun Singh, on the other hand, said that even if Vajpayee and Advani had said that the BJP was committed to the common agenda of the coalition, the Vishwa Hindu Parshad (VHP) was committed to building the temple in Ayodhya. Mulayam Singh also criticized the nuclear tests, stating that the BJP went ahead with them in order to achieve their goal of the 'Hindu Rashtra'. This line of attack would recur throughout Vajpayee's tenure.

However, the enemy was always within. No sooner had Vajpayee returned to Delhi than Jayalalithaa launched an attack on the government, calling the power sector ordinance anti-farmer and distancing her party from it. Kumaramangalam pointed out that the ordinance had been vetted by the law ministry, whose minister was Thambidurai from the AIADMK. Thambidurai, caught in this cleft, tried to wriggle out by clarifying that he had indeed seen the ordinance as law minister, but only from a constitutional angle and not from a political angle. He was absent when the cabinet discussed the ordinance and approved it. He added that he should have been consulted. I could imagine his predicament.

There was never a dull moment. One day, Jayalalithaa's representative in the finance ministry, R.K. Kumar, who was minister of state, transferred the entire income tax team probing her cases. On another day, the left parties jumped into the tainted ministers' controversy by asking both Advani and M.M. Joshi to resign, since they had been charge-sheeted in the Ayodhya case. G.K. Moopanar, the veteran Congress leader from Tamil Nadu who had broken away from his parent party in 1996, when it aligned with Jayalalithaa, to set up the Tamil Maanila Congress, expressed himself that fresh polls were imminent.

The NDA held its first formal coordination Meeting on 9 May. It was decided that only Jaswant Singh would brief the media. But that would have been boring and out of character. Mamata informed the media that Jayalalithaa had raised the issue of her income tax cases, while Jayalalithaa herself informed the media that she had raised the now contentious issue of power sector reforms. Hegde later told the media that the PM looked tired and physically weak, but not mentally. He hoped that Vajpayee would assert himself more. Little did he or the others know what was on Vajpayee's mind. Exactly a day after Hegde shared his assessment of Vajpayee's mental stress, the latter was telling the media that India had carried out three nuclear tests.

SUDDENLY, THE POLITICAL PENDULUM HAD swung Vajpayee's way. However, rather than appreciate this major step that changed India's position in the world and hinted at the country's manifest destiny, the Congress (I) was churlish in its reaction. It only cheered the Indian scientists and did not even ask why India had to wait so long to demonstrate that it is in a position to defend itself. As already described, Vajpayee invited Sonia Gandhi for a detailed briefing; later, other leaders, including the two leaders of the Opposition in Parliament, Sharad Pawar (Lok Sabha) and Manmohan Singh (Rajya Sabha), were also briefed. Though the government was a little apprehensive, President Narayanan proclaimed India's right to test 'as directed by its security needs and developments in the region'. This, he added, could not be questioned.

Routine governance could not take a back seat. Vajpayee visited Kerala in mid-May. The visit was arranged by the veteran journalist T.V.R. Shenoy, with help from E. Ahamed of the Muslim League. He was received at Kochi airport by the state's chief minister, E.K. Nayanar. This surprised some in the PM's large group, including journalists, since Nayanar had just written an article in a local CPI(M) paper attacking Vajpayee. This, I had to explain, should not be taken seriously, as Nayanar, in his article, was addressing a pure party audience.

Nayanar came across as someone who was completely grounded, with absolutely no airs. I remember he once limped into the room, and on Vajpayee's query, slightly pulled up his mundu, rolled down his socks and showed his varicose veins. He must have been in some discomfort but he laboured on. I was very impressed with his simplicity.

Jyoti Basu, the veteran Marxist leader and long-serving chief minister of Bengal, called on Vajpayee as soon as we were back from Kerala. If I recall correctly, this was Basu's first visit since Vajpayee became prime minister. State finances being what they were, he too had a long list of demands. Being pillars of their respective parties who had collaborated in the past during the Janata experiment (1977–80) and later when both their parties supported V.P. Singh's minority government, Vajpayee and Basu shared a decent comfort level but without the bonhomie that I saw between Vajpayee and Karunanidhi, Nayanar and Jag Pravesh Chandra (Congress leader of Delhi) to name a few. Despite this, Mamata was always suspicious that the Vajpayee government gave the Left Front government of West Bengal too much leeway.

A few weeks after this meeting, in the West Bengal panchayat elections, the TMC–BJP alliance actually did well. They restricted the Left Front (LF) to 58 per cent of the gram panchayat seats, the only level where voters directly participated. This was their lowest achievement in two decades in office. The TMC–BJP alliance did very well in the areas surrounding Kolkata. Since the LF had put up a good show at the two higher levels (panchayat samiti and zilla panchayat) due to the indirect nature of these elections, there was a feeling that the LF had swept the polls. It must be remembered that the panchayat elections in West Bengal see massive use of force by the ruling dispensation, including intimidation of workers of the Opposition, who are prevented from filing nominations, and violence to scare away voters likely to vote for the other side. Murders are not uncommon. This is probably the only elections in India where the brutal power of the government is on full display.

The results of the panchayat elections led to panic and anger in the TMC, and their senior leader, Ajit Panja, even announced the withdrawal of support to the Vajpayee government. Mamta toned down that decision: she would boycott the budget session. The reasons for the ire were obvious. Vajpayee had rightly ignored her pleas for clamping President's rule before the panchayat polls. Mamata's reaction to the election results was that her party had 'fought the CPI(M) and BJP as equal enemies'. She accused the BJP of having a secret understanding with the CPI(M). The BJP, particularly the West Bengal unit, was equally upset with Tapan Sikdar making it clear that they had had enough of Banerjee's arrogance. He had added that they would fight future elections separately.

Later, during the Parliament session, Mamata explained the rationale for the temporary suspension of support to the government. The ostensible reason the TMC was boycotting the budget session had to do with what she thought was the BJP government's indifferent attitude towards its allies. According to her, Panchayat polls had led to tensions among the allies, and she demanded immediate imposition of President's rule. She warned that her strength went beyond seven (TMC) MPs, claiming the support of all twenty-nine MPs of the north-east. Earlier, she had said that she would not withdraw support, but she was now cautioning the BJP to not take the TMC's support for granted. She would subsequently withdraw her suspension of support and come up with fresh demand for an eight-point package for Bengal, including big-ticket investments in railways, highways, ports, etc.

On the Tamil Nadu front, things became curious and then farcical. R.K. Kumar, as minister of state in the finance ministry, was moving heaven and earth to help extricate his boss, Jayalalithaa, from the plethora of tax cases against her. However, by the third week of May 1998, Kumar, who was diabetic, was hospitalized in Chennai, but the first news was that it was for political reasons that he got into hospital. There was speculation that it was not so much her unhappiness at his handling of her tax cases as her perception that Kumar did not do enough to fix Chidambaram and DMK leaders like Murasoli Maran. Kumar soon resigned from the government, on medical grounds, and was publicly upbraided by his leader. He never fully recovered and, sadly, passed away in October 1999.

K.M.R. Janarthanan, another Jayalalithaa nominee who was minister of state for personnel, was given the additional charge of MOS (Finance). He held both jobs till the AIADMK withdrew support from the Vajpayee government. Newspapers reported that Janarthanan, immediately after assuming office in the finance ministry, told the income tax department and Enforcement Directorate that they needed to consult Central government counsels during their investigations, clearly intended to shield Jayalalithaa. This looked to be in violation of Supreme Court directives, and in the case of Jayalalithaa, it was now her pick of lawyers who were the Central government counsels in Chennai.

With a number of senior BJP leaders either drafted as ministers or unavailable for party work, the new party president, Kushabhau

Vajpayee releasing P.V. Narasimha Rao's book, *The Insider*, at Delhi's India Habitat Centre on 20 April 1998. The easy camaraderie between the two leaders was on full display at the function.

At Governor's House, Lahore, 20 February 1998. With journalists Ishan Joshi, Sheela Chaman and Priya Sahgal.

First moments in office on 19 March 1998, having just signed papers appointing Brajesh Mishra as principal secretary to prime minister, and me as private secretary.

Vajpayee being introduced to the Pakistan team, at the India–Pakistan hockey test at Delhi's National Stadium (now Major Dhyan Chand National Stadium). This was his first official function, barely hours into office.

When Jayalalithaa came calling, on 2 April 1998, after the government had been formed. Easily the most challenging of Vajpayee's alliance partners in the March 1998–April 1999 government. Vajpayee's gaze says it all.

With Chandrababu Naidu on 3 April 1998. Even when Naidu's demands were unreasonable, which kept Finance Minister Yashwant Sinha under pressure, Vajpayee's personal equation with him was always pleasant.

Vajpayee at the CII Annual Meeting on 28 April 1998, trying to revive the 'animal spirits' of Indian entrepreneurs. He inherited a floundering economy. Government formation and the initial weeks in office were mired in controversies. The overall mood was gloomy.

Vajpayee making the historic announcement of India's nuclear tests (Operation Shakti) on 11 May 1998. Even as Pramod Mahajan and I stood away from the rostrum, so that only Vajpayee appeared in the frame, we were caught on camera. A very momentous birthday for me.

Vajpayee at Pokhran with the heroes of Operation Shakti, Dr R. Chidambaram and Dr A.P.J. Abdul Kalam, on 20 May 1998. Defence Minister George Fernandes is sitting next to Vajpayee.

Vajpayee hosted a successful meeting on the resolution of the Cauvery River water dispute, with chief ministers of Tamil Nadu (K. Karunanidhi), Karnataka (J.H. Patel), Kerala (E.K. Nayanar) and Puducherry (R.V. Janakiraman), on 7 August 1998. Jaswant Singh was there to help Vajpayee shepherd the CMs towards an agreement. A youthful Siddaramaiah, then a minister in Karnataka's Janata Dal government and later Congress chief minister, can be seen standing quite prominently.

Vajpayee with the prime minister of Mauritius, Navin Ramgoolam, flying back from Durban after the Non-Aligned Meeting on 3 September 1998. Mauritius was the next port of call, and the only way Ramgoolam could play host was by travelling with us. On landing at Port Louis, Mr and Mrs Ramgoolam exited the plane first, in order to receive Vajpayee as he deplaned.

On 28 September 1998, Vajpayee shocked his American audience at Asia Society (New York), as well as most of his own team, when he referred to India and the USA as natural allies. Kissinger was in the audience. A bold and audacious move at a time when India was facing the brunt of American sanctions and lectures on good behaviour, post-Pokhran.

Yevgeny Primakov, received here by Vajpayee at Hyderabad House on 21 December 1998, made an equally bold announcement, asking Russia, India and China to act together as a strategic triangle in order to balance America's unipolar dominance of the world. This embarrassed China, which wanted to do nothing that would upset the USA. The idea also did not find favour with Primakov's boss, Russian President Boris Yeltsin. Jaswant Singh is partially visible in the photo.

Greeting Sri Lanka's President, Chandrika Kumaratunga, at Hyderabad House, prior to the signing of the India–Sri Lanka Free Trade Agreement on 28 December 1998.

With Brajesh Mishra, flying to Rabat from Port of Spain.

Vajpayee at Minar-e-Pakistan in Lahore on 21 February 1999. It was at this place in 1940 that the Muslim League, led by Muhammad Ali Jinnah, adopted its famous Lahore Declaration, asking for autonomy for the Muslim-majority provinces of British India, which was seen as a precursor to the demand for a separate homeland/s for Muslim Indians.

Photographs courtesy of Photo Division

Thakre, formed a new team, though he could only do so some time after he assumed charge. Not unexpectedly, Narendra Modi, after his success in Himachal Pradesh as the party's *prabhari*, was made the general secretary. This choice, not entirely unexpected, stood vindicated when shortly after, the BJP–HVC alliance swept the polls to the four Himachal assembly seats, polling for which could not be held with the general election because these areas were snowbound. The BJP had now a majority of its own in the assembly and was no longer dependant on HVC's Sukh Ram for his support.

THE ISSUE OF THE construction of Ram Mandir in Ayodhya suddenly came to the forefront when a news report, authored by Prakash Patra ('The Ram Temple Agenda'), appeared in the *Hindustan Times* of 25 May, detailing how temple components were being fabricated/carved and kept in a godown in Karsewakpuram, Ayodhya. According to the report, work had picked up momentum since BJP came to power. Sonia Gandhi wrote to Vajpayee, wanting to know whether the government would uphold the sanctity of the judicial process; Vajpayee's reply was quick, confirming that it would. The timing of the report, with the budget session of Parliament only days ahead, meant that the issue was frequently in the news. It was first raised in the Rajya Sabha.

The Opposition demand that, given the past record of the BJP in not keeping its promises, off-site preparations for the construction be stopped. CPI's Gurudas Dasgupta said that 'one section of the BJP was attempting to appease the secular parties, while another led by the VHP and Bajrang Dal whipped up communal passions'. It was left to veteran BJP parliamentarian V.K. Malhotra to state that the status quo would not be changed. The BJP's position was that the temple would 'only come about when it is permitted by court'. Alternatively, it would need the BJP to get sufficient majority to get a bill passed to overcome legal hurdles. At that moment, nobody could visualize such a situation arising.

Mamta, too, raised the Ayodhya issue in the Lok Sabha. Not to be outdone, the AIADMK resorted to a walkout on this issue. Later, the BJP vice president, K.L. Sharma, also jumped into the fray and said that the party could bring legislation on the Ram Mandir issue as well; in effect, do a Shah Bano. Vajpayee attempted to tone down the temperature by clarifying that they would wait for the court orders. However, the Opposition was up in arms, calling the two statements—Vajpayee's and Sharma's—contradictory. Later, Pramod Mahajan had to correct his party colleague Sharma and remind him that the BJP lacked the numbers to bring in legislation.

Ayodhya was only one of the many points of controversy and tension in the run up to, and during, Parliament's budget session. Others included the nuclear tests, petrol and urea hike announced in the budget, the power sector reforms, the sending of Central government teams to West Bengal and Bihar in order to mollify allies and the brinkmanship by members of the ruling coalition. The media often commented that with friends like these, Vajpayee did not require enemies.

The Congress launched its attack on the government. Both Sharad Pawar and A.K. Anthony said that the nuclear tests were done to cope up with tiffs within the ruling coalition. Earlier, immediately after the tests, Salman Khurshid had said that the Congress was upset with Vajpayee for naming Pakistan and China in his letter to Clinton justifying the tests. On the opening day of Parliament, Vajpayee read out a detailed statement explaining the rationale behind the tests. A lot of effort had gone into preparing the statement, with Vajpayee correcting drafts and making changes. But it seemed to be of no avail. Or could it be that the Opposition, with honourable exceptions, was not prepared to give credit where it was due? Perhaps the latter! The columnist Swapan Dasgupta

(*India Today*, 8 June 1998, 'After Summer, the Fall') quoted the American senator Diane Feinstein as saying that the nuclear tests would not have happened in a Congress regime. He then went on to quote *Newsweek*, a prestigious American news magazine, which said that Clinton's anxiety was for 'a more predictable party to take power in India'.

Former prime minister Chandra Shekhar accused the Vajpayee government of having invented a threat, rather than discovering it. He said if China was not a threat when I.K. Gujral demitted office, how could it have become one later. The Opposition had this common theme that they talked about repeatedly, which was that the BJP government was essentially guided by its political compulsions, rather than reasons cited, in reversing the nuclear policy followed since 1974.

After Pakistan tested, the left was quick to blame Vajpayee for initiating an arms race in the subcontinent. The Congress (I) also got into the act and blamed India for the Pak tests. Sharad Pawar, agreeing that it was the Indian government which had 'initiated a nuclear arms race', advised that the government should not panic now and advocated restraint. It was left to Dr Raja Ramanna—former chairman of the Atomic Energy Commission who had also been minister of state for defence in V.P. Singh's government and was now a nominated member of the Rajya Sabha—to bring in a sense of realism, moving away from petty politicking. Among other reasons, he cited the need to keep the morale of the army high.

Advani reminded the Congress that its 1991 manifesto had spoken of the dangers of Pakistan's nuclear programme. Vajpayee also explained that the Pokhran tests had actually pre-empted Pakistan's tests. There was no way that Pakistan could have tested just in reaction to the Indian tests if it did not have an advanced nuclear programme and had made preparations for a test already. There were stories in the media that the Akalis were uneasy about the tests because Punjab would face the brunt of the damage in the event of an India–Pakistan war. Later, Sukhbir Badal cleared the air and said that Parkash Singh Badal had, in fact, congratulated Vajpayee after the tests. With so much rumour mongering and speculation in the air, the truth was always the first casualty, and people were prepared to believe the worst.

Another rumour doing the rounds was that Vajpayee, fed up with his allies, was exploring the formation of a national government. Some of the Opposition parties were up in arms, seeing this as a ploy to wean away members from their side. The government was peeved as this seemed a signal to their smaller partners that they could be dumped. It was frustrating to function with such daily misunderstandings, tantrums and lack of desire to develop a common perspective towards governance.

Nitish Kumar presented his rail budget, and this prompted the Biju Janata Dal (BJD) to stage a walkout, and even threaten to withdraw support. The BJD was undergoing a serious crisis, and with six out of its nine MPs in a rebellious mood, it seemed that Naveen Patnaik would lose control over his fledgling party. Later, when the budget was presented, the BJD expressed its unhappiness that Odisha had not been given special status. Not to be left behind, the Samata Party demanded that in view of the governor's report on the deteriorating law-and-order situation in Bihar, if President's rule was not imposed, its ministers (George Fernandes and Nitish Kumar) would withdraw from the government. With the AIADMK (perpetually), TMC, BJD and Samata Party in different stages of rebellion, no wonder Subramanian Swamy wrote to the President to ask Vajpayee to submit a list of supporting MPs. And not surprisingly, rumours that Vajpayee was exploring the formation of a national government gained currency.

Yashwant Sinha, finance minister for the second time—he had been one in the short-lived Chandra Shekhar government as well—presented his first full budget. It was fairly pedestrian, which in hindsight was not a bad thing. He did miss out on addressing structural issues like the company law and Income Tax Act, but to be fair, at this stage he was a political lightweight in the party and possibly did not have the kind of rapport with Vajpayee that would have allowed him to be bolder. The budget also did not explicitly factor in the effect of economic sanctions that were imposed on India after the Pokhran tests. Sinha would go on to present a much better budget the next year, by which time he had developed a comfort level with Vajpayee that allowed him to be more forthright. In fact, Sinha had warned much before he presented his first budget in 1998 that he wanted to but could not present a 'dream budget'. It was a bad choice of words, for the dream budget of 1997–98 had only pushed the economy downwards.

The strength of the budget was that it tried to correct the serious fiscal crisis that India was facing. A high fiscal deficit and high inflation meant that the lending rates of banks would remain high. The result was that, as Bimal Jalan, the then governor of Reserve Bank of India, explained, he could do nothing to reduce interest rates, out of fear that inflation would go out of control. High interest rates meant that productive investments, required for creating jobs and powering the economy to a higher growth rate, could not take place. The 1997–98 budget had exacerbated the situation, as it had led to fiscal deterioration.

Unfortunately, this piece of sensible decision-making had to be substantially undone. The budget had proposed a petrol cess of Re 1 per litre, which would be used for highway construction. Urea prices were also set to go up by Re 1 per kg, which would have the added advantage of preventing the soil deterioration being caused by unbalanced use of fertilizers. The allies were extremely sore over the petrol and urea hike. In addition, the finance ministry either goofed up on the petrol price hike or was caught out as they attempted to raise far more revenue than what Yashwant Sinha had declared, for the excise duty on petrol was also hiked from

20 per cent to 35 per cent. The result was that the actual hike was not Re 1 per litre but Rs 4 per litre.

There was an immediate uproar, and the finance minister was forced to say that the petrol hike would be limited to Re 1 per litre. The second rollback was in respect of urea, where he announced that the hike would be limited to 50 paise per kg, not Re 1 per kg. In fact, the Akalis were not satisfied with this and wanted that there should be no hike in urea prices. With these two withdrawals happening in less than a day, the media named Yashwant Sinha as 'Rollback Sinha', a moniker which stayed with him. As a result of pressures from Jayalalithaa and the Akalis, the Power Sector Reforms Bill, which was introduced in Parliament to replace the earlier ordinance, was toned down. It did away with the requirement for state governments to pay upfront for subsidies and establish State Electricity Regulatory Commissions (SERCs).

Not unexpectedly, the markets turn jittery, a reaction to the combined effects of sanctions, budget rollbacks and the government under constant attack by allies. Mamata did end her suspension of support to the government, but the markets shrugged it off. The budget rollbacks made the government look vulnerable. The economic situation was itself uncertain, and the budget was unable to inspire confidence among investors, locals and foreign. In Prem Shankar Jha's analysis, referred to earlier, the top priority of the government should have been to energize the economy in the shortest time; but that didn't seem to be the case.

It was not that the Vajpayee government did not mean well. In some cases, it did achieve success. The way the unnecessary spat between the government and Suzuki, over management control over Maruti Suzuki, created during the UF government, was sorted out was commendable. Industry Minister Sikander Bakht never got the credit for unravelling the mess. If India wanted FDI, it needed to show that it would not interfere in commercial enterprises. Maruti Suzuki was a joint venture between two equal partners, the government of India and Suzuki Motors. But it could be nobody's case that it was a commercial success because the government ran it!

But such wins were relatively few, and this period was mostly consumed by managing the alliance. Vajpayee, who popularized the phrase 'coalition dharma', was still learning at that time, and his learning curve was uncomfortably steep. Senior leaders of the AIADMK accused the BJP leadership of colluding with the DMK. In protest over the non-dismissal of the DMK government, they staged walkouts in both the Lok Sabha and the Rajya Sabha, and, in one case, after a breakfast meeting with Vajpayee. No wonder there was an editorial comment in the *Hindustan Times* of 10 June 1998 saying that the 'AIADMK has been on good behaviour for only one week following Pokhran'.

The changing situation in Sri Lanka gave the Tamil Nadu politicians another chance to put pressure on the government. This time, the memorandum asking for India's intervention was signed by Jayalalithaa and leaders of the alliance, including Kumaramangalam. Fortunately, the intervention sought was not military but moral. The AIADMK made it clear that the Lanka issue was a new time bomb. Swamy called upon Jayalalithaa to withdraw support from the government. He was quoted as saying, 'The only way to get the DMK out of Chennai is to get the BJP out of Delhi.' Petroleum Minister V.K. Ramamurthy said that they (the people of Tamil Nadu) would not wait indefinitely and that their patience was running out. He added, however, that he would not withdraw support because of that.

In order to queer the pitch, Jayalalithaa launched a strong direct attack on Vajpayee and Advani. She accused Karunanidhi of being a threat to national security. She once again delivered what she called a friendly warning to the BJP to not take their support for granted, adding that her party would not take a hasty decision. She alleged that there was a secret understanding between the DMK and the BJP to replace the AIADMK, therefore the BJP was not making up with her and not dismissing the state government in Tamil Nadu. Rajiv Gandhi had given her a lot of respect, even though he had the support of over 400 MPs, while Vajpayee did not have even half the number. Jayalalithaa accused Vajpayee of refusing to realize the importance of allies even when they were partners in government. She was critical that on Pokhran, Opposition parties had been briefed but not allies.

But Jayalalithaa's control over her alliance was slipping. Vaiko (MDMK) made it clear that he was against the use of Article 356 for sacking the DMK government. This was remarkable when one considered that Vaiko was seen as a protégé of, and possible successor to, Karunanidhi; the two had a falling-out, and Vaiko founded the MDMK in 1994. Despite this background, he held that the demand to dismiss the state government was unreasonable and went against his party's ethos. As he later elaborated, the alliance 'secured votes for a stable government. So it is not proper that such a government suffers from repeated pinpricks.' Even the PMK maintained silence on Jayalalithaa's demands.

There was something about BJP governments that led its critics into thinking that the worst was just waiting to happen. In this case, there was a hue and cry that the Indian Council of Historical Research (ICHR) had been recast to 'give a communal spin to history'. It was said that this was an attempt by the RSS to legitimize its own interpretation of history, and that Gandhi and Nehru would be replaced as 'central icons' by ideologues like Golwalkar and Savarkar. All that had happened was that the government had filled up a few vacancies in the governing board of the ICHR, and Professor S. Settar, appointed by Deve Gowda, remained its chairman.

Meanwhile, the law-and-order situation in Bihar continued to deteriorate. The prominent CPI(M) MLA Ajit Sarkar was shot dead on 14 June 1998. His party called for the dismissal of the Bihar government, but other Opposition parties did not endorse this demand. Nitish Kumar demanded the sacking of the Rabri Devi government, explaining that the situation in Bihar was different from that in West Bengal or Tamil Nadu; Bihar was characterized by 'financial anarchy, maladministration, corruption and breakdown of law and order machinery'.

THERE WERE NOW THREE STATES where the demand from allies for dismissal of state governments had gained traction, viz., Tamil Nadu, West Bengal and Bihar. In relation to the first (Tamil Nadu), the government had already burnt its hands. The issue then was—could the Vajpayee government impose Article 356 in the other two states? It was, therefore, decided to send Central government teams to West Bengal and Bihar. The team to West Bengal would look at alleged violations of law by state government authorities during the panchayat polls. The team to Bihar would study the general law-and-order situation.

In view of President Narayan's track record, there were doubts whether he would easily go along if the government were to try and use Article 356 to dismiss a state government. There were also members of the NDA, like the Akali Dal, Shiv Sena, National Conference, AGP, MDMK, PMK, Lok Shakti, HVP and the TDP, who on different occasions had expressed themselves against using Article 356. And between the two states, arguably Bihar was a far more suitable case for the use of Article 356 than either Tamil Nadu or West Bengal.

The central team that was sent to Bihar met the governor, Chief Minister Lalu Yadav, senior officials and leaders of different political parties. Though the Samajwadi Party had set up a Rashtriya Loktantrik Morcha with Lalu Yadav's RJD, it representative from

Bihar, Papoo Yadav, demanded the dismissal of government. On the other hand, the West Bengal government snubbed the home ministry team, who could not meet official functionaries. Their stand was that law and order, and the panchayat elections, were state subjects, and the Central government had no business sending a team to assess the situation. The Congress and United Front slammed the government, calling the move unconstitutional, one that meant to undermine the federal structure of the Indian Constitution. Jaipal Reddy, then still in the Janata Dal, called it the 'weakest central government in free India . . . such flexing of muscles is a demonstration of weakness not strength.'

Apparently, the critics of the government had not read the Constitution. Articles 355 and 256 are essential features of the Indian Constitution. Article 355 casts a duty on the Union government 'to ensure that the government of every State is carried on in accordance with the provisions of this Constitution.' Hence, sending a team to check on the actual situation was well within the powers of the Government of India. Article 256 is even more significant to the sending of the team. It requires the Government of India to issue instructions to state government/s 'to ensure compliance with laws made by Parliament and any existing laws, which apply in that State'. The direction issued under Article 256 is an essential component before any action can be taken under Article 356 to dismiss a state government, which allows the Union government take over the functions of a State government, if it is satisfied 'on receipt of report from the Governor of the State *or otherwise*' that 'the government of the State cannot be carried on in accordance with the provisions of this Constitution' (italics added). Sending a team to the concerned states was meant to allow the Union government the opportunity to assess the situation and to determine whether in fact the powers under Article 356 should be exercised. Unfortunately, even the home ministry was either unaware of these provisions of law or was unable to muster the argument that sending the team was a legitimate exercise of sovereign function. Instead, it was the Vajpayee government that was put on the defensive. As the Kashmir situation continued to deteriorate, with mostly targeted killings of Hindus south of the Pir Panjal—e.g., Prankote (17 April, twenty-six killed), Dessa (19 April, thirteen killed), Surankote (20 May, four killed) and Champnari (19 June, twenty-five killed)—Jyoti Basu taunted Advani in the most callous manner: 'Why don't you do something in Kashmir? After all you have the bomb.'

Looking back, it was clear that coalition dharma was still in its early stage. The Akalis were upset, as the Planning Commission had withheld clearance of Rs 12,000 Bathinda Refinery that Hindustan Petroleum had proposed setting up, holding it to be unviable. However, based on earlier assurances, the Punjab government had already acquired 2000 acres of land and spent Rs 80 crore. Akali support was not to be taken for granted, was the message coming from them. I could understand the logic of the Planning Commission. Neither were there any oil fields nor a port for importing petroleum nearby, so it made no economic sense to have a refinery in Bathinda. It is always cheaper to transport a value-added product like petrol, LPG or fertilizer than feedstock like petroleum.

Years later, as power secretary in the Delhi government, I was witness to the situation where Delhi power distribution companies were faced with the dilemma of buying power from the Jhajjar Thermal Power Station, which cost 50 per cent more than comparable power from other plants. Jhajjar got its coal from the Mahanadi coalfields of Odisha, while the Bhatinda refinery gets its feedstock from the Persian Gulf, via the Mundra port in Gujarat. However, when politics drives economic decision-making, which was the case in the Soviet-style planning model that we followed, then decision-making cannot be rational. This was not the first time that the Akalis had felt slighted. Earlier, Badal had reacted strongly to Advani's statement in Parliament that there was no immediate plans to hand over Chandigarh to Punjab. Badal had said that Chandigarh was Punjab's by right.

THE SECOND COORDINATION COMMITTEE MEETING was scheduled for 27 June. It was not even 100 days into the government, and the NDA coalition looked ramshackle. The only issue before the meeting was whether Jayalalithaa would attend. She did not, and nor did two of her allies, the PMK and TRC, but the former was quick to clarify that they would not withdraw support. Interestingly, Ramamurthy (TRC) and the AIADMK ministers continued to attend office, take part in cabinet meetings, etc. Hence, every time Jayalalithaa demanded President's rule or laid down an ultimatum, one was not sure whether 'this' was to be the last time. It was clear that the government would fall if she withdrew support. The question was when would she do it.

Vajpayee was not the only leader in crisis. In fact, with the election of Jaswant Singh and Pramod Mahajan to the Rajya Sabha, there was panic in Congress (I) ranks when Sonia Gandhi's close confidant Ram Pradhan failed to get elected from Maharashtra. Sharad Pawar, then holidaying in London, became a target of attack, and show-cause notices were issued to Datta Meghe and then to Praful Patel. Pawar defended his supporters and called them loyal and active Congressmen. Indeed, Pramod Mahajan may well not have been elected, but on his way to the airport to fly to Mumbai and file his nomination, he was tipped off by a senior Congress leader that his position as adviser to the prime minister could get him into trouble, since it would be affected by the bar on those holding 'office of profit' from contesting elections. Till then he had not resigned, and his ticket to Mumbai was bought through the PMO. I advised him not to panic and to send his resignation by fax. His office was told to withdraw the ticket requisition, and it was paid for by a member of his personal staff. The result was that by the time he filed his nomination, he was all clear. It would take Vajpayee months before he could induct both Jaswant Singh and Pramod Mahajan as ministers.

The month of July was consumed by two big-ticket activities. These were the attempts by the home ministry to create new states of Uttaranchal (Uttarakhand) and Vananchal (Jharkhand), and to upgrade Delhi and Pondicherry as states. The BJP, and earlier the Jana Sangh, had been a persistent votary of small states. However, due to lack of homework, so much energy went into sorting out Uttarakhand and Delhi that ultimately nothing came out of it all.

The Akalis were up in arms against incorporating Kashipur (now Uddham Singh Nagar) in Uttarakhand, since they were led to believe that their vast landholdings would face land ceiling issues. Kashipur was in the Terai part of the Jim Corbett territory, where Corbett used to hunt man-eating tigers. Post-Independence, large numbers of Sikh refugees from what became Pakistan were settled in the Terai and given land. They cleared the forests, worked hard at growing sugarcane and prospered. Later, many other Sikhs from Punjab also bought land here. The pressure to retain Kashipur in UP was so strong that eventually the proposal could not go further. Ultimately, Uttarakhand became a state only five years later, in 2003. But back in 1998, the Vajpayee government could not push the Akalis into accepting its position.

The BJP/Jana Sangh had been promising statehood to Delhi for decades, partly because their victory in the 1967 general election, when they won six out of Delhi's seven parliamentary seats, gave them a sense that it provided easy pickings for them. Though the successes of the Jana Sangh/ BJP in the metropolitan council (truncated legislative assembly) elections were limited, they controlled the municipal corporation almost always. Promising statehood is one thing, but delivering it to the capital of a federal republic is not easy.

In July 1998, the home ministry initially proposed granting statehood to the whole territory; it later modified it to take out the New Delhi Municipal Council (NDMC) area, where the Government of India was generally located. They further proposed that the NDMC area would get its own police force. This was to see that the security of the VVIPs and ministers was not in the hands of the Delhi state government. A few ministers pointedly asked about access to, and control of, the airport. Seeing that the going was not smooth, the Central government withdrew the proposal. Later, under pressure from the BJP government in Delhi, the home ministry announced that pending statehood, the control of Delhi Police would be transferred to the Government of Delhi from the home ministry. At the time of writing (October 2020), more than twenty-one years after this suggestion, the Delhi Police continues to be controlled by the home ministry.

As if to prepare the ground for Delhi to become a state, the Vajpayee government announced that Pondicherry, another union territory with a legislature, would also become a state. Unlike Delhi, there had not been much of an issue about statehood in Pondicherry, which, as a former French colony, had an additional complication. Pondicherry has three enclaves located some distance away. While Karaikal, like Pondicherry, is Tamil-speaking, Yanam is Telugu and faraway Mahe (Mayyazhi) is near Kannur in Kerala, and therefore Malayalam-speaking. At the time, Jayalalithaa thanked Vajpayee for agreeing to provide statehood for Pondicherry, but like Delhi, it remains a union territory with a legislature, and this is unlikely to change.

But, it was not all gloom all the time for Vajpayee's government. Vajpayee's most underrated and least talked-about achievement in this period was the setting up of an institutional framework for dealing with regular disputes among the riparian states, particularly Karnataka and Tamil Nadu, on the Cauvery River. Neither the origins of the dispute nor the relative merits of the party should concern us here. The Cauvery Water Disputes Tribunal had passed an interim award on Tamil Nadu's plea in 1991, which had been notified the same year but had not been implemented. The matter was pending in the Supreme Court, where it was agreed that the prime minister should call the four chief ministers concerned—Kerala and Pondicherry being the other two states—and try to find a solution.

Karnataka's chief minister, J.H. Patel, who had succeeded Deve Gowda when the latter moved to Delhi as prime minister, was facing dissent from Gowda's followers. His relationship with Ramakrishna Hegde was complicated, but they had come on the same side because of Gowda's politics. The Karnataka BJP, particularly Ananth Kumar, now a minister in Vajpayee's government, was keen on strengthening Patel. On the other side, Karunanidhi was looking for a solution so that paddy cultivation in the Cauvery delta did not suffer. Since the meeting was to take place in a living room and not in a conference hall, at Ananth Kumar's suggestion, I put the name tags of Patel and Karunanidhi next to each other on a sofa. However, when the delegations arrived, each chief minister sat with his team members on both sides for support!

I have always held that the Indian bureaucracy, if given clear directions by the political executive, delivers, and this was shown in the way the Cauvery meeting proved productive. Once it became obvious that the prime minister and the chief ministers, particularly of Karnataka and Tamil Nadu, were looking for a solution and willing to move beyond stated positions, the senior officials of the Centre and the states found solutions. The result was the establishment of the Cauvery River Authority (CRA), with the prime minister as its chair and the four chief ministers as members. While decision-making would be by consensus, in the event of a deadlock, the chair could decide. This saving clause would be used in the future, when differences became unbridgeable. The officer-level body, the

Cauvery Monitoring Committee (CMC), would feed the CRA. The CRA was able to find a sharing mechanism that helped tide over the 1998 crisis, and everybody went home happy.

The Cauvery farmers welcomed the decisions taken and all was well. Rather, all should have been well but this agreement left Jayalalithaa unhappy. She saw in it a conspiracy to strengthen Karunanidhi's position. That the Cauvery delta farmers were celebrating only seemed to make her angrier. At least, she should have been informed that an agreement would be arrived at, so that she could have broken the news and taken credit. But how does one predict an agreement till it is agreed upon by all the parties? When an understanding was reached with the three states and Pondicherry on 7 August, Jayalalithaa warned the government of 'disastrous consequences' if the original tribunal award was not notified. But she did not move beyond, though Subramanian Swamy had promised that Vajpayee would not be PM on 15 August.

Jayalalithaa did use an interesting analogy when she said that in 'a boxing match, the knock-out punch is not delivered in the first round itself'. When George Fernandes and Pramod Mahajan went calling on her, she made them wait for half a day, and then launched into a diatribe. One of her representatives in the Vajpayee government, K.M.R. Janarthanan, described the Cauvery agreement as 'a wedding without a Mangalsutra'. Fortunately, Jayalalithaa just threw a tantrum and did not move to withdraw support. What made her even more upset was that two of her Tamil Nadu allies, Vaiko and V. Ramamurthy, seemed to be moving away from her.

Vajpayee went ahead and calmly notified the new agreement. Neither the sky nor the government fell.

What made this 7–8 August agreement all the more commendable was that Vajpayee had not been at his best since mid-July, physically. Doctors treating VVIPs are prone to over-medicate. Vajpayee, who, for his age (sevety-four years at the time), was quite fit even if overweight, now looked bogged down and often sluggish. The burden of office and the uncertain nature of his position could not have made things any easier. I am convinced that it was over-medication that made life more difficult for Vajpayee than just the psychological burden that he was carrying. Fortunately, it was a passing phase, but at that moment, it seemed quite troubling. The journalist Saba Naqvi, who covered the BJP, wrote that while Vajpayee was previously described as 'wise, witty and charming', the adjectives had now changed to 'tired, exhausted, listless'.

If this was not enough, Vajpayee seemed overwhelmed about speaking from the Red Fort on 15 August and spent lots of time agonizing over the many drafts that he got prepared from different persons. Our best efforts to make him feel that it was no big deal, that it would be child's play for him, did not succeed. His simple reply was, '*Bolna toh mujhe hai* (I have to speak).' So how would others know the pressure? This, from a person whose eloquence was legendary, who had a way with language and was never at a loss for words in any verbal duel. Since the Independence Day speech by the prime minister at the Red Fort was traditionally part feel-good exercise, part exhortation to the Indian people, part reporting on the government's achievements and part announcement of new schemes, Vajpayee was clear that it had to be a written one. Even Arun Shourie's point, that if he read out the speech it would be like a major medieval warrior riding a scooter, did not move him.

The fifteenth of August was a wet morning, and our first port of call was Raj Ghat, where Vajpayee paid his tribute to Mahatma Gandhi, as all prime ministers had done before him. We left our shoes in the car and walked in our socks over the wet cemented pathway, to the spot where flowers are offered and back. Vajpayee was distinctly nervous. At the Red Fort, the car stopped. Vajpayee got down and was walking towards the honour guard to take salute when he told me that he had forgotten to slip on one shoe, which had been left in the car. I quickly retrieved it from the car and, as innocuously as possible, placed it next to him so that he could slip it on. Even though we were in a relatively secluded spot, a press photographer captured the shot, which was carried by the *Indian Express* the next day. To me, that shot signified the position that Vajpayee found himself in. Would this state of affairs continue or would it change? That was the question we were looking at after Independence Day in 1998.

6

Vajpayee Asserts

'Evidently concerned by the effect that her charges would have on the party's image, BJP spokespersons momentarily gave up their self-imposed restraint and deplored Jayalalitha's outbursts, which they said were 'unbecoming of an alliance partner'. Push had come to shove, and the BJP perhaps felt that it had for far too long been seen to be appeasing Jayalalitha and that it was time to assert itself.'

—'Survival Stakes', *Frontline*,
29 August–11 September 1998

It was clear by August 1998 that things had to change, and they indeed did. But most people did not notice, since the change was incremental and subtle, not unidirectional, with frequent sidestepping and occasional retreats. The Cauvery decision was a case in point, since it could even have endangered the life of the government. Yet, Vajpayee risked becoming the first prime minister not to address the nation from Red Fort on Independence Day.

The economy was in a downslide, and though a five-month-old government could not really take the rap for it, it was nevertheless held responsible. The Confederation of Indian Industry (CII) reported that out of eighty-two sectors, thirty-one reported negative growth and another thirty-two reported an increase of less than 10 per cent. The capital goods sector, considered the base on which other sectors depend, was particularly hard hit. Even the services sector, seen as dynamic, recorded negative growth figures. Export growth in the first two months of the financial year (April and May) was negative and trade deficit was up. Inflation, which normally moderated after the monsoon, was running at 8 per cent, as compared to 4 per cent a year back. Reflecting the sentiments of the investor community, market capitalization was down by 30 per cent. The rupee was holding up despite pressures, and even corporate profits were up, yet there was a feeling of despondence and of drift.

THE POST-POKHRAN BOLDNESS WAS MISSING. Yashwant Sinha's budget had made the right noises, but the confused handling of the petrol price hike, the rollback of fertilizer price, etc., drowned out all the other sounds and feelings, especially the positive ones. Analysts, including those who were usually sympathetic, concluded that with all attention on foreign policy, the economy was not a priority for the government. This general despondency was despite an increase in the rate of growth of agriculture and the relatively low real interest rates.

In fact, the effects of the East Asian crisis were being felt by India, particularly the global headwinds that constrained export growth. Compounding this was the poor state of public finances, which, after the decision on the Government Employees Pay Commission by the UF government, meant that not just the Centre but the states, too, were scraping the bottom of the barrel. The post-Pokhran sanctions, and the resultant stoppage of funds from bilateral donors and multilateral institutions, deprived many state governments of money to fund critical interventions, the difference between business-as-usual and making a difference. Worse, the negative sentiment this conveyed prevented foreign investors from coming to India and discouraged domestic investors from taking decisions.

Much as Vajpayee was uncomfortable with the details of economic policies, these could no longer be ignored or left to individual ministries to initiate. The economy needed both structural reforms and also short-term remedies to fix specific problems and boost investor confidence. Manmohan Singh as finance minister had famously declared that he did not let the stock markets disturb his sleep. The economic leadership of the Vajpayee government decided that while targeting equity levels was not what the government should be looking at, creating a sense of confidence and unleashing the animal spirits was decidedly a priority. There were changes made at secretaries-level of the finance ministry among others; two advisory groups were also created in the prime minister's office to provide suggestions for improved economic policymaking, though the move was controversial as it was seen to be undercutting the finance ministry.

The very first shot fired against bureaucratic changes was by Jayalalithaa. Protesting the transfer of the enforcement director, she alleged that a top media group was behind this particular change and demanded that the change be reversed. Jayalalithaa condemned what she called a 'cunning attempt' to make it appear that the transfers had been effected to placate her, since some of her close associates were facing investigations by the ED for alleged violations of the Foreign Exchange Regulation Act. She distanced herself from all the transfers and said that when George Fernandes and Pramod Mahajan called on her, she had not broached 'any subject other than the Cauvery River water issue'.

To deal with this, Vajpayee tried a different tack this time and got Brajesh Mishra, as principal secretary to the prime minister, to write to Jayalalithaa and request her to produce 'all evidence' in respect of her allegation that 'hefty bribes' had been given to 'persons very close to the Prime Minister' to get the ED transferred out. Not to be outmanoeuvred, Jayalalithaa got her office secretary, P. Mahalingam, to reply to Mishra immediately, demanding an inquiry by the Central Bureau of Investigation into 'the furious lobbying' by the media group she had blamed for getting the ED transferred. According to Mahalingam's letter, 'Such an inquiry will reveal the motives behind the shifting of an upright officer more than two years before his tenure was completed.'

Despite the domestic shenanigans, the Vajpayee that we saw in action at the NAM summit in Durban, which ran from 2–4 September 1998, was self-confident and assertive. The summit was part of a week-long tour which took Vajpayee to Oman, Namibia and Mauritius, besides South Africa. The first hop was to Salalah in Oman, where the sultan used to spend his 'monsoon months'—this being the only part of the Arab peninsula which is touched by the monsoons. Though it is located on the Arabian Sea, it has territory overlooking the entrance to the Persian Gulf. Oman is culturally very close to Kutch, practising a heterodox version of Islam. The Sultan was a Western classical music buff, and the military band regaled us with various compositions at the state banquet. However, it was not the weather or the culture that had brought Vajpayee to this place.

Oman had displayed a nuanced strategic sense. It had controlled Gwadar in Balochistan, across the entrance to the Gulf, giving it control over access into this very important body of water. However, it was forced by the United Kingdom to surrender it to Pakistan in 1957. Oman was generally helpful to India at the Organisation of Islamic Cooperation (OIC), when it discussed

Kashmir. It was also the first country in the Gulf with which India had established joint ventures. In fact, Vajpayee, in his remarks, pointed out that two of India's largest joint ventures were with Oman: the Oman–India Fertilizer Project (OIFP) and the Bharat–Oman Refinery Project. Oman had also signed a twenty-year contract for the supply of 1.2 million tonnes of liquefied natural gas per annum to India.

Flying to Namibia from Oman meant covering almost the entire length of the continent, with the Horn of Africa clearly visible from 40,000 feet. The South African winter had still not withdrawn, and Windhoek, Namibia's capital situated in the highlands, was chilly at the time. The cityscape of Windhoek is quite European, except for the dry climate. Though the visit was a bilateral one, Namibia's President, Sam Nujoma, hero of the armed struggle of his people against the South African rulers, infused excitement into the visit when he suddenly brought into the room Laurent Kabila, President of Congo. Still to recover from the collapse of the Mobuto regime and the civil war, Congo had been invaded by Rwandan and Ugandan armed forces. South Africa and Zimbabwe were also involved as peacekeepers and mediators. In other words, Central Africa and the Great Lakes Region was a mess. This had led to a lot of bad blood that would be pumped into the NAM summit at Durban.

The crisis in Central Africa, terrorism and nuclear proliferation were the issues that dominated the Durban summit. Kabila also made a dramatic last-minute appearance in Durban and stole the show. Nujoma allowed the time allotted for him to be transferred to his friend Kabila. The bitterness between Kabila, Mandela, Robert Mugabe and Kofi Annan (secretary general, United Nations) was obvious. Kabila and his allies wanted an outright criticism of the 'aggression' on Congo by Uganda and Rwanda. Mugabe refused to be photographed with Mandela, and Kabila walked out when Annan was to speak.

Vajpayee received a warm hug from Mandela on the opening day, but the mood quickly turned sour. Mandela's long speech at the inauguration touched upon Kashmir. He said, 'All of us remain concerned that the issue of Jammu and Kashmir should be solved through peaceful negotiations and called the members to lend all the strength we have to the resolution of this matter.' This was the first time that the issue of Kashmir had ever come up in a NAM chairman's speech. Vajpayee was not about to let Mandela off the hook. But this was not it. Mandela also mentioned his concerns about nuclear proliferation, saying that 'the critical question of nuclear disarmament had to remain high on the list of NAM's priorities'. South Africa also tried behind the scenes to push a critical statement on the proliferation scenario in South Asia. Vajpayee was furious, and he expressed his annoyance to Mandela at the evening reception.

The South Africans tried to make amends. Thabo Mbeki, then vice president and later President, met Vajpayee in the morning. The atmosphere was tense; it reminded me of the lashing that Kadirgamar had got from Vajpayee after the Pokhran tests—controlled and focused anger. Mbeki, in effect, apologized for Mandela's Kashmir reference. The result was that in the final NAM statement, the India–Pakistan tests were not condemned. Instead, in the context of nuclear apartheid and the failure of disarmament, it noted the 'complexities arising from the tests in South Asia. They considered positively the commitments given by the parties concerned in the region to exercise restraint . . . to discontinue nuclear tests.' The reversal was total. After the summit, Mandela's spokesperson said that South Africa would prefer that India and Pakistan resolve their outstanding issues bilaterally. Vajpayee had successfully defended India's interests, even if it meant expressing annoyance at Mandela's comments.

The role of the then Indian high commissioner to South Africa, L.C. Jain, also complicated matters. A Gandhian economist, he was sent as an envoy by the Gujral government. When the government changed, all such envoys appointed by Gujral from outside the Foreign Service were withdrawn. Jain was still there in South Africa, and reportedly shared Mandela's distaste for the nuclear tests, and apparently did not hide it. I remember Brajesh Mishra was livid about it; he mentioned it to all concerned, and Jain was recalled almost immediately after Vajpayee's return from Durban.

I was acquainted with L.C. Jain, had met him at his Barakhamba Road office a few times and knew that since he was a Gandhian, the tests would not have made him happy. If memory serves me right, he had resigned from the Planning Commission in 1990, in protest against Chautala's reported rigging in a Haryana assembly (Meham) by-poll. Knowing Jain's strong convictions, the Vajpayee government should probably have withdrawn him much earlier.[1]

Vajpayee, in his address to the summit, strongly rejected any third-party role in the Kashmir dispute, 'however well-intentioned'. He said that Jammu and Kashmir was an integral part of India, and that the real problem there was cross-border terrorism. Therefore, what was needed essentially was a concerted action against terrorism. Just before the summit, in reaction to massive truck-bomb attacks on the US Embassies in Dar es Salaam and Nairobi, the Clinton administration had fired missiles at a pharmaceutical factory in Sudan and at a terrorist training facility in Khost, Afghanistan. Thus, while terrorism as an agenda was very much on everybody's lips, there was still inadequate appreciation of India's concerns and experiences. Sudan and many others wanted outright condemnation of the United States' action, but this would have been one-sided. The final declaration of the

---

[1] In 2018, his sons, Sreenivasan Jain and Gopal Jain, filed a defamation suit against one R. Mantri, who'd called L.C. Jain a 'certified traitor' for his anti-nuclear stance.

summit emphasized its opposition to 'selective and unilateral actions' and underlined that 'international cooperation to combat terrorism should be conducted in conformity with the principles of the U.N. Charter'. Again, India had reasons to be satisfied, as it had long argued for the convening of an international summit to formulate a joint global response to terrorism.

INDIAN POLITICS, MEANWHILE, CONTINUED TO fester. The Congress (I) did some brainstorming at Pachmarhi. Even as it decried coalition politics, calling it a temporary phase, it agreed that 'coalitions will be needed'. However, the party added, somewhat contrarily, that it should not compromise on its basic philosophy. What the newspapers focused upon besides the substance of the decisions, was the complete sidelining of Sharad Pawar, though he was the leader of the Opposition in the Lok Sabha and had successfully dented the BJP–Shiv Sena's newly acquired strength in Maharashtra in the 1998 elections, denying Vajpayee a comfortable majority he would have otherwise got.

Vajpayee also faced challenges from within the larger Sangh Parivar, specifically from the Swadeshi Jagran Manch (SJM), which dubbed some of the Centre's economic policies as 'anti-people and anti-swadeshi' and criticized the government for following the National Agenda of Governance rather than the BJP's own manifesto. It was critical of the composition of the two advisory committees that Vajpayee had formed to deal with economic issues, pointing to the exclusion of any known proponent of Swadeshi. It was also upset with Vajpayee retaining certain bureaucrats, who, according to the SJM, 'are habituated to compromise national interests'. This was strong language, but Vajpayee remained unruffled, or so it seemed to us around him.

Vajpayee's strength within the larger ruling alliance was increasing, in an incremental manner. On 15 September, Vaiko organized a grand rally and public meeting in Chennai. His party, the MDMK, had split from the DMK and Vaiko was keen to show how much it had grown. Though Jayalalithaa avoided the rally by organizing one of her own at Tiruchi the same day, her Tamil alliance partners, S. Ramadoss and V. Ramamurthy, were present at the Marina in Chennai. It was a grand show with floats and party units marching down, culminating in a massive public meeting. Top leaders present included Advani, Parkash Singh Badal, George Fernandes and Farooq Abdullah. Since the ostensible reason for the rally was the celebration of Annadurai's ninetieth birth anniversary, Vajpayee reminded the audience that in 1947, when Periyar, the founder of the Dravida movement and Anna's guru, described 15 August 1947 as a black day, Anna welcomed the departure of the British. Vajpayee also recalled how the 1962 war so upset Annadurai that he gave up his demand for Dravida Nadu.

On his part, without referring to Jayalalithaa, Vaiko said that in the Lok Sabha elections, the people of Tamil Nadu had given a mandate for a stable government under the leadership of Vajpayee. He assured the audience, and Vajpayee, that the MDMK would not do anything to betray the trust of the people and would provide unconditional support to the BJP government. Earlier, when Vajpayee had alighted from the plane, Karunanidhi, the chief minister, was there to receive him, along with Vaiko. The latter was really excited, and not just because of his rally. He repeatedly mentioned that he and Karunanidhi were meeting after a long time. Anybody familiar with Dravida politics would remember how the two had been very close before Vaiko fell out with him, when the DMK started morphing into a family-run entity.

Buoyed by this turn in domestic politics, which provided the government with a little more stability and assurance, Vajpayee set off for what was till then the most important overseas trip of his tenure. He was headed to New York to attend the meeting of the United Nations General Assembly (UNGA), an occasion that allows for a large number of other engagements. The fiftieth-floor suite of the Plaza Hotel provided the perfect platform to make the world understand the New India that Vajpayee had effectively launched by going through with the nuclear tests.

Vajpayee gave two important speeches, one at the UNGA and the other at Asia Society, where he addressed the US strategic community. Vajpayee, true to form, had asked different people for draft speeches, and we had to fashion coherent messages out of those. The UNGA speech was delivered in Hindi, following a tradition that Vajpayee had himself initiated in 1977, when, as foreign minister, he chose to address the UNGA in Hindi. It was, however, his speech at the Asia Society that got more attention, though this attention was not all positive. Vajpayee mentioned that on a number of occasions when India wanted to open up to the US, the latter had either walked away or actually spurned India. There was no rancour in his tone, and yet, a few Americans at my table were upset with what they felt was a harangue. Vajpayee then dropped his bombshell when he said that India and the US were natural allies. He was criticized for drawing this parallel at the time, but history, and the not-so-peaceful rise of China, has proven him right.

After that, there were numerous meetings, with leaders ranging from Nawaz Sharif to Benjamin Netanyahu, with important US advocacy groups like the B'nai B'rith, and with the Indian diaspora. The days and evenings were packed, but Vajpayee had an able support team—Jaswant Singh, Brajesh Mishra and Foreign Secretary K. Raghunath. Vajpayee was in his element in New York, and went through all the programmes with aplomb.

An interesting aspect of the New York visit was that Jaswant Singh was provided security cover by the US Administration, guarded by no less than the famed Secret Service. In the Indian hierarchy, he enjoyed a minister's rank by virtue of being deputy chairman of the Planning Commission, but in the Indian pecking order, rank comes with office and responsibility. Singh's security detail always referred to him as minister, which we found amusing.

Paris was next on the schedule, where we had productive meetings with Prime Minister Lionel Jospin and later with President Jacques Chirac, followed by a five-course meal at the Élysée Palace. France had been extremely supportive in the immediate aftermath of the tests, and while it could not stop the sanctions, it did its best to limit them. Due to shortage of time, Jospin dispensed with interpretation, but Chirac, after his initial welcome notes in English, said that he would speak in French so that he could accurately convey his thoughts—so accurately, in fact, that he had to correct his interpreter more than once when she used words that he felt were not appropriate. For me, the high point of the visit was staying at the historic Ritz and listening to the fascinating conversation between Vajpayee and the French leadership. Vajpayee also met a group of French Indologists and thinkers. Their depth of scholarship made me regret our monolingual academic system that has denied us access to their works and that of others who do not write in English.

The after-effects of the sanctions were slowly tapering off, not just strategically but economically as well. This was reflected in the overwhelming response from non-resident Indians (NRIs) to the Resurgent India Bonds (RIB) scheme, launched to avoid a run on our foreign-exchange reserves post-sanctions. The response to the scheme, worth US\$ 4.18 billion, helped restore a measure of confidence in the Indian economy, which, as we saw in the CII report, was in dire straits. The economy, and the government, desperately needed this reassurance because of what was happening in the Unit Trust of India (UTI), which was till then Indian society's primary vehicle for participation in the capital market through investment in mutual funds. Its flagship venture, the Unit Scheme 1964 (US-64), which has a corpus of over

Rs 22,000 crore, was under tremendous pressure. Its sale price was higher than its net asset value. Public acknowledgement of this led to a stampede, causing the collapse of the Bombay Stock Exchange Sensitive Index (Sensex), which fell by 224 points in a single day (5 October). This put on hold government's hopes of raising revenues through disinvestment of its holdings in public sector undertakings. The situation called for demonstrating decisiveness and leadership.

Vajpayee used the forum of the annual session of the Federation of Indian Chambers of Commerce and Industry, on 24 October, to announce different steps aimed at the revival of the economy. There were two separate components to this stimulus package. The first was changes to the Companies law, using the ordinance route. The amendments would allow corporates to buy back, and boost, their own shares, and to make it harder to allow creeping takeover of companies. The changes also allowed for much higher levels of inter-corporate loans and investments, which were meant to facilitate fresh investments. Recognizing that IT sector had emerged as an important player, with the potential to drive economic growth, we pushed through a provision to allow for 'sweat equity', which would let companies reward good performers by giving them stock options.

In fact, these proposals—to allow corporates to buy back their own shares from the market and on liberalizing rules governing inter-corporate loans and investments—were not strictly new. They were part of the companies law amendment bill, introduced by the UF government, but which was still to be cleared by Parliament.

A valid question may be asked here: What was the big deal about these changes? The answer is, politics. The minister for corporate affairs, Thambidurai of the AIADMK, was presumably under strict instructions to do nothing that would enhance the reputation of the Vajpayee government. T.S. Krishnamurthy, later to become chief election commissioner, was the secretary of the ministry concerned, and though he was ready with the proposal, the ministry just stonewalled it. It took all of Vajpayee's persuasion and cajoling to get it out from the ministry to the cabinet. It was easy for us to blame Thambidurai then, but I can only guess at the kind of tightrope he must have had to walk. The compromise he made was that he would oppose his own ministry's proposal but not obstruct it. Vajpayee had to later convince the President to go along with the Ordinance. Technically, the President can always return any cabinet proposal that goes to him for reconsideration, but if the latter resubmitted it without changes, the President would have to go along. However, governance is not just about technicalities, and governments do not usually act to overrule any President's advice unless it is really important. Vajpayee was therefore keen to avoid such a situation.

The second part of the announcement has actually had a much greater impact on India in general, and not just on its economy. Persuaded by an internal discussion that India must learn something from the US Interstate Highway system, Vajpayee announced a massive highway project which aimed at developing highways from north to south, from east to west, with the Golden Quadrilateral linking the four metros. The plan was to have main grids with spur roads to link interior areas to metros. The total length would be 12,000 km, and it was estimated to cost approximately Rs 50,000 crore.

In addition to budgetary support and private partnership, money would be made by charging a cess on petrol sales. The costing was tentative but, to be fair, no cost-benefit analysis was done. Not that governments in India actually look at policy alternatives or even cost-benefit analysis before taking major decisions, but in this case, the government's gut feeling, that reducing logistical costs would give a big boost to growth, would be vindicated many times over. But where would the funds come from? The private sector was roped in as a partner in this scheme, something

which was happening in India for the first time. Funds raised by
the Resurgent India Bonds were seen as another source. Lastly,
the funds that the government could release from disinvestment
of PSU shares and buybacks were other alternatives. In fact, it
assumed that the construction phase of the project would itself
push up demand for steel, cement and labour.

DESPITE THE STOCK MARKET REACTING positively to these
announcements, the overhang of poor economic outcomes
threatened to sink Vajpayee. The high price of onions in 1979
brought Indira Gandhi back to power in the January 1980
elections; it was threatening to be equally unsettling in late 1998.
Though there was a poor onion harvest in December 1997, about
15 per cent lower than usual, neither the UF nor the Vajpayee
governments imposed a ban on onion exports, since such drastic
actions would not have been good for farmers and for the reputation
of India as a reliable trading partner. There were onion exports of
2,50,000 tonnes or 8 per cent of the depleted harvest during the
year. This led to an increase in prices, and by the time the export
ban was imposed, on 8 October, the retail price of onions was
over Rs 40 a kg in several centres in the north. It later scaled an
all-time high to Rs 60. Though import norms were liberalized,
onion imports did not total more than 500 tonnes. It was not just
onions; prices of vegetables and fruits also went up and remained
high. The consumer price index was in excess of 15 per cent by the
end of October, the highest in five years.

Vajpayee decided that the time for audacity in economic
reforms had come. On 23 November, the cabinet decided to go
ahead and open up the general insurance sector to foreign investors.
Chidambaram, as finance minister in the UF government, had
attempted to do this but, in the face of strong opposition from the
BJP and his own allies, had to withdraw his bill from Parliament.
Vajpayee now decided to take up from where Chidambaram was

forced to abandon his plans. This decision took the BJP by surprise, and the party president, Kushabhau Thakre, publicly complained that they had not been consulted.

The bill was slated to be introduced in Parliament in the winter session, but there were doubts about its fate. A vocal section of the BJP was completely against it. In fact, Vajpayee had his back to the wall since the opposition to his economic policies, and even his governance, ran strong. The RSS and its affiliates (BJP, BMS, ABVP, VHP, SJM, etc.) held their *chintan baithak*, a regular event, in Nagpur, early in December. The message was that the Parivar was not happy with the government because 'the Vajpayee government is giving in to immediate constraints, including pressures from the international agencies, without considering the long-term implications'. Not only had the BMS publicly opposed the Insurance Regulatory Bill, but its convenor, Dattopant Thengadi, had also resigned from the government taskforce on employment generation in protest against Montek Singh Ahluwalia being made the chair. Thengadi, a senior RSS functionary, also attacked Vajpayee later at a public event in Nagpur. But there was an acceptance that other parties in the NDA would rally around Vajpayee. The general acceptance in party circles was that ultimately, there would be a compromise and the opening in insurance would be restricted to domestic investors only.

There is a cliché that Indians do not cast their votes but vote their caste. While this may have been true in parts of the country, it seemed absent in November–December 1998, when legislative assembly elections were held in Rajasthan, Madhya Pradesh and Delhi (Mizoram, too, went to the polls at the same time, but the issues there were different). Rajasthan and Delhi were ruled by the BJP, and Madhya Pradesh by the Congress. The elections in the Hindi heartland were seen as a referendum on the Vajpayee government, which faced huge challenges, mostly home-grown.

In Rajasthan, the Shekhawat government was skating on thin ice. The BJP had been blown away in the parliamentary elections in terms of seats and could not do worse, but it did. It polled a mere 32 per cent, 10 per cent less than its share in the parliamentary elections, held barely six months prior.

In Madhya Pradesh, the BJP won 39 per cent of the popular vote, exactly the same as in the previous assembly elections in 1993, so it remained in the Opposition. Surprisingly, the BJP had swept the parliamentary elections in 1996 and 1998, polling 46 per cent and 48 per cent respectively. The state BJP was faction-ridden, and it was said that each faction leader was happier seeing Digvijaya Singh of the Congress (I) in power as chief minister than any of his rivals. Singh, on his part, did not allow anti-incumbency to harm him by denying tickets to a large number of incumbents. His re-election was a big shock to the BJP.

But the BJP's performance in Delhi was probably worse. The party had removed Madan Lal Khurana from chief ministership because his name had figured in the Jain hawala scam. Sahib Singh Verma took over as chief minister, but when Khurana was found to be innocent, he saw that his way back to the office of the chief minister was blocked. High food inflation, prolonged infighting and a perceptible lack of governance forced the BJP leadership to replace Verma with Sushma Swaraj, but not without drama. Verma switched off his phone and went underground. When forced to quit, he walked out of his official house and boarded a city bus. Swaraj took office just forty days before Delhi went to the polls.

The BJP was wiped out, with the Congress (I) winning fifty-two out of the seventy seats; its earlier tally was fourteen. The BJP's vote share fell 17 per cent, from over 50 per cent in February to 33 per cent, and it had only fifteen MLAs as against the forty-nine seats won in 1993. Interestingly, the BJP's share of votes in the Delhi assembly polls has, over the years, remained in the

32–34 per cent range, depriving them of the right to form the local government. It won thirty-two seats and almost formed the government in late 2013, and one and a half years later, got wiped out, wining just three seats, but with almost the same number of votes. What determines the number of seats the BJP wins in Delhi is how well or badly others perform.

Were these late-1998 state assembly elections a referendum on Vajpayee? The Centre for the Study of Developing Societies (CSDS) had conducted a pre-election survey in Delhi. According to its findings, '63.5 per cent of the respondents considered price rise as the biggest electoral issue, 47.8 per cent said that the law and order situation in Delhi had deteriorated during BJP's five-year rule, nearly 50 per cent were unhappy about the shortage of drinking water, and 57.7 per cent had a similar opinion about electricity supply.' Responsible or not, Vajpayee's government had to take a beating that pushed it on to the back foot.

Before Parliament met, there was further pressure on Vajpayee, this time from the Christian community, which on 4 December, held a nationwide day of protest. The protest was directed at the attacks that were said to have taken place against members of the community. Christian institutions, including schools, remained closed for the day. They said that there was propaganda against the Christian community that it was 'pursuing an aggressive campaign of proselytisation'. A delegation of Church leaders and laypersons met Vajpayee on the day of the protest. Vajpayee deprecated all incidents of violence against the community, but he strongly refuted any suggestion that the BJP might have been involved in them. The issue would, of course, continue to dog Vajpayee for much of his tenure as prime minister.

Vajpayee was carrying too much of the burden of governance and needed effective support. Even though Parliament was in session, he expanded his ministry, which was unusual timing since the new ministers would have to answer questions in Parliament even before they could settle down in office. The induction of Jaswant Singh and Pramod Mahajan as ministers was proof that Vajpayee had indeed come into his own and would not allow himself to be boxed in easily. Further, he needed a full-time foreign minister, and the government's bench strength needed credibility. Singh had the gravitas, Mahajan brought in political skills, and Jagmohan, also sworn in, was acknowledged as possessing formidable administrative capabilities.

It was widely expected that Sushma Swaraj would be back in government after her stint as Delhi CM, but this was not to be. She had just been elected to the Delhi assembly from the Hauz Khas constituency, and since she was a member of the Lok Sabha, she was required to resign from one seat. She asked Vajpayee, who wanted her to remain in the Delhi Assembly. However, Vajpayee either changed his mind or was persuaded to do so, for Swaraj resigned her Delhi assembly seat, but she did not become a minister in the Vajpayee government for another two years.

WITH PARLIAMENT ON AND A visible need to push the legislative agenda, Vajpayee, an economic liberalizer at heart, came out very strongly in favour of the decision to allow FDI in insurance. He understood that business-as-usual would drag India down and that bold steps were necessary to reverse the decline in the country's fortunes. He also seemed determined to establish his authority and would not let the conflicting pulls and pressures of his disparate alliance to hold him back any longer. He had to live up to the expectation that his government would be different from the others and would deliver. Therefore, to quote *Frontline* (19 December 1998), 'Vajpayee put his personal prestige on the line, warning that any hint of prolonged turbulence over a crucial policy issue would deal a fatal blow to the Government's credibility.'

The party and the alliance, by and large, rallied behind Vajpayee. The only notional concession was that no amount collected as insurance premium would be allowed to be invested overseas. On the other hand, the government maintained the equity ceiling for foreign investors at 26 per cent, with another 14 per cent permitted for NRIs. There would be an Insurance Regulatory Authority, vested with wide-ranging powers to ensure the security of insurance funds. This was done despite continued opposition to this measure from the Bharatiya Mazdoor Sangh, part of the larger Sangh Parivar.

It would take Vajpayee another year to get the insurance law through, but that was because his government fell and there was no Parliament for six months. Fortunately, the Congress (I) and BJP shared the understanding that this reform was necessary. Similarly, the Congress (I) went along with the government in the passing of the amendments to the patent law to make it compatible with a ruling of the World Trade Organization in a case that India lost. There was, however, still considerable opposition to the proposed changes, from both the left parties and from within the BJP and its ideological partners like the Bharatiya Mazdoor Sangh. The Cabinet discussed the proposed legislation a number of times but eventually agreed that it had become necessary to amend the law without further delay. This legal change would be approved in another three months, in the budget session of Parliament.

There was consternation in the non-Congress Opposition ranks that the government's legislative agenda was moving so smoothly. Could the Congress's attitude have anything to do with its expectation that it would soon be running the government and therefore considered it better that the BJP government took the initiative to get these controversial laws through Parliament? There was no political capital to be gained if the BJP government succeeded in pushing these changes through, which the Congress agreed with in any case. However, if the government failed, it would stand exposed as ineffectual. Arguably, the Congress (I) would not want to be seen as being led by other Opposition parties. Instead, it would prefer to lead the alternative government as the largest non-BJP outfit in Parliament, and to reclaim its base in UP, where it was increasingly becoming irrelevant.

There was one piece of legislation that Vajpayee set much store by. Though the Congress (I) was in agreement with it, the legislation still went nowhere. This was the bill to reserve one-third seats in Parliament and state legislatures for women. The UF government had taken the initiative, but with large-scale opposition in its ranks, the bill it introduced lapsed when Parliament was dissolved in December 1997. There were, no doubt, practical difficulties with the proposal in a constituency-based first-past-the-post system. Fixing some seats for women, as is done for scheduled castes/scheduled tribes, would not work, because in the latter case, it was done on the basis of the relative strength of the SC/ST population in individual constituencies. The other option, of rotating seats, as is done in municipalities and panchayats, was also not found feasible, since MPs would not be sure that in the next election they could even stand from their own constituencies. Vajpayee felt that the option of increasing the number of seats in Parliament and state assemblies could be explored. However, opposition from Lalu Yadav, Mulayam Singh Yadav and Sharad Yadav, backed by members across parties, made even the introduction of the Constitution Amendment Bill, providing reservation for women, almost impossible. Vajpayee's symbolic success was that the bill was introduced at all, with no hope for any further movement.

The relative success of the government in pushing its agenda somewhat in the winter session of Parliament ensured that there was no immediate threat to it. However, this did nothing to shore up the inherent instability of the Vajpayee government, which meant placating Jayalalithaa. The DMK government had filed cases under the Prevention of Corruption Act (PCA) against her. It had also set up special courts under PCA to expedite the disposal of the cases. Contrary to popular wisdom, the CBI and PCA are the responsibility of the Ministry of Personnel, and not of the home ministry. The minister in charge has always been the prime minister. However, the day-to-day management rests with the minister of state, who, in this case, was K.R. Janarthanan of the AIADMK.

Jayalalithaa wanted the government to intervene and found a legal loophole, which was that it was only the Central government that had the powers to establish and transfer cases under the PCA to special courts. After many discussions, including lengthy consultations with Attorney General Soli Sorabjee, the Ministry of Personnel issued a notification transferring the cases back to the regular court. This was despite the fact that the Madras High Court had upheld the creation of the special courts by DMK government, and though the Supreme Court had admitted Jayalalithaa's appeal, it had not issued any stay orders. While politics is not about ethical behaviour, however desperate the circumstances, this was a cynical move that neither enhanced Vajpayee's image nor, in the final analysis, prolonged the life of his government. Even if it was Vajpayee acting on legal advice, it was not a happy occasion.

IT IS NOT EASY TO understand the full scope of a prime minister's responsibilities. Vajpayee had to grapple with insurgencies in Assam that seriously threatened the stability of the state. Unlike in the smaller states of the north-east, reports of insurgency from where could be kept away from the mainstream, Assam is a big state and effectively controls all access to the other states in the region. Vajpayee had been given an extensive brief on the Assam situation by the state's governor, Lt Gen S.K. Sinha, right at the beginning of his tenure. Armed insurgents of the United Liberation Front of Asom (ULFA) and of Bodo groups had cross-border sanctuaries in Bangladesh, Bhutan, Myanmar, etc.

The Bhutanese government finally agreed with the Indian assessment that such sanctuaries needed to be destroyed. Around December 1998, the Bhutan Army started joint operations with Indian security forces against ULFA and Bodo rebels in the hills and forests of southern Bhutan. The then king, Jigme Singye Wangchuck, put his personal weight behind these flushing operations, with reports emerging that the crown prince and present king, Jigme Khesar Wangchuck, led the operations. Encouraged, Bangladesh too started putting pressure on camps in its territory.

The Russian prime minister, Yevgeny Primakov, visited India in early December 1998, the first high-level visitor from any major power to visit India since the Vajpayee government assumed office. In fact, no high-level visitor from any Western country visited India in Vajpayee's first term. Primakov, was a stand-in for Yeltsin, who wanted to visit India but his health was failing. The evening meeting at Hyderabad House, followed by dinner, was a raucous event by diplomatic standards, since the meeting kept getting postponed while the visitors quenched their thirst. However, there was also a lot of substance to the meeting. India's recent experience with Primakov had not been very pleasant, when post-Pokhran, he bluntly told Brajesh Mishra that India must sign the NPT and CTBT. Still, it was easier to talk to him than to his boss, Yeltsin. Vajpayee's phone conversations with Yeltsin were nightmares for us. They were long, rambling monologues, which, because of translation, made it hard for Vajpayee to recall all the points and nuances later, when we made notes.

Primakov was a realist who had thought long and hard on re-positioning a declining Russia in the world. Russia and China had started moving closer to each other, partly as a response to Clinton's unilateral actions in the Balkans and West Asia. The Russia–China relationship could be described as hardcore strategic, with a total absence of ideology. Primakov loudly wondered whether India and

China might develop a similar tack. A 'strategic triangle' between Russia, India and China would, in his eyes, be the best way to prevent the continuance of the post-Cold War unipolar world.

His suggestion, though tantalizing, could not be endorsed easily. Vajpayee responded by pointing out that while India's relations with Russia had stood the test of time (after all, Russia sold more defence supplies to India than to the rest of the world), post-1991, their non-defence economic ties had collapsed. In the case of China, Vajpayee was defensive and agreed that bilateral relations must improve. He, however, made it clear that India would not like to be in any bloc, not even in a partnership that could be seen as directed against any other country, certainly not the US. In any case, their bilateral relations with the US were most important for all three countries. Vajpayee wanted India and Russia to sign a strategic partnership agreement, whose contours were broadly agreed upon. These would be long-term military cooperation, possible purchase of important defence platforms (like the incomplete aircraft carrier 'Admiral Gorshkov'), advanced jet trainers, mid-air refuelling planes, T-90 tanks, the joint manufacture of silicon chips and cooperation in hydrocarbon exploration and development (including in Sakhalin). Russia also categorically confirmed to India that it would not sell defence equipment to Pakistan. India and Russia further shared concerns over the evolving situation in Afghanistan and decided to continue to collaborate over it. There were obvious disagreements on the NPT and CTBT, with Primakov arguing that India must sign the former if it wanted to join the UN Security Council.

The month of December was almost done with. It was on a cold and misty morning that Vajpayee waited in the forecourt of Rashtrapati Bhavan, where Sri Lanka's President, Chandrika Kumaratunga, was to be given a ceremonial welcome. Kumaratunga, who was staying at Rashtrapati Bhavan itself, was late. We had been informed by those who knew her that she was always late, and she lived up to her reputation. The visit was an important one. Later that day (28 December), the India–Sri Lanka Free Trade Agreement was signed. This was as much political as economic. The hope was that it would lead to the economic and political stabilization of Sri Lanka. The economies of the two countries were not very complementary from the point of view of bilateral trade, since both were interested in the export of garments and tea. Though limited in its ultimate impact, the Agreement helped cement India–Sri Lanka relations.

On 30 December, the Vajpayee government threw a bombshell. It issued an order for the dismissal of the navy chief, Admiral Vishnu Bhagwat. It was a simple order which read, 'The President is pleased to withdraw his pleasure for the continuance of Admiral Vishnu Bhagwat . . . on account of the loss of confidence in his fitness.' This was done under Section 15(1) of the Navy Act, 1957. It was possibly the most difficult decision that Vajpayee had to make. I realized this because for Vajpayee, and indeed for the BJP, the armed forces were an exalted institution, which they worshipped. In their eyes, for history to reverse itself and for India to emerge as a world power, we needed a strong military. Their main grouse against Nehru was for his failure to defend India in 1947–48 in Kashmir, and for failing to build up a strong army that could have avoided the humiliation of 1962. Despite all their differences with Indira Gandhi, who sent them to jail during the Emergency, she was still an admired figure for many in the BJP and the larger Sangh Parivar, because of her dissection of Pakistan in 1971. However, contrary to legend, Vajpayee never called her Durga!

In the Admiral Bhagwat case, the issue had been building up for months. Bhagwat would not accept government rules on promotions or on the appeal process of performance appraisal of individuals. He'd had a running battle with the navy's hierarchy, with even a past chief recommending his dismissal from service.

Bhagwat himself had argued that in the case of promotions and appraisal, the navy chief could only propose, and it was for the government to decide. Despite repeated counselling, including by Brajesh Mishra, and using the good offices of Sharad Pawar, Bhagwat was not prepared to accept orders passed by the defence minister.

Something had to give, but it wasn't Vajpayee. My own hunch is that with the government almost on permanent crisis mode, and with allies and party colleagues putting relentless pressure on Vajpayee, Bhagwat's assessment was that the government would back off. This was a mistake. A reluctant Vajpayee was forced to accept an unpalatable truth that Bhagwat's misdemeanours had crossed all limits of discipline. There was confusion on who could sack a serving chief. Since the President is the ceremonial head of the armed forces, it was suggested that the matter be taken up with him. It was left to me to point out that as per the 'Transaction of Rules', which governs government functioning, it is the minister concerned who exercises the powers of the President. Even the most minor of government orders—for the purchase of pencils, for example—are issued in the name of the President. As are all appointment orders. Ministers, in turn, delegate financial and administrative powers to different levels below them. As a matter of caution, the cabinet committee on security endorsed the decision to sack Bhagwat.

Bhagwat did not take this lying down. Niloufer Bhagwat, his wife and also his advocate, used rather strong language, alleging that Bhagwat's successor, Admiral Sushil Kumar, was unfit. She even accused the government of acting on communal lines. Three of the key players in this issue—George Fernandes, Admiral Sushil Kumar and the then defence secretary, Ajit Kumar—were all Christians. Since Bhagwat had a running feud with one senior naval officer, Vice Admiral Harinder Singh, a Sikh Officer, whom the Akalis were said to be supporting (a claim made by Niloufer

Bhagwat), this Christian angle was missed by many. On New Year's Day 1999, as if to emphasize that he did not regret his decision, Vajpayee paid an unscheduled visit to a naval warship in Port Blair on his visit to the Andamans, where Vice Admiral Singh was the local fortress commander. However, despite the sacking and the lack of any legal intervention to reverse it, *l'affaire* Bhagwat would not go away.

The coming year, it was hoped, would to be different. But how different? From Port Blair, Vajpayee went to Bengaluru via Chennai, where he inaugurated the Indian Science Congress, keeping up the tradition of past prime ministers. Vajpayee also launched his dream project, the National Highways Development Project, in Bengaluru. The full impact of this initiative would be visible only in the future; Vajpayee had to demonstrate similar vision and leadership politically.

This opportunity came to him at the BJP National Convention, which was what Vajpayee had primarily come to Bengaluru for. This meeting was being held in the context of the drubbing the party had received in the legislative assembly elections, the concerns that Christians were being targeted, and the controversies within the BJP and the Sangh Parivar over economic reforms. Kushabhau Thakre, in his presidential address, mentioned that the perceived delay in containing the price rise had hurt the party in the assembly elections. The backlash was swift. Madan Lal Khurana, a minister in Vajpayee's cabinet and member of the party's national executive, strongly defended Vajpayee and blamed his attackers in the Parivar for blocking government decisions and obstructing smooth administration. He was scathing in his criticism of the Bajrang Dal, Swadeshi Jagran Manch and Vishwa Hindu Parishad. Khurana also announced his resignation from the BJP's national executive.

It was time for Vajpayee to assert himself. He said that while 'widest consultations are both desirable and necessary, decisions of the government are final'. He was not going to accept any back-seat driving by people outside the government. A draft resolution on economic matters had been prepared by K.R. Malkani, an RSS veteran who edited many publications. This draft was not taken up, and instead, the party adopted a fresh resolution prepared by Finance Minister Yashwant Sinha. The party agreed that the 'government is the best judge of the country's economic situation and is best placed to take appropriate steps'. The resolution endorsed the IRA and Patent Bills. Sinha added that there was 'no contradiction between economic reforms and Swadeshi'. The political resolution did not blame the BJP government for losses in the Rajasthan, MP and Delhi assembly elections. It described the violence against Christian places of worship in Gujarat as extremely unfortunate and agreed that the party should speak with one voice. The clear message was that the continuance of the government would be given precedence over the priorities of the party.

Vajpayee followed up this public acknowledgement of concerns of the Christian community, particularly about attacks on places of worship in Gujarat, by visiting the Dang district of that state. We saw damage—broken tiles, parts of the roofs of those temporary (*kucha*) structures had been destroyed—and also met with members of the community and others. In some areas, we were told that reconversion efforts had been started. The Christian population of this predominantly tribal district had gone up by 416 per cent since 1981, and their total number had reached 30,000 due to evangelical efforts. We were told, and I later read about it in the *Economic and Political Weekly*, that in a particular village, Christian tribals refused to contribute to the traditional village feast, which led to large-scale resentment. In one of Vajpayee's meetings with members of the civil society, two Sarvodaya leaders, Chunibhai Vaidya and Ghelubhai Nayak, opposed the violence strongly but also said that they were upset by the conversions, quoting even Gandhi. They sought a debate on conversions, which Vajpayee endorsed in all sincerity. This endorsement was to come back to haunt him in ways wholly unexpected.

ON THE NIGHT OF 22–23 January 1999, in a heinous crime that put the country to shame, an Australian Christian missionary, Graham Staines, and his two young sons, were burnt to death as they slept inside their station wagon, by a mob in Manoharpur village of the Keonjhar district in Odisha. The mob was said to have been led by a member of the Bajrang Dal named Dara Singh. Staines had gone to conduct a jungle camp, where he would preach the Bible. Tensions had been brewing in this village and neighbouring areas between the converted Santhals and the non-converted, with the former said to have tilled land when it was not supposed to be tilled and taken a few other steps that went against tribal culture and practices. The state of Odisha was ruled by the Congress (I), and while there were multiple allegations against Dara Singh, there appeared to be no formal cases charged or being pursued by the police.

Vajpayee was shocked and horrified. I never saw him look so perturbed. The murders had, in fact, shaken the entire country. Vajpayee immediately condemned the murders, said that a judicial enquiry would be appointed and sent three ministers, George Fernandes, Navin Patnaik and Pramod Mahajan, to the spot. Fernandes, on his visit, questioned why the state government had not taken action against Dara Singh. According to Fernandes, 'After Pokhran, there are many forces that don't want this government to remain . . . Someone had decided at some point of time that Staines had to be killed.' The Bajrang Dal denied that it had any link with the murders. Advani backed them, for which he received a lot of flak. Dara Singh was apprehended, convicted and given the death sentence, which was reduced to life imprisonment later, but the Bajrang Dal connection could never be established.

Vajpayee was so affected by the brutality that he sat on a one-day fast on 30 January, Gandhi's martyrdom day. But this got no traction. On the contrary, some analysts attributed his talk of national debate on conversions as encouraging such violence, for it delegitimized the work of missionaries—a conclusion which could not have been more distorted and wrong. In fact, Vajpayee's sadness about this and many other such incidents was well recorded by *India Today* (18 February 1999) when he said, 'The outer shell of democracy is no doubt intact, but it appears to be moth-eaten from inside.'

Simultaneously, the Khurana issue was coming to a boil. He wrote a letter to party president, Thakre, resigning from the national executive—something he had said in his speech at Bengaluru. He also said in the letter that he was 'shaken over the killing of the missionary'. He sought 'permission to atone for the countrywide anti-minority attacks'. He added that he considered 'Hindutva to be nationalism . . . The meaning of pseudo-Hindutva for some could be destroying cinema halls, digging up cricket pitches, but not that Hindutva which I believe in.' More than the language used, the fact that the contents of the letter reached the media before it reached Thakre, could not go unchallenged. Thakre accepted his resignation, and when Khurana dropped in to see Vajpayee, presumably seeking help for the second and last time, I was the harbinger of bad news.

Khurana had been waiting in my room when I came back and conveyed Vajpayee's terse message that he should submit his letter of resignation. I knew Khurana well, from his days as the chief minister of Delhi. He was always warm and supportive of my maverick ways, and whenever I came up with a bold proposals on education, he counselled me to seek the advice of Jag Pravesh Chandra, former chief executive councillor (like chief minister), a Congressman to his bones and then sitting on the Opposition benches. I felt terrible as I handed Khurana a blank sheet of paper, on which he wrote his letter of resignation.

What probably made it worse for Khurana was that he was basically reflecting what he thought was Vajpayee's angst, partly personal and partly structural. The first as represented by the ideological issues with the Sangh Parivar, which sometimes resulted in direct attacks on Vajpayee. It was also structural, as neither did the BJP have the numbers to push its agenda, nor did the alliance have the cohesion to be able to deliver on good governance. Khurana, unfortunately, had crossed the line and tarred the reputation of the party and the government comprehensively. Disagreements and arguments are fine, but his attacks deteriorated into becoming unguided missiles that worked against Vajpayee, against what Khurana himself was arguing for and ultimately, against the BJP as well.

Khurana, however, did not relent easily. In an interview after his resignation, he was quoted as saying, 'There are elements in the RSS which want to remote control this government and tarnish its image . . . A section of the RSS is hell bent on destroying Vajpayee.'

Within a couple of days of the Staines murders, on 25 January, twenty-five Dalits, including women and children, were massacred by the Ranbir Sena in Shankarbigha village of the Jehanabad district in Bihar. Reports suggested that this terrible violence arose from land-related tensions. The Naxalites had effectively taken over thousands of acres of land of the upper castes, with both sides resorting to violence. The Dalits were identified as supporters of Naxalism. The brutality of the violence, which for the first time targeted women and infants, was meant to send a message to anybody with Naxalite sympathies. It was chilling. Unfortunately, the Rabri Devi-led Bihar government was either ineffective or had a stake in inter-caste tensions. The tragedy was that nationally, this massacre soon became a non-event.

Continuing his political offensive, at the end of January 1999, Vajpayee attended the Swadeshi Mela organized by the Swadeshi Jagran Manch (SJM). He'd probably decided to make up with the SJM, many of whose leaders he knew well and, by and large, shared a common world view with. He said that they all belonged to the same family, and he welcomed their suggestions but added that he may not be able to accept all of them. It was reconciliation but on his terms. Similarly, he reached out to different parties within the ruling alliance. He was very keen on Mamata joining the cabinet, but she wanted only railways, and the Samata Party (SP) could not be asked to accommodate her at their cost. The SP also wanted their senior leader, Abdul Ghafoor, made a minister. Jayalalithaa wanted some more of her nominees, including Ramamurthy, to be made ministers (Ramamurthy was in the government from her quota). She also made it clear that just because her nominees were made ministers, it should not be taken to mean that she would cease her onslaught of criticisms. Internecine conflict within the Akalis meant that their nominee Prem Singh Chandumajra withdrew his candidature. Vajpayee effectively said a no to the allies by simply not including anyone. They would have to wait.

Vajpayee, it seemed, was always under attack, from different sides at different times. Even the activist role of the National Commission for Minorities (NCM), post-March 1998, indicated the kind of pre-conceived notions and biases that Vajpayee had to encounter. The NCM sent its team to Gujarat as early as August 1998, as if predicting that there would be trouble in that state. There had been no violence till then, only sporadic, localized tensions, no different from the past or elsewhere.

The team was composed of the NCM's vice chairperson, Reverend James Massey, and member Marzban Patravala, a Samajwadi Party activist who had lost the 1996 parliamentary elections on that party's ticket. The team was also accompanied a lawyer, Y.M. Muchala, and two journalists, namely John Dayal (general secretary, All India Catholic Union, who had authored a pamphlet for the Catholic Bishops Confederation of India in 1997 on the occasion of the fiftieth year of India's independence, arguing for reservation for 'Dalit' Christians); and Javed Anand (who later attained prominence along with his wife, Teesta Setalvad, in the aftermath of the Gujarat riots of 2002). The NCM submitted its first report on Gujarat in September 1998. Its chairman, Tahir Mahmood, was quoted in *India Today* (18 February 1999) as saying that the 'problem in Gujarat is based on a central theme: alleged conversions.' He did not present any facts in support of his claim and completely ignored the census report of Dang.

Massey wrote to the chief minister of Gujarat, Keshubhai Patel, and to Advani in December, saying, 'To an impartial observer it appears that the control of the entire country, particularly the state of Gujarat, has been mortgaged to the activities of the VHP, the Bajrang Dal and the RSS.' Again, a case of judgement without evidence! Tahir Mahmood happily informed the media that he saw his tenure as chair, NCM, divided into two phases—pre-March 1998 and post-March 1998. Mahmood was the person who wrote the legislation (Muslim Women's Act) that overrode the progressive Supreme Court judgment in the Shah Bano case. The NCM submitted two more reports on Gujarat, in January and February 1999, the latter report was presented to the President himself, possibly to get greater media attention.

Despite the fact that constitutional bodies like the NCM had started behaving in this cavalier manner, Vajpayee was still able to assert his authority and tried to ensure a sense of balance. However, whatever he did was never enough to silence those who were determined to show him in a bad light, even by misrepresenting his position. To wit, the historian K.N. Panikkar, who wrote, 'The response of Prime Minister Vajpayee, who is considered a good man and a liberal by many, was the most devious. By calling for a public debate on conversions, he suggested that the blame, in fact, rests with the victims.' As Panikkar wrote in 'Towards a Hindu Nation' (*Frontline*, 30 January–12 February 1999), this 'anti-Christian tirade' was '. . . another example of the unfolding of the fascist agenda of the Parivar'. He concluded that 'the BJP leadership, including the Prime Minister, has not unequivocally condemned it is reflective of its tacit acquiescence'.

7

The Bus Ride

*'My message to the people of Pakistan will be short and simple.
Put aside the bitterness of the past, together let us make a
new beginning.'*

—Atal Bihari Vajpayee at Atari border, 20 February 1999

*'De-freeze the Kashmir problem, weaken Indian resolve,
and bring India to the conference table without provoking a
general war.'*

—Maj. Gen. A.H. Malik, XII Div., who planned
Operation Gibraltar

Even as India was trying to navigate the international arena
and establish its position as a responsible state, domestic
developments were a perpetual cause of distraction. The issue of
violence against Christians had suddenly acquired salience with
the brutal murder of Graham Staines and his two sons in Odisha.
With this incident, India was once again on the back foot globally,

with an extremely high level of negative reporting. The general trend of the reports was that the minorities were being persecuted and that India was close to becoming a genocidal state. So much so that even the friends of India raised alarm. Congressman Gary Ackerman, co-chair of the now emergent India Caucus, said in an Indian event in the US that 'I must warn all of you that unless the Government of India does act firmly, showing the whole world that it won't tolerate attacks against religious minorities . . . New Delhi may have serious problems on the Hill. Not merely image problems but legislative sanctions as well.'

Simultaneously, and almost as a complementary to this negative publicity, the US nuclear non-proliferation pressure on India was upped considerably. From Strobe Talbott to his boss, Madeleine Albright, the message they gave to the US Congress and to the world was that India was ready to sign the CTBT, following which sanctions would be lifted. As if to soften the blow, or conversely, to put us on the defensive, they said that Pakistan, too, was readying itself to sign the CTBT.

In parallel, Russia's attempt to reframe international order, by creating a strategic triangle involving Russia, China and India, had run into a wall, an idea which Prime Minister Primakov had pushed in his December visit to Delhi. Primakov was assured that India valued friendship with Russia and would strengthen it. In early February 1999, China formally rejected Primakov's idea of a strategic alliance between Russia, China and India, more or less deploying the same logic as India.

According to the Chinese foreign minister, Tang Jiaxuan, China had 'always adhered independently to a foreign policy oriented towards peace'. He made it clear that while China had a strategic partnership with Russia, this 'includes neither alliances, nor confrontation with third countries such as the United States'. In any case, he said that his country's relations with India were 'far from ideal'. In the context of the present times, it is clear that

China has completely given up such objections, while it is India that keeps emphasizing that its approach towards the Indo-Pacific in general, and the Quad in particular, is aimed at confronting, or isolating, China. However, if Tang's successor in 2019 was to say that India–China relations were 'far from ideal', he would not have been wrong. Some things, it seems, never change.

Vivek Katju, who enjoyed, and rather continues to enjoy, the reputation of being a hawk in the Indo–Pakistani strategic circles, rang me on 2 February 1999, around mid-morning. What he said challenged my own understanding of Vivek's world view; for him, defending the national interest was the driving force, and if that made him appear as a hawk, so be it. In fact, Pervez Musharraf in his memoir, *In the Line of Fire*, blames Vivek for the failure of the Agra talks—a remark easy to make but wholly inaccurate.

Going back to that winter morning of 1999, Vivek said that the *Indian Express* had carried a long interview of their editor-in-chief, Shekhar Gupta, with Prime Minister Nawaz Sharif. The short point of the interview was that Sharif was inviting Vajpayee to Pakistan. Vivek worried that the response the Ministry of External Affairs had finalized, was going to be a damp squib. The ministry spokesperson was going to say that the 'government would give an appropriate answer as and when a formal invitation was received'. Vivek argued with me that our response should be a positive one and that we should not worry about formality. Unfortunately, Vivek said, even Brajesh Mishra had gone along with the ministry's position. Could I reach out to the PM, who, by the way, was away in Lucknow, his parliamentary constituency? Vivek felt that this was an opportunity that had to be grasped. I spoke to Vajpayee, who agreed that we should send out a positive message. As Shekhar Gupta subsequently wrote, Sharif himself was apprehensive that his invitation might be snubbed by Vajpayee.

Sometime later that day, while addressing a press meet in Lucknow, Vajpayee said, 'I would like to have a bus ride from Delhi to Lahore.' Since this was a bombshell, the media wanted more information. At that stage, all Vajpayee could say was that the details would be worked out between the two governments. Since it wasn't Delhi, Vajpayee could get away with such cryptic answers. He did clarify, however, that some progress has been made but added that 'much ground [is] yet to be covered before India becomes a signatory to the CTBT'. He made it clear that there were obviously a number of steps required before this could happen.

As expected, this announcement of the Lahore visit set off a multitude of reactions from analysts and commentators. Significantly, the impending visit was generally seen as an indication that India and Pakistan were moving on the road to signing the CTBT. This was because the US specifically, and the West in general, maintained that 'only close and friendly relations between India and Pakistan can avoid effectively a suicidal nuclear race in South Asia'. This was despite India shouting from the rooftops that its security concerns went beyond Pakistan.

There were a number of reports in the media that Western and Japanese sources believed that India would sign the CTBT by end of April or early May. This belief was based on a read-out of the Jaswant–Talbots talks, as briefed by the Americans. To strengthen this narrative, the State Department spokesperson, James Rubin, on 2 February, said that the US had not diluted its commitment to the CTBT, in order for India and Pakistan to sign it. The unambiguous message was that it was India, and not the US, which was making major concessions in moving ahead with improving relations. The US made it explicit that the CTBT would come into effect as per the treaty; in other words, India and Pakistan would sign up. For India and Pakistan, the expectation was clear. They needed to have a number of mechanisms in place, namely a nuclear weapons and delivery system restraint regime; a stringent export control system; a moratorium on fissile materials production pending agreement on the FMCT; direct India–Pakistan talks on all outstanding bilateral issues, including nuclear. It was obvious that the US was targeting to get India on board for not just the CTBT but also for the NPT.

Editorial comment in India was more upbeat and less about the international ramifications. It was suggested that the bus trip showed a new mood of bonhomie, suggesting 'a distinct thawing of relations'. There were references to the idea of a common destiny of both India and Pakistan, despite the three wars, Pakistan's proxy war and terrorist activity elsewhere. Analysts remembered that it was Vajpayee as foreign minister who had opened up to Pakistan. There was a general feeling, which exists even now, that in dealing with Pakistan, the BJP in power would be much less constrained.

The news from Pakistan was somewhat different. Sharif was seen as acting under economic compulsions, in addition to pressures from the US. After all, Pakistan was economically much weaker than India. There was appreciation that both leaders were aware of the limitations of confrontation. With this move, Nawaz Sharif was signalling a shift away from Kashmir and towards investments and trade, recognizing that resources should not be wasted on an arms race. There were concerns in both countries, more so in Pakistan, that signing the CTBT was a pre-condition for lifting economic sanctions.

What made things worse for Sharif, though, was that in terms of Pakistan's power structure, his position was weak. As a Pakistani commentator, Rasheed Rahman, bluntly explained, 'The terms of "endearment" between the military and civilian spheres, are still heavily loaded in favour of the former.' According to him, and to the agreement of many, none of the civilian governments had established that they hold power, 'and not merely occupy offices'. The Pakistan Army had a powerful instrument of ensuring this, which was that the electoral process was less than credible. This instrument is as potent at present as it was two decades ago, with the electoral victory of Imran Khan in 2018 a powerful reminder of it, if any was needed.

With the confirmation of Vajpayee's Lahore visit, there was palpable excitement, and unrealistic expectation, in the air. It was said that Sharif would be visiting Delhi for the India–Pakistan Test match due in a couple of days. That the visit did not happen was understandable. But Vajpayee did go to the Feroz Shah Kotla stadium in Delhi, met both the teams, spent some time watching the match and later hosted a reception for the teams at 7 RCR. On that day, I enjoyed my conversation with Raj Singh Dungarpur, the then president of the Board of Control for Cricket in India, about cricketers of yore, including the American fast bowler John King, who scored over one thousand runs and took over a hundred wickets in one season playing for an English county in the early twentieth century.

Slowly, the officialdom got into the act. The Ministry of External Affairs (MEA) hailed the proposed Lahore initiative as a path-breaking exercise, as something that 'will be one more manifestation of India's abiding desire to build peaceful, friendly and co-operative relationship with Pakistan'. Vajpayee would become first Indian PM to visit Pakistan since Rajiv Gandhi's visit for the SAARC summit in 1988. At the same time, the MEA also cautioned that Pakistan was yet to convey its acceptance, or rejection, of the proposed dates (17–20 February) for the meeting between the foreign secretaries of both countries. A series of meetings at the foreign-secretary level had been mandated at the Vajpayee–Sharif talks in New York in September 1998. That meeting had identified a set of six issues as the agenda of these talks.

The Pakistani establishment now warmed up to Vajpayee's proposed bus ride. Their foreign ministry said that this 'is a welcome step and would go a long way in establishing good ties with India'. As with all bureaucracies, including our own, they added that they were still waiting for official communications from New Delhi that Vajpayee would indeed travel to Lahore. One side wanted a written invitation, while the other wanted a written confirmation.

When asked about the visit, Jaswant Singh, who was in London for not very pleasant talks with the British government, explained that Vajpayee had decided on taking the inaugural bus to Lahore months ago, 'but the announcement had come only now'. He was right that the idea of the bus service was mooted in New York but had since moved rather slowly. In fact, all actual approval and agreements were finalized in the two weeks between Vajpayee's public acceptance of Sharif's invitation and the actual travel.

Interestingly, at this time, the Vajpayee government also decided to grant a visa to Salman Rushdie to visit India. This announcement was made by Jaswant Singh in London. The Vajpayee government would later allow him to take possession of his ancestral house in Solan, to my mind, by taking a liberal interpretation of the law governing evacuee property.[1] Singh held talks with both Tony Blair and Foreign Minister Robin Cook, whose encounter with I.K. Gujral in 1997 has been referred to earlier. Singh explained in detail how the India–Pakistan agenda was developing and went beyond just the bus service. There was the resumption of officer-level talks; India was interested in the supply of power from Pakistan; it had purchased sugar from Pakistan; and their discussions would cover nuclear issues also. Singh later told the media that on the CTBT, India would not stand in the way of its coming to force, 'provided all other Article 44 countries

---

[1] The Evacuee Property Act was legislated to deal with property left behind in India by those who had migrated to Pakistan at the time of Partition, and to settle the property claims of those who had to leave what became Pakistan.

agreed to it'. He also made it clear that he was in London not to make a case for lifting sanctions but to see that our position is better understood. Cook's gratuitous advise on Lahore was that Kashmir be discussed too, which was obviously on the table.

It was not as if there were no discordant notes in India or in Pakistan. Bal Thackeray thought it was futile for Vajpayee to attempt to improve relations with Pakistan. He was clear that 'Vajpayee's bus travel to Lahore will not help him in either improving India's relations with Pakistan or get extra votes back home for his party'. For some time, Thackeray had been targeting Vajpayee and the BJP over Pakistan, despite the fact the Shiv Sena and the BJP had been allies for a long time, jointly running the government in Maharashtra, besides being in the NDA.

In order not to disrupt Pakistan cricket team's first tour to India in over a decade, in the face of very strong objection from the Shiv Sena, the government agreed not to schedule any match in Maharashtra, remembering how the 1991 tour was disrupted when the Wankhede pitch was dug up. Not satisfied with Maharashtra being kept out of the tour, Shiv Sena workers this time attacked the pitch in Delhi's Feroz Shah Kotla stadium. Fortunately, the damage was minor. Then, on 18 January, when Advani was in Mumbai, over seventy Shiv Sena workers vandalized the office of the Board of Control of Cricket in India (BCCI) in Mumbai, damaging, in the bargain, even the 1983 World Cup won by India. It was left to Advani to sue for peace; Thackeray announced that the Shiv Sena was ending its agitation against the Pakistan tour because he did not want the Congress (I) to benefit from these public differences. However, he continued to use rather strong language against Vajpayee and Advani on this issue.

ON THE OTHER SIDE OF the border, there were reports that the Lashkar-e-Taiba (LeT) would disrupt the proposed Lahore–Delhi bus service. Of all the jihadi groups that have emerged out of Pakistan, LeT was, and is, seen as an arm of the army, rather than an entity supported by it. The Jamaat-e-Islami youth wing (Pasban) also announced that they would 'not allow Vajpayee to enter Pakistan as his visit will harm the cause of Kashmir'. Later, the Jamaat-e-Islami and Imran Khan's Pakistan Tehreek-e-Insaf (PTI) opposed the visit, with the former sending its storm troopers in the streets of Lahore at the time of the visit. But no major political party joined in this opposition. In a sense, these opinions reflected the misgivings the Pakistani establishment harboured at the bus initiative, in opposition to the positive sentiments on the Indian side.

Veteran broadcaster David Frost's interview with Jaswant Singh and the Pakistani foreign minister, Sartaj Aziz, brought out this contradiction quite starkly. For Singh, Vajpayee's bus ride to Lahore was part of confidence-building measures. He explained that talks had been going on, and both the PMs had issued a joint statement. Aziz, on the other hand, talked about India's 'inflexibility on Kashmir', mentioning the 'high-level deployment of troops and the number of civilian casualties'. He conceded that both PMs were talking to help build a better world and that the US had been helpful.

These differences in approach would be on full display in the days immediately prior to Vajpayee's travel dates, when parliamentarians from both sides met in Islamabad. Pakistan's finance and commerce minister, Ishaq Dar, was a rare public figure in that country to have a different take on the matter. At a SAARC ministerial meeting in Dhaka, he said that political conflicts between India and Pakistan should be no bar to increasing trade, because 'the governments of India and Pakistan were firm on improving the situation'.

In case anybody thought that with the Lahore bus yatra in the offing, all else was forgotten, discussions in the US Congress on the

Christian issue reminded us of the need for continuous vigilance, early action and persistent balancing act. The US Congress wanted India to protect minorities and mentioned what it saw as a sharp increase in violence. It specifically wanted the Indian government to 'check burnings, beatings, assault, rapes'. It appreciated the government's condemnation of violence, Vajpayee's visit to Gujarat and the arrest of the main accused of Graham Staines murder in Odisha, but was 'concerned about your government's inability to protect the basic human rights of Christians in India . . . while political organizations such as the World Hindu Council, which has been allied with your political party, continues to foment violence and call for a ban on conversions'.

Taking his mind off the domestic and international pulls and pressures, which were becoming immense at that time, Vajpayee travelled to the Caribbean and to Morocco in the first fortnight of February 1999. It was the first prime ministerial visit to Trinidad and Tobago since 1968. Our host, Basudeo Panday, was the first prime minister of Indian descent in Trinidad and Tobago and had been the chief guest at the 1997 Republic Day in New Delhi. It was moving to hear the local band play 'Suhani Raat Dhal Chuki' at the airport welcoming ceremony.

The dynamics of race politics and tensions that Trinidad was grappling with came to the fore when Vajpayee laid the foundation stone of the Government of India-funded Mahatma Gandhi Institute of Cultural Co-operation, on a site donated by the local government. Prime Minister Panday, to balance this, announced at the function that his government would establish a research centre on Trinidad and Tobago Carnival in order to satisfy the Afro–Caribbean community. Incidentally, when Panday had visited India in 1997, the Indian media generated a wholly unnecessary controversy on whether he was a Brahmin.

For me, the highlight of that visit was meeting an elderly lady, who was born in India and had moved to Trinidad in

the 1930s. She was an exception, for the present-day Indo–
Trinidadians are the descendants of indentured labour taken by
the British Raj to different parts of their empire, largely to grow
sugarcane. This was necessitated by British economic interest,
hamstrung by the abolition of slavery. The terms of engagement,
or agreement, were legally governed by an agreement, hence
they referred to themselves as *girmityas*, which was slavery in
all but name.

From Trinidad, we hopped over to Montego Bay in Jamaica
for the G15 Summit. It seems an embarrassment to remember
but once upon a time, India and a large number of developing
countries worked hard to try and restructure what was called
'global financial architecture'. The G15 was the most important
such platform. Vajpayee had been unable to attend the previous
iteration in Cairo (May 1998), because of the nuclear tests. The
expectation this time was that India would offer major inputs in
this restructuring exercise.

The Malaysian prime minister, Mahathir bin Mohamad,
fresh from the setbacks he'd suffered during the East Asian crisis,
when his country's economy went into free fall, was in full flow
and had the hall at his feet with his denunciation of global capital
flows. On the other hand, there were countries like Brazil and
Peru, plugged into global financial markets and worried about
doing anything that would upset their access and therefore
threaten their growth story. In between was Vajpayee, trying a
balancing out. So on the one hand, he called for transparency in
regulations governing financial markets, and linked booms and
busts to massive capital flows ('hot money'). The reality was that
such turbulence even affected countries not directly involved due
to global interdependence, recalling the adverse effect of the 1997
Asian crisis on India.

On the other hand, Vajpayee was clear that 'India remains
committed to continuing with our economic liberalization

programme at a pace and in a manner that we consider is best suited to our needs'. Ultimately, all these efforts at restructuring came to nothing as the largest and fastest-growing developing country, China, stayed out, preferring to link its fortunes with the supply of its manufactured products to the developed world and later to all of us. Ultimately, most of these countries needed financing from the World Bank/IMF; where they did not, they still needed to meet the financial ratios laid down before they could access global financial markets. The limited restructuring which happened was in reaction to the North Atlantic financial crisis of 2008 and the need to make China a larger stakeholder in the system.

On our return, we stopped in Morocco for a day—a whirlwind of a day at that. Breakfast on the plane, lunch in Rabat, evening tea in Marrakesh and dinner in Casablanca. The last one was only for a few of us, but it had been a gruelling day and Vajpayee was up to it. The formal meeting with the Moroccan prime minister, Abderrahmane Youssoufi, was in Rabat, where we stayed. The king, who ran the show despite an elected government, wanted a meeting, but he was in Marrakesh, so we were flown there on a windowless plane. Before meeting the king, we were taken on a quick tour of what was supposed to be the most expensive hotel in the world, La Mamounia. Then, without any warning, the king promptly awarded a medal to Vajpayee, possibly some kind of national honour.

India's relations with Morocco were on the mend at this time. India used to import phosphates from Morocco for conversion into fertilizers. India was also negotiating setting up a joint venture fertilizer plant in Morocco. Bilateral relations had worsened since India had recognized the Polisario Front as the government of newly decolonized, disputed territory of Western Sahara. But India was now moving away from that position. The formal dinner, hosted by the Moroccan prime minister was in Rabat, but it was likely to be long and boring, like all such dinners, so off a few of us went to Casablanca. We covered the hundred-plus kilometres in less than an hour.

THINGS WERE MOVING RATHER WELL on the Lahore front, if less well on the domestic political front. All formal approvals of the bus service were in place. It would run point-to-point between Delhi and Lahore, a distance of around 500 km, with three technical halts, taking a total of fourteen hours. The flagging off would be held at Ambedkar Stadium, New Delhi, on 20 February at 6 a.m. Though Vajpayee was to travel on the initial run, the plan was wisely modified to the extent that he would board the bus at Amritsar airport and travel the thirty-seven kilometres to the Attari border on it, where he would be received by Nawaz Sharif. In fact, the official agreement between the two sides on the establishment of the bus service was formally signed by High Commissioner G. Parthasarathy and the secretary, communications ministry, Government of Pakistan, barely two days before the actual visit.

For the US and most developed countries, every step towards Lahore and the establishment of better bilateral relations seemed to revolve around the nuclear issue, and the false India–Pakistan equivalence. Strobe Talbott chose the impending visit to affirm that the Clinton administration was determined to see India and Pakistan sign both the CTBT and the NPT. He added that the US position 'remains that neither India nor Pakistan should possess or deploy any nuclear weapons' and 'any number higher than zero' would not be fine. Yet he let on that the US had accepted that 'neither India nor Pakistan is likely to abandon its nuclear program any time soon'.

Talbott hinted that both PMs were building domestic consensus in favour of signing the CTBT. At that time there was a G8 meeting in Tokyo, which made it clear that there would be no lifting of economic sanctions till India and Pakistan 'demonstrate more willingness' towards moving to signing the NPT. If the US was serious about India signing the CTBT/NPT, statements like these were certainly not the best way to help the cause. Today, the CTBT is one forgotten treaty, while the NPT is better known by its failure to stop proliferation even by those countries who have signed it.

Building on the momentum to improve bilateral relations, Pakistan's Jang Media Group, organized an India–Pakistan Parliamentary Forum meeting. The Indian side was full of heavyweights, including past and future ministers. It was led by former speaker of the Lok Sabha, Balram Jakhar. Other members included Sushma Swaraj, Arif Mohammad Khan and K.R. Malkani. There was lots of bonhomie, people quoting poetry, etc., but the 'K' word divided the sides. Indians, irrespective of their political affiliations, said the time had come to look beyond Kashmir and solve other issues. They specifically suggested that if goodwill was developed, Kashmir could be sorted out. The Pakistani side wanted Kashmir on the agenda as the top priority. Their minister for parliamentary affairs said that the Lahore bus service was a good beginning to solving Kashmir.

Sartaj Aziz urged India to focus on 'the core issue of Kashmir' rather than lay emphasis on peripheral areas of the relationship between the two countries. He warned the meeting that 'unless we move forward towards a settlement of the Kashmir dispute on the basis of respect for the inherent right of self-determination of the Kashmiri people, peace will continue to elude South Asia'. Benazir Bhutto came and told the meeting that she was 'unable to pray at my grandmother's grave in India' and brought in Kashmir. Gohar Ayub spoke only about Kashmir. It was left to Sushma Swaraj to point out that there was a lot of misinformation about Kashmir.

Nawaz Sharif, in his interview with Shekhar Gupta, had set a very ambitious agenda. He said that if sincerity and reasonableness were to prevail, India and Pakistan should be able to resolve the Kashmir problem as well as other outstanding issues by the end of 1999. The veteran diplomat Mani Dixit, someone Vajpayee was quite fond of, wrote a newspaper article in support of the initiative and raised the important issue of whether this meant that there would be a qualitative change in the negotiating stands of both countries and in the mindset of the power structures of both countries; because only then could the atmospherics change for any progress to take place.

Dixit underscored the fact that Pakistan was facing political and economic dilemmas, and needed a working relationship with India. He acknowledged that Vajpayee was practical, sober and had a non-confrontational approach to foreign policy. But would domestic political compulsions in both countries allow relations to move towards finding solutions? Dixit's view did reflect the general perception that the visit might just provide the right environment to move ahead. However, there were also fears that 'without some substantial progress on substantive issues, the whole exercise might go waste'. One of Dixit's predecessors as foreign secretary, the redoubtable A.P. Venkateswaran, unfairly sacked from his job by Rajiv Gandhi, was sceptical, arguing against the perils of 'instant' diplomacy, since what would be achieved by it was unspecific.

In hindsight, it should have been clear that any road to peace with Pakistan was going to be a long and hard one. But those were heady days, when the sheer audacity of the initiative made all obstacles look manageable. In fact, the only prominent person in Pakistan exhibiting any ambition about the effect of the visit was Nawaz Sharif himself. Initially, he even announced that he would travel back in the bus to Delhi. Pakistan Tourism, who would run the bus from their side, said that the PM's office had asked them to be ready for it. Sharif then told the Pakistani parliament, 'We are not afraid to take bold decisions. I will use my mandate to ensure that.' He urged India to go beyond stated positions for a meaningful dialogue and not to let the opportunity go waste.

It was at this moment that the IMF board considered Pakistan's loan proposal. The US, UK and Canada abstained, a technicality that ensured that the loan went through. India did not oppose the proposal, indicating that it wanted an economically stable Pakistan. We could hardly have acted otherwise, considering that two of our joint secretaries in the Ministry of External Affairs—Vivek Katju (looking after Pakistan) and Rakesh Sood (disarmament)—were on their way to Islamabad, finalizing the agenda and negotiating a joint statement and an agreement on nuclear issues with Pakistan, necessary to make the Lahore visit a substantial one.

Vajpayee's bold initiative seemed to be paying off. Japan, ever so gently, shifted its stand. It 'urged Pakistan to ensure progress in the nuclear field and with the CTBT before India'. Japan also asked Pakistan to show adherence to the NPT, tighten its nuclear export controls, and expressed concerns 'over the co-operation between Pakistan and North Korea in the nuclear field', making it clear to Pakistan how this might affect its ties with Japan. Unfortunately, Indian analysts don't seem to have even noticed this clear signalling about the 'help' that Pakistan received in its nuclear and missile programmes.

The changed sentiments were not limited to the Japanese alone. As if on cue, the World Bank approved a US$210 million loan, for the restructuring of Andhra Pradesh's power sector, the first Indian loan to go through after the Pokhran-II tests. Though the sanctions had exempted poverty-related loans, the World Bank management was obviously under US pressure not to act till they saw some progress, in terms of the reduction of tensions, in South Asia. Further, Frank Pallone, the Democrat Congressman and co-founder of the India Caucus in the US House of Representatives, came out boldly in favour of US–India relations. He said that the US should move away from a confrontation with India and that instead, the US should try 'to make India a partner in American foreign policy goal of minimizing the threat of nuclear war'.

The campaign to demonize India as a country which had initiated a nuclear arms race in South Asia was beginning to come apart. Pallone endorsed India's candidature for permanent membership to the UN Security Council, the first time that a US policymaker had taken such a position. No wonder that the Vajpayee government decorated Pallone with a Padma Vibhushan in 2002.

Yet Sartaj Aziz remained sceptical. Even as Vajpayee was packing his bags for Lahore, Aziz cautioned that 'India must go beyond its present emphasis on peripheral areas of our bilateral relationship and demonstrate its willingness to work for the resolution of our fundamental differences'. By contrast, Jaswant Singh was magisterial. Vajpayee, he said, would 'carry the message of peace, of India's desire for an enduring relationship of mutual confidence, peace, and multi-faceted co-operation between the two countries'. Since the US was seen to have, directly or indirectly, pushed India and Pakistan to meet, Singh clarified that 'there has been no pressure. India and Pakistan do not require the services of an interpreter in their dialogue.' It was Jaswant Singh at his best.

A few days prior to the visit, some of us were bogged down in tying up the visit of the non-official delegation that would accompany Vajpayee to Lahore. A very efficient foreign service officer in the PMO, Satish Mehta, sat with me in my room as we contacted everybody selected to go along, and where needed, added names. If I remember correctly, they included the evergreen peace activist Kuldip Nayar; poet Javed Akhtar; actor Dev Anand; BJP leader Vijay Kumar Malhotra; economist-administrator A.M. Khusro; heads of Indian chambers of business, Rajesh Shah and K.K. Poddar; cricketer Kapil Dev; singer Mahendra Kapoor; journalist-parliamentarian Indrajit; actor-politician Shatrughan Sinha and others. It was not an easy task as we were running short on time. Passports had to be collected, travel plans arranged and visas stamped. To be fair, the Pakistani high commission was most cooperative. Farooq Abdullah, who was at his aggressive best during the visit to Pokhran the previous year in May, declined the invitation. One name I completely missed was Muhammad Ali Jinnah's grandson, Nusli Wadia—a fact he reminded me of when we returned. Taking him along would have been a coup.

On the official side, Jaswant Singh would come along. Brajesh Mishra had gone to Lahore a day ahead, to finalize the text of whatever was to be released by both prime ministers. From Vajpayee's family, his adopted daughter, Namita Kaul Bhattacharya, her husband, Ranjan Bhattacharya, and their daughter, Niharika, would accompany us. This indicated how much Vajpayee was personally invested in the visit, raising the tenor of the occasion by a few octaves.

The excitement at Race Course Road on 20 February was infectious. As Vajpayee was to say on crossing the border later that day, he saw it as a defining moment in South Asian history, which he hoped he and Sharif would be responsible for. It all seemed unreal, as if there was nothing else left to do, now that peace with Pakistan was all dusted and ready to be launched. What could go wrong?

PRAMOD MAHAJAN, WHO WAS THE minister of information and broadcasting, organized live coverage of the visit on Doordarshan, at a time when only cricket matches were covered live. But life can be difficult. The burdens of office and unrealistic expectations are not easy to handle. On our way to the airport, Vajpayee turned to me and nervously told me that he had left his hearing device at home. He had been checking his pockets and found them empty! Fortunately, we had cell phones by then, so I quickly rang back and asked for it to be sent pronto. But while the PM's motorcade gets a free pass on the roads, a car carrying the PM's hearing aid does not. Once again, fortunately for us, the PM's plane, operated by the air force, always has sufficient margin, a fact I knew by then. This I found out early, when one day, while flying back from the north-east, I was told somewhere above Lucknow that we would be landing in Delhi an hour later and not 35–40 minutes as I expected. That knowledge gave us breathing space.

The airport send-off was touching, with L.K. Advani, M.M. Joshi, Ranga Kumaramangalam, Ananth Kumar and Pramod Mahajan among the ministers, the service chiefs and the Gandhian activist Nirmala Deshpande present to wish Vajpayee the best. We boarded but could not leave immediately since the car with the hearing aid was still on the way. But we were lucky that the traffic was light and the delay was a manageable twenty minutes.

The welcome at Raja Sansi Airport (as it was called then) in Amritsar was raucous. After Vajpayee alighted and was received by the governor of Punjab, General B.K.N. Chhibber, and Chief Minister Parkash Singh Badal, all discipline broke down. There were people milling all over—a veritable monsoon wedding in February. It was a relief to get on the bus, named Sada-e-Sarhad, and move on. Earlier, speaking to the media on alighting, Vajpayee had said:

> I am going with a message of peace (*aman*) and friendship (*dosti*). The approximately 100 crore people of India want relations with Pakistan to improve, trade between the two nations to increase and travel to be made easier. There are some issues of Punjab I would take up with them.

The journey to Attari passed off quickly. The bus had two seats on either side of the aisle. Vajpayee was on the first seat on the left side of the bus, all by himself. Throughout the short forty-minute journey, we provided an opportunity for each member of the delegation to sit with Vajpayee and chat for a while. Kapil Dev came across as the most gracious, quickly moving out when it was the turn of somebody else to sit with Vajpayee. With some of the others, I had to almost physically evict them; they shall not be named as they are not with us any more.

On reaching Attari, the Indian side of the border, the bus slowed down, as bhangra dancers moved in front of it and there were cheering crowds everywhere. Eventually, the bus stopped and Vajpayee got down to address the media and the country. Unlike at Amritsar airport, this time he used a prepared statement, as he was conscious of history in the making. To quote:

> I am visiting Pakistan today at the invitation of Prime Minister Nawaz Sharif. When I cross the gate and throughout my visit, I will draw inspiration from the knowledge that the prayers and goodwill of the people of India are with me. My message to the people of Pakistan will be short and simple. Put aside the bitterness of the past. Together, let us make a new beginning.

The message was brief but succinct, anticipating the 140-character Twitter generation.

Vajpayee then boarded the bus and it crossed over to Wagah, Pakistan. In fact, the entire bus was not even through the gate when it stopped. Nawaz Sharif was at hand with half his cabinet and the governor of Punjab, our host, to receive Vajpayee. The two prime ministers hugged each other, with Sharif taking the lead and Vajpayee being, as always, the more publicly reserved. Dev Anand, who stood next to them, started reminiscing about the time when he left Lahore for Mumbai and would have carried on till we gently guided him away.

What does one say about the atmosphere? Adjectives failed us but yes, it was Amritsar's chaos multiplied a few times. Much as I admire the professionalism of our security set-up, especially of the SPG, for those ten minutes, it was the almighty or pure chance that ensured things went well. Even the guard of honour, though correctly conducted, was so squeezed for space that when the guard commander lowered his sword to convey his acceptance of dismissal, Vajpayee was well within striking distance. There had to be a discordant note, and that was the absence of Pakistan's three service chiefs at the reception line-up.

Vajpayee again read out a written piece as his message and did not speak extempore.

> I am grateful to Prime Minister Nawaz Sharif for his kind invitation. I bring the goodwill and hopes of my fellow Indians who seek abiding peace and harmony with Pakistan. I am looking forward to a substantive programme and talks with Prime Minister Nawaz Sharif and am conscious that this is a defining moment in South Asian history and I hope we would be able to rise to the challenge.

Vajpayee's long years in diplomacy, mostly as observer and discussant, had taught him the importance of being specific. Ambiguity had its purposes but had to be ditched when one wished to achieve specific goals. This visit was a big risk, possibly the biggest of his political career, and he wanted to send a clear message—that India wanted peace and was willing to stake its reputation to achieve it. Again, in retrospect, a well-thought-out and thought-through move, contrary to many who missed this paradigm shift engineered by Vajpayee because they were blaming him for his lack of short-term achievements.

The brief helicopter ride from Wagah to Governor's House in Lahore brought us face to face with the realities of the deep state. The three chiefs of the army, air force and navy were on hand at the helipad to receive Vajpayee; the army chief was General Musharraf, whom Sharif had appointed after removing the very professional Jehangir Karamat, the last time any Pakistani PM would even contemplate such a move. Yet this was a show of pettiness, as the chiefs seemed prepared to salute

Vajpayee in private but not in public. In fact, as a uniformed officer once taught me, for a person in uniform a salute is a proxy for a greeting and nothing more. The city of Lahore was more or less under a lockdown, with a rampaging group of Jamaat-e-Islami going around the old city, forcing shops to shut down. In fact, the Jammat had given a call for a *hartal*, but the only way it could enforce it was by force.

After our arrival, I remember a very casual evening tea session with Sharif, his key ministers, service chiefs and a few of us. It was a surprise to see the wife of our host in a saree, but then history tells us that till 1971, that was the norm in Pakistan's elite circles. Photographs of Musharraf's wife in his memoir would show the transition from the saree to salwar-kameez, once the former was declared un-Islamic. Noticing that Namita was accompanying Vajpayee, Sharif sent word to his wife, Begum Kulsoom Nawaz, who was in Islamabad to drive down to Lahore.

The motorway from Lahore to Islamabad, a creation of Sharif initiated in an earlier stint, was discussed. Apparently, the planners told Sharif that the road made no economic sense. Sharif countered: Did Shah Jahan calculate the costs and benefits before he built the Taj Mahal? A practical difficulty with the motorway, we were told, was that since it was so prestigious that all leading Chaudharies wanted it to go through their *pind* (village). The result was that the roadway did not take the shortest alignment between the two cities, running rather in a zig-zag manner to cover as many pinds as possible!

The atmosphere was relaxed. I did notice, though, that the chiefs were not in their ceremonial dress but in their official uniform, a boorish act at best. None of this registered very strongly, since the mood was exuberant. But it was not meant to last. The departure for Lahore Fort for the grand dinner kept getting postponed because it was said to be chaotic outside. As we found out later, the numbers of Jamaat workers roaming the streets were in dozens, but the police gave them kid-glove treatment, something which those who follow Imran Khan's accession to power would understand.

The Jamaat-e-Islami leader Qazi Hussain Ahmad had vowed that 'we will not allow Vajpayee to walk the streets of Lahore'. The general understanding was that the Jamaat was acting on instructions from the army. Suddenly, the repeated use of the 'K' word by Sartaj Aziz—'Settlement of the Kashmir issue will be accorded the highest priority'—began to make sense, though to be fair, Aziz personally was in favour of improved relations. He had become the foreign minister, even though Finance was his natural home, after Sharif realized that relations with India could not improve with Gohar Ayub as foreign minister. Few remember that Sharif actually campaigned in 1997 on making peace with India, a position he has stuck to since then at tremendous personal costs.

The Punjab governor had graciously put a bottle of whisky each in the rooms of those of us who were put up in the Governor's House. But as the evening wore on and the large delegation kept waiting, the supply proved inadequate. It must have been past 9 p.m. when we received the all-clear to move for dinner. Throughout, Vajpayee was a picture of calmness and patience. His reminiscence about his visit to Lahore pre-Independence, specifically about going to Anarkali, the heart of culture and entertainment in the old city, reminded us how recent the political divisions were. Vajpayee looked happy but was not exuberant.

We first drove to Maharaja Ranjit Singh's samadhi and the gurdwara, and then went to the Lahore Fort. Sharif had laid out a red carpet, the likes of which most of us had not seen before. Sharif and Vajpayee rode on a horse carriage into the fort. The dinner was overshadowed by the music. The band played Hindi songs throughout. With great difficulty and after much persuasion, we managed to convince them to play a few Pakistani numbers, which was a bad idea.

WHILE THE MOOD IN LAHORE was stratospheric, the news from India was extremely dispiriting. Late the previous night, there were three horrific, targeted massacres of Hindus in the Jammu region, and in all, twenty Hindus were killed. In normal circumstances, this should have led to the cancellation of the visit, but Vajpayee was truly invested in it, and he could not let down Sharif, who, it subsequently emerged, had staked so much more on it that cancellation could not have been an option. But it did point to the limitations in terms of what the visit could achieve in concrete terms. Sharif was battling those who were determined to see the collapse of his outreach to India. So while the American scholar Dennis Kux could say that Vajpayee's Lahore visit was as dramatic as Egyptian President Anwar Sadat's visit to Israel in 1977, the fact that Benazir Bhutto endorsed Vajpayee's visit but did not turn up for the banquet demonstrated that in Pakistan it was unrealistic to expect dramatic results, since the forces against the normalization of relations with India were very powerful.

If I'd thought that dinner meant the end of my working day, I was wrong. Vajpayee was tense about his speech at the next day's public reception and wanted to go over some of his poems, to decide which one he could use. My colleague, Venkat—who is now in Washington, D.C.—and I, spent the best part of the night with our Hindi stenographer in Delhi, going over Vajpayee's poems and having them faxed to us.

If 20 February was all about euphoria, the next day was one long grind, but one should not complain. To us, at Ground Zero, it was history in the making. There were official meetings of the prime ministers, the Lahore Declaration was signed, a press conference in which both PMs were grilled and a relaxed lunch. However, the two public events, one in the morning and the other in the evening, were the highlights, which would be remembered for a long time.

The first one was a visit to Minar-e-Pakistan, a column erected to commemorate the 1940 Pakistan resolution of the Muslim League. If memory serves me right, the idea of visiting the Minar was Vivek Katju's. He thought that it would send a good signal that India had in fact accepted the reality of Partition. What Vivek had left unsaid, though, was that with the BJP supposedly committed to an 'Akhand Bharat', a Vajpayee visit to the Minar would make for powerful optics. Some of us were very enthusiastic about it, but there were contrarian views. The idea was debated in Delhi quite a bit, and Vajpayee agreed that his visit to the Minar would be in order, though initially he was not very convinced.

The line between a politician and a statesman can actually be quite thin, and I realized that Vajpayee had the skill to make the transition when required. His comments at the Minar, and later, while referring to his visit at the civic reception, were proof of that. It was a learning experience for me. 'From this historic Minar-e-Pakistan, I wish to assure the people of Pakistan of my country's deep desire for lasting peace and friendship. I have said it before and I will say it again that a stable, secure and prosperous Pakistan is in India's interest. Let no one in Pakistan be in any doubt of it, India sincerely wishes the people of Pakistan well.' This was direct and forceful, yet conciliatory, taking on all the naysayers in Pakistan who liked to indulge in misinformation about India's intentions. Vajpayee also needed to play to the gallery a little, which he did at the public reception later that afternoon. He opened the subject by mentioning that 'I was told that my presence at the Minar would put my seal of approval on the creation of Pakistan' but then added with a flourish, 'Pakistan does not run on my seal. It has its own seal.' The effect was electric. Unfortunately, the word 'seal' does not quite convey the effect of its Hindi equivalent, *mohar*.

At the public reception held on the lawns of the Governor's House, even as Vajpayee worked the crowd, there was no ambiguity in his message. He said that he was not in favour of Pakistan and that Partition had left a scar, but added that 'we have no option but to live together and work jointly. One can change history, not geography. One can change friends, not neighbours.' Without bringing in China, he explained that Pokhran-II was not done with an aggressive intent but was an act of self-defence. Vajpayee, far from making light of the threat of nuclear war, warned his audience that 'a small spark can cause a huge fire'. He emphasized that there was no option available to us but peace and hoped that both sides would respect a mutual moratorium on further testing. And then he unleashed his most potent weapon, reading out from his poem, 'Jang Na Hone Denge'. The general buzz in the audience was that if Vajpayee were to stand for election from Lahore, he would sweep the polls!

Earlier in the day, the two countries had signed a number of agreements, some symbolic and others of substance. The prime ministers joined in signing the Lahore Declaration, a detailed statement intended to meet the needs and requirements of all concerned. It condemned terrorism in all forms and committed the two sides to promoting and protecting human rights and fundamental freedoms. It spoke of implementing the 1972 Simla Agreement, in letter and spirit. With an eye on the international community, particularly the US, Japan and the UK, it specifically spoke of 'Confidence Building Measures in nuclear and conventional spheres in order to prevent conflict.'

Even the memorandum of understanding (MOU) signed between the two foreign secretaries was finely detailed. One could call it the operational manual of the Lahore Declaration, which if implemented would have allowed the two sides to actually get into a strategic dialogue (though the word 'strategy' has lately got debased in the academic discipline of international relations, since it is used rather casually). The MOU, without using the term 'strategic', had got it right when it said that the 'two sides shall engage in bilateral consultations on security concepts, and nuclear doctrine, with a view to developing measures for confidence building in the nuclear and conventional fields aimed at avoidance of conflict'. It talked about setting the stage for a regular security dialogue covering disarmament and non-proliferation. It was agreed that the foreign ministers would meet periodically to discuss all issues of mutual concern, including those falling in the nuclear domain.

The MOU was also about brass tacks. For example, it said that 'the two sides undertake to provide each other with advance notification in respect of ballistic missile tests and shall conclude an agreement in this regard'. Both sides agreed to have an immediate exchange of information about any accidental, unauthorized or unexplained incident that could create the risk of a (nuclear) fallout or an outbreak of a nuclear war between the two countries. An appropriate communications mechanism would be established to eliminate possibilities of misinterpretation by either side of any action or incident.

Sharif was open and very positive in his meeting with the media. He said that in the near future, Pakistan would extend the most favoured nation (MFN) status to India, reciprocating India's action of 1996. MFN is possibly the most misunderstood word in international trade; all it implies is the lowest level of normal trading relations by which countries agree not to discriminate against any trading partner. Before China joined the World Trade Organization, the USA would give it MFN status on an annual basis. Since people wondered why China was being singled out for favourable treatment, the US administration replaced MFN with NTR, or normal trading relations. Twenty-one years after Sharif's announcement, till the Pulwama attack led to almost a complete cessation of India–Pakistan bilateral trade, Pakistan had yet to actually extend MFN status to India.

Sharif confirmed to the media that the Kashmir issue would be discussed with India, but there seemed to be a certain amount of disbelief, so Vajpayee was also asked this question. He confirmed that Kashmir was indeed on the agenda. It was clear that most of the local press were unaware of India's persistent complaint about Pakistan-backed terrorists operating in Kashmir, or about the Indian Parliament's unanimous decision on Pakistan Occupied Kashmir. Therefore, India did want to talk about Kashmir with Pakistan.

Vajpayee was effusive in his praise of Sharif and the hospitality. Left unsaid was his acknowledgement of Sharif's bold but risky gamble. The body language and comfort level between Vajpayee and Sharif was to be seen to be believed. That Begum Kulsoom Nawaz reached Lahore to play formal host to Namita was a touching gesture. Sometime in the course of the day, there was an informal interaction between the two prime ministers in the first-floor living area of the Governor's House, the same place where we had tea the previous evening. A few of us were present there. The singer Mahendra Kapoor, in a mustard-coloured suit, dropped in. He wanted to go back early. Sharif told his people to arrange for a car to take Kapoor to the border. It felt like the morning after a grand subcontinental wedding.

The chief ministers of both the Punjabs met separately. Parkash Singh Badal's emphasis was on the need to have an institutionalized arrangement for cultural exchange. He expressed his concern about the upkeep of Sikh shrines in Pakistan and suggested that the Amritsar-headquartered Shiromani Gurdwara Prabandhak Committee (SGPC) could do it. Incidentally, the head of the Pakistani version of the SGPC had been invited for the Vajpayee functions. He was a non-Sikh army officer. But unlike Badal's forward-looking approach, his counterpart, Shehbaz Sharif, brought in Kashmir and bilateral trade. Of the Sharif brothers, Shehbaz remained less inclined to take on the

Pakistan Army, always looking for a compromise with them, and therefore the mandatory reference to Kashmir.

We returned to Delhi that evening buoyant and hopeful. Parliament was to convene the next day, and since it was the first session of the calendar year, it would begin with the President's address to the joint sitting of both the Lok Sabha and Rajya Sabha. Though the President reads it out, the address contains the government's agenda. The speech had been finalized before we'd left for Lahore, but it would need revision. I was asked to write out one paragraph, get Vajpayee's approval and have it translated into Hindi before sending it to Rashtrapati Bhavan. I alerted Gopal Gandhi, the principal secretary to the President, and set to work. The next few hours went into that one paragraph, because the President himself, being a former diplomat, was very particular about the use of language. My day ended late, but it was with a sense of achievement, bordering on euphoria.

Still, scepticism persisted in both countries about the usefulness of this high-level initiative. Going further, people questioned the motivations of both countries for what was seen as a high-risk gamble, which, while raising expectations, could simply fail to deliver. Indian analysts were more or less in agreement that with the economy in Pakistan floundering, Sharif's options were limited. Pakistan, much more than India, wanted the sanctions lifted, and assuring the West that the 'dangers' of a nuclear conflagration in South Asia had lessened would help in achieving this objective. Peace with India and signing the CTBT were seen as key to this. Sharif was also constrained in that his space for manoeuvre domestically was limited, though the full extent of how limited it was did not become apparent immediately.

While Pakistan kept its options open to resort to multilateralism in case the bilateral approach towards India failed, there was a realization that the Kashmir issue had lost traction internationally. Despite this, the Pakistan foreign office had to clarify within a day of the summit that they have not accepted that Kashmir was an integral part of India, pointing that the 'Declaration testified to the fact that Kashmir is an issue between the two countries, to be discussed and resolved . . . We will rightfully expect a genuine and positive movement towards the final settlement of Jammu & Kashmir.'

India's position was much better, but there was a lot that had to be done, and getting the US sanctions lifted would help, financially, psychologically and strategically. India's problem was—and largely remains—that it needed to regularly demonstrate its autonomy. This meant that there was a strong aversion to third-party intervention, particularly if this had to do with the dispute with Pakistan. It is not as if third-party intervention hasn't been used in sorting out India–Pakistan disputes before. This happened in the 1950s, when the World Bank, under US instructions, brokered the Indus Water Treaty; and again in 1965–66, when the Tashkent agreement was midwifed by the Soviet Union. Both parties in 1999 came to the conclusion that they would have to sign the CTBT to get the sanctions lifted, and the leaderships felt that domestically, it would be easier to sell this in the context of a bilateral peace deal than concede that it was due to any perceived American pressure.

In those days, it was difficult to keep America out of any India–Pakistan conversation. In the context of Lahore, President Clinton commended 'the two Prime Ministers for demonstrating courage and leadership . . . addressing difficult issues'. He called on both to curb competition in nuclear arms, prevent nuclear and conventional conflict, and resolve tensions and disputes, including Jammu and Kashmir. The US State Department added that they were 'pleased that they discussed steps to address nuclear concerns, including CBMs'. In case somebody had missed the story, it added that the two prime ministers 'met on their own, not under pressure'.

There was already considerable opposition to India moving away from the national convention on not signing the CTBT. In fact, even as preparations for Lahore were on, the analyst Brahma Chellaney wrote that 'the blame for providing resuscitation and respectability to the loophole-ridden treaty goes to Prime Minister AB Vajpayee's government, which began talking about CTBT in a disjointed manner after the tests'. He pointed out that initially, Vajpayee had said that India was 'prepared to consider being an adherent to some of the undertakings of the CTBT'. Later, he said, Vajpayee moved further and asked that the US should match India's steps, hinting at his readiness to make concessions in his UN speech. However, the US backed out and started helping Pakistan. Chellaney's criticism, in retrospect, has its merits. There was a lot of confusion on the CTBT, and India did seem on the road to signing this highly flawed treaty. Fortunately, this was not to be, as other developments overtook it.

In the Indian establishment, George Fernandes was consistent in his opposition to signing the CTBT under pressure, arguing that India would do so only if its security concerns were taken care of. Post-Lahore, Jaswant Singh, largely seen by the strategic community as pushing the CTBT agenda, had to clarify that there was no secret pact with the US on the CTBT, that no other country could determine India's level of minimum nuclear deterrent and that there was no arms race in the sub-continent. He emphasized that India would never compromise on fundamentals and that he would not respond to claims by US officials that India was on the verge of signing the CTBT. Talks with the US were focused on converting voluntary moratorium into de jure obligation, and no decision had been taken about entering into negotiations over the CTBT. Soon, this debate would get sidelined as the region faced new challenges.

The story of Lahore was to end, but in very different ways from what any of us could have envisaged. Vajpayee's position as prime minister had strengthened substantially over the past few months, and Lahore only added more weight. Yet there were many in India who were unhappy with this, and they realized that if Vajpayee were to continue, their agendas may well be over. On the other side, would the Pakistani establishment allow any substantial move towards normalizing India–Pakistan relations?

The ferocity of the backlash in both cases was unbelievable and unexpected.

8

The Fall

'Since the BJP is at the core of the alliance, it shall make every effort to ensure that the prestige and cohesiveness of the coalition are not diluted by organisations belonging to its ideological fraternity.'

—Resolution of the NDA Coordination Committee,
2 February 1999

After the horrible months of most of 1998, with Vajpayee gradually clawing back his autonomy but with the situation mostly in crisis mode, it was difficult to believe that the Vajpayee government had any other way to exist. It was a constant struggle to set the new agenda—meant to lift the trajectory of the country so that it would be recognized as an emerging powerhouse. Not that the external environment was particularly hospitable, despite Vajpayee's best efforts to tell the 'free world' that their hopes of China evolving like one of them was going nowhere; instead, it was with India that there was a convergence of interest and values.

If Vajpayee was not taken as seriously as he should have been, it was not just because of the minuscule size of the Indian economy but also because of the doubts about Vajpayee's longevity as a PM and his ability to push India forward, weighed down as he was by the political baggage of a fractious alliance and intra-party challenges. Lahore and his assertion domestically was potentially a game changer.

The NDA Coordination Committee met yet again on 2 February 1999. This was meant to be one more attempt at trying and salvaging the government. On the one hand, there was a certain ambiguity about what the stance of the BJP's ideological partners—the members of the Sangh Parivar, like the VHP, Bajrang Dal, Swadeshi Jagran Manch or even the RSS—would be on economic policies. Even before the terrible murder of the Staines had occurred, the narrative that minorities, especially the Christians, were under attack had gained considerable traction. The level of communal violence was actually quite low, but perceptions are important and the BJP was lagging in this. The Coordination Committee made it clear that the onus of keeping its ideological cousins under control was on the BJP. However, the meeting balanced this by calling upon all coalition partners to ensure that none of them 'shall publicly voice its opposition/dissent to any policy or order of the government'.

As expected, Jayalalithaa did not attend the meeting, and Thambidurai, who did, was not authorized to sign any document. A few days later, when Fernandes met Jayalalithaa, she refused to endorse the agreed statement of the meeting, highlighting the part about partners agreeing not to go public with their disagreement about government policies and actions. She clarified that she did not object to it but had her reservations. However, though Chandrababu Naidu also did not attend, he was not about to withdraw his support to the government. Mamata Banerjee had walked out of the Coordination Committee in November 1998 in protest against the 'neglect' of West Bengal, particularly in terms of railway projects, and refused to budge. But she, too, was not likely to pull down the government. Responding to the demands of its allies, the government had rolled back wheat and rice price hikes in the public distribution system (PDS) for the below-poverty-line (BPL) families but managed to retain it for others. The extra burden was a steep Rs 1800 crore.

Though Vajpayee's Lucknow press meet was noted more for his announcement of accepting Nawaz Sharif's invitation to visit Lahore, he had also used this platform to inform the media that there were to be no further rollbacks. He called for a fresh look at the economics of subsidies and clarified that the government was willing to take tough decisions. Vajpayee was forced to say this, as there were persistent questions about his government's inability to say 'no' and stick to doing what it had announced. The tensions within the coalition were best expressed in a *Hindustan Times* editorial of 4 February ('Back from the Brink'), which said that this was a case of one step forward, two steps back. The editorial also said that there was a distressing pattern of the allies and the organizational wing of the BJP pushing the coalition to the edge of the precipice and then pulling back in the nick of time.

With the pendulum poised to swing to the other side, no wonder Sonia Gandhi wrote, in an article published in the Congress's in-house journal and widely reported in the media, that the government was in danger of collapsing and that her party was ready to discharge its responsibilities to the country, which, she said, 'would fall on the Congress (I) sooner than later'. She also wrote that there was 'competitive populism' between the BJP and other members of the Sangh Parivar, that the government's credibility was at its lowest ebb and that Vajpayee's one-day symbolic fast, prompted by the Staines murders, was not going to solve anything as 'fundamentalism was an inherent part of the ruling party.'

The gossip in the media was that the Congress (I) would prefer to form a government with or without the participation of other 'secular' parties, and then go in for a mid-term poll, the assumption being that the BJP's graph would only go down. The composition of the Lok Sabha simply did not allow for a stable government to emerge. And yet, few would have bet that the government would go so soon.

Vajpayee decided to call a meeting of the National Development Council (NDC) on 19 February in response to Naidu's request, or should one say 'demand'. The NDC was chaired by the prime minister, and its members were key economic and development ministers of the Union government and all chief ministers. The main official agenda was to discuss and approve the draft Ninth Plan and criteria for the allotment of funds under major rural poverty alleviation programmes. Naidu's main focus was to discuss issues such as the price of rice and wheat in ration shops under the public distribution system as well as the contentious issue of urea and fertilizer prices. Of the parties supporting the government, from within or without, it was actually Naidu who put the maximum pressure on the government, but it was never a public tantrum. In fact, it was never public at all. But he would always have a list of demands and grievances ready. Likewise, Yashwant Sinha used to have a note ready on all that had been done for Andhra Pradesh, or what could not be done. The pressure was relentless, even unfair, but the government's handling of it was sophisticated.

Mamata was mollified by a number of railway projects announced for West Bengal. She expressed happiness and said that her party would continue to extend support to the NDA. Not just that, she added that 'no political party or group is in a position to replace this government and nobody wants another election'. What was left incomplete was Mamata rejoining the Coordination Committee, but that had to do with her becoming the railway

minister in Vajpayee's government, which would have to wait
for some time. Similarly, Pawan Chamling, the chief minister
of Sikkim, clarified that his party, the Sikkim Democratic Front
(SDF), was not withdrawing support from the NDA, but he
wanted a complete rollback on wheat and rice prices, and not just
the limited one announced by the government.

Even as the supporting parties were pressuring the government
to go slow on economic reforms because of the short-term costs, the
others were highlighting ideological issues. Jaipal Reddy accused
the government of saffronizing broadcasting. The Congress (I)
agreed with this charge and added that Prasar Bharati was being
converted into 'Prachar Bharati'. It was a relief to see some creativity
in politics, even if those making the allegations always judged
the usefulness of state organs in relation to their commitment to
the ruling dispensation. When Advani met VHP leaders Giriraj
Kishore and Ashok Singhal at his office, the Congress (I) smelt
a hidden agenda. Predating Arnab Goswami by decades, their
spokesperson was clear that the 'Nation has a right to know what
transpired at the meeting'.

The pressure on Vajpayee was not just domestic. The US
Congress wanted India to protect minorities. It appreciated
Vajpayee's visit to Gujarat, the arrest of the accused in the Odisha
murders case, the government's condemnation of violence, but
was 'concerned about your government's inability to protect the
basic human rights of Christians in India . . . while political
organizations such as the World Hindu Council, which has been
allied with your political party, continues to foment violence and
call for a ban on conversions'.

The poet Javed Akhtar said in an interview that he had told
Vajpayee, 'You may intend to have a secular society, but will the
forces you have released, allow you?' Vajpayee had replied that he
would manage. Akhtar was sceptical and told the interviewer to
see the headlines all over the front pages. He clarified that he had

accepted the Padma Shri earlier that year, in January, because this honour was from the government of the country and not from the BJP. He would soon accept Vajpayee's invitation and travel to Lahore on the bus.

Deve Gowda publicly called upon the Congress to pull down the NDA government and said that he would support an alternative, despite his differences with Lalu Yadav and the RJD. The media reported that the Congress was confident that Mamta would ditch the government; P.A. Sangma and Santosh Mohan Dev were reportedly in touch with her. The Congress's assessment was that the government's announcement of railway projects in West Bengal would only slow her departure but not stop it, since she was basically afraid of losing Muslim votes.

The Jayalalithaa saga, too, continued to dog the government. Despite the Ministry of Personnel's order transferring Jayalalithaa's cases from special courts to regular courts, the judges trying the cases decided to ignore the notification. The special courts judges said that the Madras High Court had upheld the Tamil Nadu government's decision to set up special courts, and though an appeal was pending before the Supreme Court there was no stay. The DMK was quick to jump into the fray, saying that the PM had been bullied into agreeing to this order by Jayalalithaa. Despite the Centre going out of the way to help Jayalalithaa in her legal travails, she still refused to either attend the Coordination Committee meeting or sign its statement. The left parties and the Janata Dal attacked the BJP, calling the action unprincipled. It was, they said, the government choosing both the judge and the court. Interestingly, the Congress was mum on the issue. Their stand was that the matter was sub judice and that, therefore, it would not be correct on their part to comment. In fact, the Congress (I) went further and said, 'We do sympathise with the way she has been treated in jail and outside. It is not right.'

The BJP came out in support of the government, explaining that the decision was taken at the highest level of the government after consulting with the attorney general. This did not impress the others. The Rashtriya Loktantrik Manch, a platform that brought together the Rashtriya Janata Dal and the Samajwadi Party, attacked the Congress on a number of grounds. One, that it was prolonging the life of the government. Lalu accused the Congress of being complicit in what he called 'the atrocities against Muslims and Christians'. Mulayam Singh Yadav, in fact, held the Congress responsible for the Ayodhya imbroglio, tracing the dispute back to 1949 and the installation of the Ram Lalla idol.

THOUGH VAJPAYEE TRAVELLED TO TRINIDAD, and later to Jamaica, in the second week of February 1999, political developments in India continued to occupy his mind. Om Prakash Chautala, whose party, the Indian National Lok Dal (INLD), had four members of Parliament, threatened to withdraw support if the government failed to completely roll back the price hikes of wheat, rice, urea, fertilizer and cooking gas within forty-eight hours. Interestingly, though this was an ultimatum, he said that he did not want the government to fall. However, newspaper articles reported otherwise.

It was at Montego Bay in Jamaica that we received the news of yet another terrible massacre of Dalits, in Narayanpur near Jehanabad in Bihar, where eleven persons had been shot dead. Narayanpur was not far from Manoharpur, where another massacre, of twenty-three Dalits, had taken place on 25 January. This was numbing, and the government could not just sit back and watch. Sonia Gandhi's first reaction encouraged the government that a consensus could be reached on handling this shameful incident. About the Bihar government, she said, 'Any government which is helpless in preventing such heinous acts forfeits its moral right to rule.' Ironically, the Rabri Devi government was then in minority, propped up by Congress's support.

This statement by Sonia Gandhi was seen as clearing the way for President's rule, which the Vajpayee government had attempted earlier, in September 1998, but was stymied by President Narayanan. The President had returned the government resolution on 25 September, pointing out that the government had not followed the procedure laid down in Article 256 of issuing a warning to the state government of its failure to protect the constitutional order. This time, the government obviously fell for Sonia Gandhi's statement that the Rabri government had lost all moral authority to rule, a belief strengthened by her subsequent visit to Manoharpur, the scene of the crime. In Vajpayee's absence, Advani chaired a cabinet meeting, which considered the governor's report. The cabinet's decision was sent to Montego Bay for Vajpayee's endorsement and then to the President for acceptance.

Bihar was brought under President's rule. But would Parliament ratify this decision on imposing President's rule? Pramod Mahajan, the government's crisis manager, seemed to think so. He was sure that in the changed political environment, nobody would oppose the move. Barely was the ink on the notification dry when the first rumbling of dissonance was heard, and it wasn't from Lalu, who was on the defensive then. It was the Left Front (whose component CPI was demanding just such a step only a few weeks earlier) that opposed the use of Article 356 of the Constitution to dismiss the Bihar government. It wanted to know why the government had not used this in Gujarat, and accused it of double standards. The left, it was said, was consistently against the misuse of Article 356, forgetting that it was a Union home minister, Indrajit Gupta, of the CPI, who had moved to impose President's rule in UP during the United Front government.

The Congress seemed to waver, just a bit. Senior leader Shivraj Patil conceded that the Rabri government 'was not conducting itself in the manner it should have', but Ajit Jogi, seen as very close to Sonia Gandhi, was equivocal. When Sonia Gandhi decided to visit the site of the massacre, it was reminiscent of Indira Gandhi's famous elephant ride to Belchi in August 1977, seen as the beginning of the revival of her political fortunes which had nose-dived after the Emergency and her electoral defeat just months earlier.[1] Sonia Gandhi chose a helicopter instead and while she conveyed her outrage very strongly, there was no mention of President's rule. This was despite the fact that the state Congress (I) president, Sadanand Singh, had welcomed the imposition of Article 356. Lalu, quick to sense an opening, asked the Congress to clarify its stand. Would the Congress collude with the BJP? The minority question was brought in, unsaid.

Over the next few days, Congress started distancing itself from Article 356 in Bihar. Sushil K. Shinde agreed that the Rabri government had failed to maintain law and order but added that 'the BJP invoked Art 356 for political gains. Only Congress has stood up for the people.' When the issue came up before Parliament, he said that the Congress Working Committee would decide the party's stand but reiterated that his party stood with the Scheduled Castes and Scheduled Tribes. According to Jogi, 'governor's rule is not a substitute for good governance'. The BJP tried to put the Congress (I) on the defensive and said that it owes an explanation to the people for supporting the Rabri government.

It was not as if all was well in the BJP itself or even that it was united. Kushabhau Thakre, the BJP president, had to tell the

---

[1] On 27 May 1977, fourteen persons, including eleven Dalits, were killed in Belchi village, Bihar. Indira Gandhi decided to visit the village on 23 August, almost two and a half months after the massacre. The road to the village was impassable, so she rode on an elephant. The pictorial effect across the country was electric.

media that the RSS and Vajpayee were not at war; that Vajpayee had been with the RSS since 1939; and that there was 'bound to be differences in perception amongst our leaders but that does not mean everyone is at war with each other and trying to disown our long-standing association.' Thakre clarified that the Vajpayee government was a coalition government and not a BJP one. It was guided by the National Agenda for Governance.

The Madan Lal Khurana story refused to die down as well. Thakre was clear that Khurana had resigned from the government and from the national executive of the BJP, and that these resignations had been accepted. Countering Khurana, Thakre asked, 'Why should we engineer attacks on Christians and give ourselves a bad name?' He said that there had been no deaths or even serious injury to anyone in Gujarat and that the BJP did not 'believe in vote-bank politics'. As far as he was concerned, the Khurana chapter was a closed one.

But it was not going away. The Delhi Akali Dal announced that it would not support the BJP in the two assembly by-elections scheduled for that year and in Delhi, because of the Khurana episode. They expressed anger at what they said was 'unfair treatment' meted out to him and recalled his courage in 1984. The Delhi Akalis expressed their disappointment that Vajpayee had accepted Khurana's resignation. Prem Singh Chandumajra, an Akali MP close to Gurcharan Singh Tohra and therefore a dissident, even wrote to Vajpayee on the Khurana episode. In fact, analysts now linked Chautala's threat of withdrawal from the government to Khurana, reasoning that it was the latter who was the main interlocutor with both the Akalis and Chautala, who were very close to each other.

This was a weak moment for the BJP. The party seemed to have been caught on the wrong foot. Khurana repeated his charge that he had resigned as minister and from the party's national executive on the issue of violence against Christians, and that he had been prevented at Bangalore by the BJP leadership from defending Vajpayee against attacks emanating from the RSS.

Sonia Gandhi asserted the seriousness of her response to the gruesome murder of the Staines by removing J.B. Patnaik, till then the longest-serving chief minister of Odisha (later, Naveen Patnaik broke his record and remains in office as chief minister). J.B. Patnaik had had a controversy-ridden tenure, which included multiple charges of corruption. He had a tough time dealing with the Anjana Mishra case, where he was alleged to have protected his advocate-general from allegations of rape, but he rode overall attacks till he was asked to step down. He was later able to ensure that his replacement was not among those seeking his ouster. The new chief minister was Giridhar Gomang (now Gamang), a lightweight, but who would soon emerge in the limelight for reasons that had nothing to do with Odisha.

The controversy over the Odisha attacks was not just limited to domestic politics; the UK Parliament, at the initiative of a Labour MP, discussed the subject, at which thirteen MPs were present. Mary Robinson, the United Nations Commissioner for Human Rights, would visit India soon after, for a conference organized by the National Human Rights Commission. She met Vajpayee and other leaders and, in her interaction with the media, said that she hoped 'the Indian government would take all necessary steps rapidly to stop atrocities against Christians and other minorities'. Interestingly, while Sonia Gandhi's use of the term 'merchants of death' or *maut ka saudagar* is associated with the 2007 Gujarat assembly elections, she had first used it against the BJP in February 1999 itself, at a meeting of the Youth Congress, blaming the BJP for violence against Christians.

Realizing the gravity of the political challenges facing his government, Vajpayee, on his return to India, reached out to allies. Mamata met him, assured him of her support, but she felt that it was not a good time to join the government. The reason cited was that the government was in the midst of preparing the budget and should concentrate on revenue maximization.

Before any momentum on strengthening the government could gather force, a new controversy arose. After a meeting with George Fernandes and Nitish Kumar, Home Minister Advani made an announcement that seemed eminently sensible but became a bombshell. He said that S.S. Bhandari would be replaced as Bihar governor. He explained that the government was committed 'to speeding up developmental works and show results to provide for the much-needed social harmony through a non-political dispensation based on merit and experience'.

The decision was taken 'to prevent Lalu making the point that Bhandari was a defender of upper and intermediate castes interests'. This seemingly innocuous statement implied accepting Lalu's criticism against Bhandari that the latter was out to have the Rabri government dismissed, or so the analysts and Opposition accepted. It was seen as a 'sop to the Congress' so that it would support the imposition of President's rule. Advani's meeting with leaders of the Samata Party and his announcement should be seen against the backdrop of these developments in Bihar, where Bhandari had carried out important shifts in civil service appointments. It was said that the chief secretary, director general of police and entire top brass of the Patna district were from the upper castes.

Even before firefighting could begin, there were more shocks on the way. Chautala met Vajpayee as a last-ditch attempt to find a compromise, but as Vajpayee was no longer willing to roll back the modest price increase, the INLD withdrew support. According to Chautala, Vajpayee expressed his 'helplessness' in agreeing to the demand. Chautala, however, added that his party would continue to extend issue-based support to the government.

There was considerable churn within the BJP. Four MPs, namely Madan Jaiswal, Lalmuni Choubey, P.S. Gadhavi

and Janardan Yadav, raised the Khurana issue. According
to them, the points raised by him were in the interest of the
party and the government, and should have been squarely
addressed. The reason for Chautala's withdrawal of support
was also intensely discussed. The accepted view was that it
was due to internal party pressure, specifically the continuance
of BJP's alliance with the Bansi Lal-led HVP in the Haryana
government, what with the HVP and INLD being strongly
opposed to each other. Added to this were factors like a by-
election loss in Haryana and poor performance of the BJP and
LD(D) in the Rajasthan assembly elections, with the final straw
being the increase in fertilizer/urea prices.

Ajit Jogi, commenting on the withdrawal of support by
Chautala, said that the 'government would fall under the
weight of its own contradictions'. He also said that Chautala's
reasons for withdrawal confirmed the Congress's stand that the
government was anti-poor and anti-people. He added that the
Congress was looking at an 'interim, secular government before
the general elections'.

Closer home, Dattopant Thengadi, founder-president of the
Bharatiya Mazdoor Sangh (BMS) and a senior RSS leader, said
that Vajpayee was a 'petty politician' playing into the hands of his
'policy advisers with doubtful credentials'. According to Thengadi,
previous governments had followed policies of globalization on
the diktats of Western powers and he had hoped that the Vajpayee
government would be different, but it had 'belied the expectation
of the nationalist forces'. Thengadi, who was Vajpayee's
contemporary in the RSS, repeated the allegations raised by the
Swadeshi Jagran Manch that Vajpayee was surrounded by 'self-
serving advisors' specifically when those 'top bureaucrats advising
Vajpayee were from the past regimes and had their own agendas'.
These charges were made by him in a speech at an annual meeting
of the BMS, held at the Hedgewar Smriti Bhavan, the RSS

headquarters in Nagpur. This was the second such attack on Vajpayee by Thengadi.

Even as fast-paced developments were taking place in Indian politics, and just three days before Vajpayee went to Lahore, there was a moment of personal joy and satisfaction for me. Vajpayee attended the centenary celebration of my alma mater, Hindu College, on 17 February. It provided much-needed respite from the grind of day-to-day firefighting.

IN BIHAR, BHANDARI WAS NOT one to take things lying down. He packed his bags, said his farewells, left Patna by train and quit later. He refused to use any government transport. Bhandari said that he was 'embarrassed and hurt' by Advani's statement, which he heard for the first time on TV. The Samata party had made public its preference for replacing the governor. Nitish Kumar said that he supported Advani's statement and that the governor should be a non-political man, one who 'inspires confidence with an impartial image'. According to senior Congress leader Rajesh Pilot, Vajpayee and Advani were working at cross purposes, and he said that this reminded him of the tensions between Morarji Desai and Charan Singh during the Janata days of 1978–79.

Due to these missteps by the government, the Congress was now in an advantageous position. There were serious doubts that the decision of replacing the governor would satisfy the Congress and persuade it to support the government's decision on Bihar. The Congress was quick to embarrass the government by explaining that while it was their stand that the Rabri government had lost the moral authority to rule, it had not called for its dismissal!

At a time when Vajpayee's impending visit to Lahore should have been grabbing all headlines, domestic issues refused to subside even temporarily. Vajpayee was able to persuade Bhandari, his old friend and colleague, to stay on as governor. The feedback from Bihar was that most Congressmen wanted Parliament to ratify the Article 356 proclamation because though the idea of a 'saffron' administration made them tense, Lalu raj made them afraid. There were feelers that since the Congress (I) could not be seen to act in support of the BJP, abstention would be the way out.

The National Development Council (NDC) met on 19 February, just a day before Vajpayee departed for Lahore. The one message from the states was that competitive populism had left them bankrupt. In 1997, the politically weak UF government had notified new pay scales for Central government servants, for the first time, in excess of what the Pay Commission had recommended. These new scales were gradually adopted by all the states, and because these were to come into effect retrospectively, once payments for salary arrears had been made, the states were looking at scraping the bottom of the barrel. At the NDC, Yashwant Sinha agreed to move for increased devolution of funds, but this did not satisfy the states, which wanted immediate cash. The compromise was that the RBI would allow states a higher degree of overdraft.

Politically, the situation was becoming interesting, in all sorts of ways. Jayalalithaa issued a statement, which in retrospect is intriguing. She said that their 'support is for a Vajpayee-led government and not for a BJP-led government'. She pooh-poohed the Congress claim that the government was going to fall on its own and, enigmatically, said that 'such a scenario does not exist now and the government will not fall now'.

On the day Vajpayee went to Lahore, Chautala met the President and handed over his letter of withdrawal of support to the government. It was no longer only about not supporting the government; Chautala went further and said that he would support a no-confidence motion against the government in Parliament. Reflecting the general perception of the BJP being a divided house, Chautala advised it to 'better set their own house in order as all their senior leaders including Home Minister

LK Advani are speaking in different voices even on issues of national significance'.

Interestingly, Chautala ruled out support to the Congress either and was also not in favour of mid-term polls. But he left the door slightly open in regard to the BJP, saying that while he was against the 'anti-farmer, anti-poor policies' of the Vajpayee government, he was prepared to support specific pro-farmer measures. It wasn't Chautala alone who was uncomfortable with the prospect of a Congress-led government. Sharad Pawar, still in the Congress and in fact the leader of the Opposition in the Lok Sabha, had expressed himself in favour of mid-term polls were the Vajpayee government to fall.

As part of the Opposition parties' efforts to portray the Vajpayee government as a threat to minorities, the CPI(M) organized what it called the 'People's Convention against Communalism' on 20 February, the day Vajpayee reached Lahore. There was a considerable attendance of top leaders, with I.K. Gujral, Deve Gowda, Mulayam Singh Yadav, Lalu Yadav, G.K. Moopanar and Murasoli Maran besides those belonging to the CPI and CPI(M), present at the event. The convention came to the conclusion that the 'government's complicity in deepening the communal divide, disrupting social harmony amongst people belonging to different faiths and consequent insecurity, is gravely endangering our country's unity and integrity'. It held the BJP's allies as equally guilty since they 'were also encouraging communalism by extending support to the government'. The domestic political developments seemed to remain in firm control of those opposed to the government, inspiring Jyoti Basu to predict that the government would fall any day.

ONE OF THE TRAGEDIES OF Vajpayee as prime minister was that he was denied any kind of honeymoon period, neither when he took office in March 1998 nor after his Lahore visit, which should have been followed by days of basking in the sun. Parliament was to meet from 22 February, and Bihar would be at the top of the agenda. However, the headlines of the day were not about the boldness of Vajpayee's gesture towards Pakistan but about Sonia Gandhi's decision that the Congress (I) would vote against the use of Article 356 in Bihar.

This decision seemed to bear out Mulayam Singh Yadav's prediction that the government's use of Article 356 was a blessing in disguise, since it forced the Congress to take the lead in mobilizing the Opposition parties. Arjun Singh's cynical explanation of the Congress's decision was that Sonia Gandhi's earlier position on the Rabri government having lost the moral authority to rule was essentially the expression of the party's outraged feeling over the Jehanabad killings. On the other hand, the Congress (I) saw the government's decision to invoke Article 356 as being dictated by the RSS! This was despite the Bihar Congress (I) shouting from the rooftops for the party to support the government on this.

Sonia Gandhi's decision challenged the government's ability to get the Article 356 motion approved even in the Lok Sabha. Would the TDP, Akalis, National Conference or even the Trinamool Congress vote in favour? The Akalis were historically against the use of Article 356. The Congress (I) obviously saw that the government's position was shaky. The TDP and DMK, which both used the same language, had, as members of the UF government, gone along in February 1999 with Mulayam as he went about trying to topple Kalyan Singh in the midst of parliamentary elections. In any case, it was now certain that the government would fail to get parliamentary approval since it simply did not have the numbers in the Rajya Sabha.

Yet Vajpayee was not about to go without putting up a fight. Realizing the gravity of the situation, Vajpayee saw that his partners were raising theoretical issues unnecessarily, when the survival of the government was at stake. He made it clear to the BJP and its allies that the government would fall if it did not get the Lok Sabha's backing on the Bihar issue when the voting takes place. The BJP rallied behind Vajpayee as never before. The Bahujan Samaj Party announced that it would support the government on this issue as Dalit lives mattered. Ram Vilas Paswan tried to persuade the Janata Dal not to vote against the imposition of President's rule in Bihar. The voting was set for 26 February, and there wasn't simply enough time available to satisfy every party's past stand on President's rule.

To add to the confusion, and vindicating the government on his dismissal, Admiral Vishnu Bhagwat claimed in a media interaction that on 9 May, when the three chiefs were briefed on the nuclear tests, they were specifically told not to inform George Fernandes. This was pure nonsense, since George Fernandes and other senior Ministers were also briefed about the tests. And if true, why did Bhagwat wait so long to say it? Why did he wait for the eve of parliamentary session to reveal it? The suspicion was that Bhagwat had reinserted himself into the public domain so as to allow the Opposition an issue to attack the government. He was not about to fade away that easily.

As Parliament met, there was a lot in the air. The finance ministry presented its Economic Survey, which listed the government's reform priorities. Significantly, other than promising to relook at subsidies, a task no government has attempted to do seriously, it mentioned the amendment to insurance laws to allow for private sector participation and FDI, spoke of opening up pension funds to private players and having a cap on fiscal deficit.

The general feeling, and not just among Vajpayee's acolytes, was that Sonia Gandhi's decision on opposing the imposition of President's rule in Bihar was linked with the perceived success of Vajpayee's Lahore trip. If unchecked, the optics of the Lahore initiative would have firmly established Vajpayee in office, making it much more difficult to dislodge him. There was also the lingering fear that if the Vajpayee government was beset by fewer distractions, like trying to hold its coalition together, it would focus attention on the Bofors inquiry. There were also doubts that Madan Lal Khurana would use the opportunity that Parliament allows ministers who have resigned or been thrown out: to make a statement. If so, whom would he embarrass more?

The final victory margin in the Lok Sabha, of twenty-nine votes, was almost double of what Vajpayee had secured in the confidence vote eleven months ago. This was achieved in the typical manner of Indian politics, some would say. On the one hand, it did mean that negotiations with Chandrababu Naidu, Jayalalithaa and Mamata descended to what could be described as 'the level of bazaar'. There was brinkmanship, and there was face-saving. Once it was clear that the Rajya Sabha would not endorse the government's action and that the government would fall if there was no affirmation vote in the Lok Sabha, things fell into place.

The Akalis and the Telugu Desam said they would have no difficulty voting in support of the government. Those of the allies who wanted the dismissal of state governments, like Mamata and Naveen Patnaik, seemed quite pleased with the vote; Jayalalithaa was probably not thrilled, but since she wanted Article 356 used in Tamil Nadu, she went along. Vajpayee's assertion worked and the government seemed to tide over the crisis. Rather than face even a symbolic defeat in the Rajya Sabha, the government chose to withdraw the proclamation under Article 356 and the Rabri government was restored. It was an embarrassment, and the Opposition went to town, but it was seen as a game of numbers more than that of propriety.

THE BUDGET PRESENTED BY YASHWANT Sinha was generally well received. Unlike in 1998, when the government was in its early stages and all of us were groping in the dark for some clarity, his budget preparations this time were far more thorough. Yashwant Sinha and his top officials, including Vijay Kelkar (finance secretary), Dr Shankar Acharya (chief economic adviser) and others, met with Vajpayee five or six times. Contrary to the first budget, when all Vajpayee wanted was more money for agriculture and rural development, this time around, aspects like economic reforms and taxation were on top of the agenda. This was clearly reflected in the budget, which saw an overhaul of the excise duty structure; there was an attempt to make productive use of gold, and it provided for incentives to equity-oriented mutual funds while also allowing write-offs to facilitate corporate mergers/ demergers. What was most heartening was the budget's clear indication of the direction of future trade policies. Far from giving into protectionist lobbies, it talked of bringing down customs tariffs to ASEAN levels by 2004.

Even if the high-profile anniversary event organized by Pramod Mahajan didn't go down very well, I thought that Vajpayee had achieved a lot in one year as prime minister. Domestically, the fact that he was able to balance the competing demands of the parties in the coalition, including the BJP itself, was commendable. Frustrations about the inability of the government, indeed of Vajpayee himself, were regularly commented upon, but what these criticisms did not take into account was the lack of a decisive mandate. It was one thing to say that even Jayalalithaa had campaigned for a mandate for Vajpayee, but this fact was not enough as a viable argument to counter her unreasonable demands. Vajpayee's ability to get the state governments of Tamil Nadu and Karnataka to find a solution to the Cauvery dispute has not been given the importance it deserves. The 1999 budget and the scores of economic reforms that preceded it—patents, the introduction of insurance bill, the scrapping of Urban Land Ceiling Act, share buyback, sweat equity, etc.—set the economy on a path of sustained growth that lasted till 2008.

Vajpayee's decision to go ahead with the nuclear tests and his courage in engaging diplomatically with Pakistan had suddenly lifted India's standing internationally. It was not so obvious then, with many doubting both the tests and the efforts to improve relations with Pakistan. But it was soon clear that both were required—the first, to demonstrate India's determination to defend its interest and not be boxed into a corner of the world called South Asia; and the second, to signal that India was prepared to extend its hand of friendship and not be dragged into an endless cycle of fending off Pakistan's attempts at low-intensity conflicts. Even if the effort failed, India would go on to establish its credentials very effectively, but that was not evident in April 1999.

There were disappointments too, beginning with the first, direction-less budget. The failure to control retail prices of fruits and vegetables, as exemplified by the onion crisis, was more bad luck than bad governance, but Vajpayee and the BJP had to pay a huge price. The Bhagwat affair should have been nipped far earlier and not been allowed to reach a stage where a confrontation became inevitable. Using politicians, including influential ones, to bring recalcitrant officers under control, was probably a bad idea. Lastly, so was the decision on Bihar, which was essentially sound but handled badly afterwards, with cynicism and political opportunism ultimately prevailing over any notion of justice for the Dalit victims of mass murders.

In an interview to Prabhu Chawla (*India Today*), Vajpayee, though known for his interest in international relations, listed the improved economic situation first in his list of his government's achievements. Again, on regional parties he was far more understanding than what could be expected in view of what he had been going through. According to Vajpayee, '. . . it is natural that they would seek redressal for regional grievances that have long been ignored. My job is to fit these into a mosaic of national interests.' It was this attitude that led him to lead a successful coalition for the next five years, practising what was called 'coalition dharma'. He was unsparing of the Congress (I), telling Chawla that the 'Congress is free to think that they have embarrassed us. The truth is that they have let down the Dalits of Bihar.'

Vajpayee's psychological victory in establishing his numbers in the Lok Sabha, and therefore consolidating his control over the BJP and the alliance, could not go unchallenged. The Lahore visit, efforts to get Bihar rid of the Lalu raj and a decent budget, made the government look much better than it ever had. Would Vajpayee emerge as another Narasimha Rao, who not only lasted a full term but also succeeded in converting his minority government into a majority one?

There was palpable pressure to bring down the government. With its success in thwarting Vajpayee's move on Bihar and its success in mobilizing almost all Opposition parties behind it, the Congress aggressively took up the issue of Bhagwat's dismissal. They were also helped by allegations against Vajpayee raised by Mohan Guruswamy, adviser to finance minister, when he was dismissed by Yashwant Sinha. Some of the allegations were personal, others systemic. Guruswamy specifically targeted Vajpayee's grand announcement of building the six-lane North–South–East–West corridor, the most ambitious national highways scheme of its time. Till then, most national highways were two-laned, sometimes less, and incapable of giving the economy a big push by facilitating logistics and reducing its costs. According to Guruswamy, Vajpayee 'was proposing highways from nowhere to nowhere'. He was happy that the 'highway project has now being given a quiet burial'.

As the Congress launched its aggressive attacks on the government, senior leaders like Manmohan Singh, Sharad Pawar

and Pranab Mukherjee were not seen to be involved in the daily
fracas in Parliament. They were probably viewed as old-fashioned
and not aggressive enough, so other leaders were used. It was a
novelty to see Congress MPs rushing to the well of the house and
disrupting parliamentary proceedings. Their impatience to get
power was obvious. It was no more the case that the government
would fall on its own contradictions; it needed to be pushed.

However, what complicated their calculations was that unlike
Sharad Pawar, most MPs did not want a mid-term poll. The
issue was no more about just bringing down Vajpayee, whose
government had only a slender majority (283 MPs at best), but
to win over the MPs supporting the government, including the
AIADMK. Were the Vajpayee government to fall, would its
replacement be a Congress-supported one, a Congress-led one or
a Congress government itself? The thought that it may be none of
the three was possibly too remote to consider.

THE SECOND FORTNIGHT OF MARCH saw increased political
momentum (not that the preceding year had ever been dull). And
yet, at that moment it seemed that the politics of recrimination,
positioning and jostling would just carry on. Clearly, the danger
signs were ignored or maybe had not emerged.

Rangarajan Kumaramangalam, power minister in the
Vajpayee government, organized a massive rally in Tiruchirappalli,
which he represented in the Lok Sabha. This was followed by a
public meeting, the likes of which the BJP had never organized
in Tamil Nadu. It was the culmination of the state-level party
meeting. Ranga, as Kumaramangalam was called, was exuberant
and could hardly contain himself on the viewing platform where
Vajpayee and the other leaders sat. His political base was Salem,
which had been represented by three generations of his family, but
the Congress, where he came from, had become a minor party in
Tamil Nadu, and the BJP was still a fledgling party.

The show was an impressive one. Not surprisingly, the AIADMK, the senior ally in the state, kept away. But the other NDA partners participated, indicating that Jayalalithaa had lost her ability to keep the alliance together. She was not going to take this lying down, but these three smaller parties seemed ready to stay with Vajpayee and take her on. The Trichy event and the public meeting in Kolkata, where again the local senior partner (Mamata) stayed away, demonstrated that Vajpayee's popularity was not just intact but was on the rise in states like Tamil Nadu and West Bengal, where the BJP was a minor player. This should have sounded a bell.

Bhagwat gave Jayalalithaa the opening she needed. Not satisfied with his press meet on 21 February, he released a so-called affidavit on stamped paper, listing his allegations and charges, on 14 March, the eve of the Parliament session. Was the timing simply coincidental? It gave just the opportunity that the Congress (I) and Jayalalithaa wanted, to create the perfect storm for Vajpayee to sail into. They both demanded that a joint parliamentary committee be constituted to look into the Bhagwat dismissal. The government was only open for a debate in Parliament. Vajpayee made his position very clear; Bhagwat's insubordination was too severe for any compromises to be made.

With the Congress demanding that Fernandes be sacked from the government, and Jayalalithaa demanding that he at least be shifted to a 'minor' ministry, Vajpayee saw the attack on Fernandes, baseless as it was, as an attack on the government. Though he did not say it, he was clear that there would be no compromise on these demands. It was not as if this was a case of regional/state grievance or even of helping Jayalalithaa out of some legal tangle. There would be no compromise on issues of national security, including on civilian control over armed forces, and certainly politicization was the worst way to repair the damage already done. It was clear that as far as the Bhagwat issue was concerned, there was no going back.

The situation now inexorably moved towards the climax. It was the time for tea parties, the main purpose of which lay in their symbolism and signalling effect. Jayalalithaa travelled to Delhi to, among other things, attend what would be her last meeting of the NDA Coordination Committee. Even though there was unanimity at the meeting on all issues except one, all attention was on Jayalalithaa's stand on the Bhagwat issue. All others disagreed with her, and some, like Mamata and the Samata Party, quite strongly. This was despite Mamata's earlier patch efforts to patch up with Jayalalithaa. In her meeting with Vajpayee, Jayalalithaa raised many demands—e.g., the inclusion of nine ministers from the AIADMK, including Subramanian Swamy; the sacking of Ramamurthy and his replacement as petroleum minister by one of her nominees; and the appointing of twenty-five bureaucrats in specific posts. Contrary to her public posture, she did not press either on Bhagwat or on Fernandes. On Ramamurthy, her stand being that the latter was a Minister from her quota, which was factually correct. Ramamurthy had to be made to pay a price for shifting out of her camp. Later that evening, Delhi MP and future minister Vijay Goel organized a grand tea party for Jayalalithaa, which Vajpayee and the entire BJP top leadership attended.

IT WAS THE OTHER TEA party, hosted by Swamy on 29 March, that got far more attention, since both Jayalalithaa and Sonia Gandhi were present there, though not for very long. There was no substantive discussion between the two, but that was to be expected as their intention was more about sending out a signal than anything else. Besides a whole host of Congress leaders in attendance, three ex-prime ministers— Narasimha Rao, Chandra Shekhar and Deve Gowda—also attended the party. Interestingly, the Pakistani high commissioner and Chinese ambassador were also present.

Speaking about the tea party, Jayalalithaa said that it 'can be termed as a political earthquake'. She had to later retract the statement, since it was insensitive to use the word 'earthquake' in jest, given that the Uttarakhand Himalayas had just suffered a real one at a huge human cost. Ever irreverent, Vaiko described the meeting as a 'storm in a tea cup'. Possibly indicating that the Congress (I) should not take her for granted, Jayalalithaa, at another event in Delhi, attacked Nehru's Kashmir policy, calling it a 'Himalayan blunder'.

THE BJP'S NATIONAL EXECUTIVE, WHICH met in Panaji, Goa, on 2–4 April, strongly endorsed Vajpayee's leadership. The party highlighted four key achievements of the government in the past one year: the bomb, the bus, Bihar and the budget. It was difficult to believe that less than six months back political analysts were speaking of how sections of the BJP and the larger Sangh Parivar were working at cross purposes and undermining Vajpayee.

But if in-house bonhomie was on the mend, dissensions outside were growing. Vajpayee had refused to entertain Jayalalithaa's latest and, as it turned out, last set of demands since accepting them would have meant sacrificing Samata and other allies. The AIADMK ministers stopped attending cabinet meetings and said that they would send their resignations to Vajpayee. The public attacks by Jayalalithaa and her party members, against Vajpayee and their erstwhile allies in Tamil Nadu, picked up in intensity, but there was still a perception that Jayalalithaa would continue to raise the pitch without actually withdrawing support, which would have weakened her position.

The end of the BJP's alliance with the AIADMK was actually on the horizon, and the numbers were stacked against Vajpayee. But how would events eventually unfold? Would the DMK cross the aisle and support Vajpayee, and if so, would its five MPs make up for the loss of AIADMK's eighteen? Where would the BSP go? Congress sources were confident that the Samata Party would break? What about the Janata Dal? Or the TMC? Would the Akalis split? Which way would Chautala go? And if Vajpayee fell, would Sonia Gandhi be able to meet Jayalalithaa's demands? Did the latter want an alternative government in Delhi, or did she want to precipitate state elections in Tamil Nadu? There were too many questions, and no one was able to confidently predict what would happen.

On 6 April, the AIADMK ministers sent in their resignations to Vajpayee, and after two days he sent those to the President for acceptance. Another day later, the AIADMK withdrew from the Coordination Committee. With this, the die was cast in all but name. It was clear that major changes were in the offing. I detected bad omen but kept it to myself. Vajpayee visited Anandpur Sahib on 8 April for the celebrations of 300 years of the Khalsa panth. Sharad Pawar, the leader of the Opposition in the Lok Sabha, accompanied him. I remembered Deve Gowda's last trip out of Delhi as PM about two years earlier; he'd gone to Shantiniketan, and Sharad Pawar, as leader of the Congress party in the Lok Sabha, had accompanied him. Would history repeat itself?

In Anandpur Sahib, the function itself was joyful, and the spirit of equality and participation inherent to Sikhism seemed so natural as the rich and poor mingled together. Tarlochan Singh, member of the National Commission for Minorities and later Rajya Sabha MP, pointed out a man who he said was 'California's fruit king' and who was happily serving the congregation. In his speech, Vajpayee recalled Guru Gobind Singh's fight against injustice. The shadow of Jayalalithaa was never far away. She was also supposed to visit Anandpur Sahib after a few days but cancelled her visit.

A FEW DAYS LATER, JAYALALITHAA came calling and checked into a Delhi hotel, reportedly with forty-eight pieces of luggage. There were hectic parleys over the next few days, and on 14 April, at 11 a.m., she met the President and gave him the letter of withdrawal of support. Parliament was due to resume its budget session the very next day. President Narayanan immediately asked Vajpayee to seek a vote of confidence. This, I felt then and still feel, was absolutely improper. With Parliament in session, the right way to bring down a government would be either to bring in a motion of no confidence, or, since it was the budget session, to defeat the government on any money bill due in the session.

Vajpayee's opponents cited precedents of 1990 and 1997, but in neither case was Parliament due to meet the next day, with several money bills listed to be passed. Those who felt that the government had lost majority could have moved a no-confidence motion. But this they were loath to do, since a no-confidence motion meant prior agreement among Opposition parties on alternative arrangements, which they would propose while moving the no-confidence motion. Also, if such a motion failed, parliamentary rules precluded another no-confidence vote for six months. It was obvious that if the AIADMK moved a motion of no confidence, the Tamil Maanila Congress would not go along with it. If, on the other hand, the Congress moved it, then the Forward Bloc and the Revolutionary Socialist Party would have problems going along. Similarly, would the Bahujan Samaj Party have supported any motion moved by the Rashtriya Loktantrik Manch, of which the Samajwadi Party was an important component? It was much easier for most Opposition parties to vote against any motion moved by Vajpayee than to support another party's motion.

The debate in the Lok Sabha was as thrilling as it was tense. There was forceful manoeuvring and floor management, but in the end the Vajpayee government lost by one vote. The newly appointed chief minister of Odisha, Giridhar Gamang, appeared in Parliament at the time of the vote. Though he was a member of the Lok Sabha and had not yet resigned, the fact that he had taken over a full-time political appointment in a state whose legislature he would have to be a member of, it was expected that he would not take part in a critical vote in Parliament. The speaker was asked to rule, and based on the advice given to him by the secretary general, S. Gopalan, the matter was left to Gamang's conscience. His conscience told him to follow his party's orders, and so he voted against the confidence motion. Many criticized the speaker's orders, seeing a conspiracy in Gopalan's advice. Gopalan had been appointed to the post by the previous speaker, Purno Sangma, but legally speaking, the speaker's orders were sound. At best, the speaker could have asked Gamang to withdraw but without being able to actually enforce this.

I saw a bigger role in the BJP's failure to manage small parties and in the tendency for regional parties to be converted into family-held, private companies. Three specific cases would illustrate this. The ruling party in Arunachal Pradesh had split in January 1999, and Gegong Apang, the chief minister, was unseated after a long stint in office, replaced by Mukut Mithi. Of Apang's Arunachal Congress party's two MPs, Wangcha Rajkumar was with Mithi. Rajkumar met Vajpayee and told him that though his party had split and he was only against Apang, his support for Vajpayee would remain. At that moment, there was no immediate threat to the Vajpayee government. Unfortunately, when the moment came, no one remembered to approach Rajkumar, and he voted against the government, being an old Congressman. I don't think the BJP's floor leaders were aware of his existence.

The second case would be that of the National Conference (NC). It had two MPs in the Lok Sabha: the veteran Saifuddin Soz; and the young Omar Abdullah, the son and grandson of previous chief ministers and himself a future CM. Farooq Abdullah, the chief minister of Jammu and Kashmir and head of the NC, pushed his son hard and sidelined Soz in an extremely petty manner. Every year, the Government of India sends an official delegation for hajj. Since numbers are limited, there is pressure from all sides to include persons of choice. Soz had suggested the name of a certain person, and when Farooq Abdullah found out he had the name removed.

When Vajpayee visited Srinagar on 6 December 1998, he was supposed to meet ministers of the local government at the Sher-i-Kashmir Convention Centre. Since we were running slightly late, Farooq Abdullah dismissed the meeting in what I thought was an extremely cavalier manner. Vajpayee paid the price. While Omar Abdullah voted for the confidence motion, Soz voted against.

The third case, of the Janata Dal, is the most intriguing. Former prime minister I.K. Gujral could get elected to the Lok Sabha only because of the Akalis, yet he voted to bring down the government, of which the Akalis were a part. Ram Vilas Paswan did not want the Janata Dal to vote with Lalu Yadav and play a part in bringing down the government, but the party persuaded him to be patient. He would later walk away, and with that the Janata Dal ceased to exist in its original form. Gamang wrongly got the wrath for bringing down Vajpayee; there were too many others who'd played their part. Ironically, Gamang is now in the BJP!

Two other parties were being closely watched. Vajpayee had spoken to Kanshi Ram on the phone on the morning of the second day of the debate, and the latter had told Vajpayee that he was on his way to the airport as he was flying out of Delhi, and that while the BSP could not support Vajpayee's government, it would not vote against it. Kanshi Ram did not leave Delhi and the five-member BSP voted to bring down the government. Interestingly, the person who triggered the whole process of withdrawing support, Om Prakash Chautala, came back and his party voted in favour of the government. Ultimately, it was the fear of the Congress's resurgence in Haryana that made him retreat.

I HAD NEVER SEEN VAJPAYEE more distraught than when he
walked back into his room in the Parliament House after losing
the vote of confidence. He was crestfallen and in tears. But
that moment passed, and he was off to Rashtrapati Bhavan
to submit his resignation. Very soon it became obvious that
it was easier to vote out a government than replace it with an
alternative. The questions that immediately came up were:
Which parties would come together and form a government?
Who would lead it?

His short-sightedness in asking Vajpayee to seek a confidence
vote became clear within two days of the fall of the government
when President Narayanan asked Vajpayee, only a caretaker PM,
to get the budget (not just the vote on account) and the railway
budget passed by Parliament.[2] This was bad parliamentary practice
and Vajpayee resisted, but the nationalist in him overruled the
politician, and he agreed that Parliament could meet and pass the
necessary legislation—which it did, without discussion, as agreed
by the leaders of important parties.

With the budget out of the way, efforts at formation of an
alternative government gathered steam, but the going wasn't
easy in the least. The BJP met the President and insisted that he
obtain formal letters of support, as he had done when Vajpayee
formed the government in March 1998. They also said that
they, too, should be given a chance, for which they would need
support from non-NDA parties and persons. The situation that
emerged was that other than the left, all other non-BJP parties

---

[2] A vote on account allows the government to collect taxes and spend money
     for a limited period, normally three or four months, giving Parliament more
     time to consider the full budget or allowing an expected new government
     to present its budget. This has been standard parliamentary practice. In
     fact, since a money bill is the test of a government's majority, technically,
     when Parliament approved Vajpayee's full budget, it demonstrated that
     his government enjoyed the confidence of the Lok Sabha.

were uncomfortable with the Congress (I) either forming or even leading a government.

There were further complications. The Tamil Maanila Congress, Revolutionary Socialist Party and Forward Bloc refused to be a part of, or even support, any government in which the AIADMK was involved. In fact, the RSP and FB were reluctant to even support a Congress government. For its part, the RLM, which constituted of Mulayam Singh Yadav's SP and Lalu Yadav's RJD, wanted a third-front government with the Congress's support, but they were not willing to support a Congress (I) government. Mulayam's stand showed his apprehensiveness about losing Muslim votes. A Congress–BSP combination would be a powerful force in UP, drawing support from even the BJP's 'upper-caste base', thereby making it even more attractive to Muslim voters.

The CPM/CPI were the most flexible and were even agreeable to the AIADMK's participation, though their preference seemed to be for a Congress government. The Janata Dal, for its part, was against any government which had Lalu Yadav's RJD in it. Contrary to expectations, there were no defections from the NDA. The Congress's game plan seemed clear, which was to form and lead a government—whatever it would take—consolidate, and then go in for elections by the end of the year. Unfortunately for them, only a part of their wish list fructified, and that too went against them.

On 21 April, Sonia Gandhi met the President and formally staked her claim, citing the support of 272 MPs. This was despite the RSP and FB making it clear that there was no question of supporting any Congress government, even before Sonia Gandhi had met the President. She said that she wanted some time to produce letters of support. Around that time, Mulayam had mooted the idea of Jyoti Basu as PM; and the CPM would have been willing to bite, unlike in 1996. But now the Congress wanted to lead the government.

Vajpayee kept up the pressure on President Narayanan, and the latter was forced to issue a long press note, detailing the process of consultation with different parties that he had adopted. At the same time, Vajpayee received feelers from Buta Singh and others, but I guess by then exhaustion had set in and he was not interested in petty bargaining.

The Narayanan–Vajpayee dynamic was an interesting one. Narayanan was serving as a foreign service officer when Vajpayee was the foreign minister (1977–79). Later, Narayanan quit, joined politics, became a junior minister and, later, vice president. When the presidential vacancy arose in 1997, the United Front was in government; it was not clear who was in power. Once it became clear that Narayanan would be the candidate supported by the UF and Congress, the BJP too decided to support him and filed nominations papers for him, among others.

His efforts to make it difficult for Vajpayee to form a government in March 1998 have been described before. In fact, as Natwar Singh writes in his book *One Life is Not Enough*, President Narayanan was very much involved in trying to engineer an alternative government when the Vajpayee government fell. Gopal Krishna Gandhi, then his principal secretary and a serving officer of the government, was sent to meet Congress leaders and convince them on the need to support Jyoti Basu as PM, but he was unsuccessful. Natwar Singh's point about Gopal Gandhi being used (misused?) as a political emissary to prevent Vajpayee from coming to power has not been denied by any of the protagonists.

It soon became clear that Sonia Gandhi had the support of only 233 MPs, not 272 as she had claimed. By contrast, the NDA had the support of 270 MPs. Therefore, fresh polls were the only option left. President Narayan again issued a long press note explaining how and why he came to this conclusion.

The implicit logic behind asking Vajpayee to seek a confidence vote—that those who'd organized the fall of the government would agree on an alternative—now proved hollow. Vajpayee was summoned to Rashtrapati Bhavan and asked to recommend the dissolution of Parliament; the cabinet duly complied, 'in deference to President's assessment of the situation', while making it clear that it (the cabinet) had no moral authority to do so on its own.

What I find really interesting about this period was that despite all the political upheavals, the government went ahead on 11 April with the testing of the intermediate-range ballistic missile Agni-II. Its range was 2000 km, and it used solid fuel. Vajpayee addressed the nation, since it was necessary to avoid chest-thumping, and explained that this test was a purely defensive one—a natural follow-up to the Pokhran-II nuclear tests.

And unlike the Pokhran II tests, this time around, not only were the five permanent members of the UN Security Council (the P5) informed, but so were Germany, Japan and Pakistan. In fact, the Pakistani high commissioner, Ashraf Jehangir Qazi, a professional diplomat, had been called in and told by Brajesh Mishra, in Vajpayee's presence, that the Agni-II was not directed at Pakistan. The missile had been ready for testing earlier, but things were held back because of the talks with the US, Vajpayee's Lahore visit, etc. This was India's first missile test after 1994. The missile's range covered all of Pakistan, the Chinese provinces of Yunnan and Qinghai as well as Tibet and Xinjiang. In seeking minimum deterrence, this was a good restart to India's missile programme, but it was clearly not enough.

The Pakistani response was quick in coming. On 14 April, it fired the Ghauri-II, and a day later, the Shaheen. The claimed range of Ghauri-II was 2300 km, but experts said that the actual figure was 1500 km. The claimed range of Ghauri-I was 1000 km, but the actual range was 700–800 km. On the other hand, the range of Shaheen was put at 600 km. This meant that other than extreme south and the north-east, the rest of India was now within the range of these missiles. There was, and remains, a general belief based on good evidence that the Pakistani nuclear and missile programmes are not home-grown. Its missiles are largely of North Korean origin, with the Ghauri-I identified as the Nodong-1. The Ghauri-II was probably the Taepodong-1 or Nodong-2, and the Shaheen was a Chinese M-9, a well-documented transaction that Pakistan had entered into a few years ago.

Unlike the hysterical reactions of less than a year ago, at the time of the Pokhran-II tests, the Agni-II tests were greeted by China and the big powers most calmly. India's argument, that it needed a minimum deterrence, was accepted by all. Only Japan was an outlier, understandably concerned because of its fears over the North Korean missile programme.

The domestic reaction was even more surprising. Sitaram Yechury thought that Vajpayee's motivations were similar to Bill Clinton's, when the latter ordered the bombing of Iraq when he was faced with impeachment proceedings. He was possibly half-right. There was no doubt that the Indian test date had been postponed after the Lahore visit, and could have been further postponed but for threat to the government. But here's what Yechury got wrong. For years since 1994, successive Indian governments had held back the missile development programme because of American pressure. There was legitimate fear this time that if India did not test, future governments could be browbeaten into holding back the programme, a key element of India's security preparations.

THE STORY OF THE FALL of the Vajpayee government couldn't be complete without the mention of some other developments that flowed from the circumstances of its fall. Becoming wiser by experience, the NDA decided to fight the elections as one entity with one manifesto. Vajpayee also made it clear that Sonia Gandhi's foreign origin would not be an issue, nor would the NDA run a personality-based election; he said that it should, instead, lay emphasis on the real issues and on the achievements of the Government. Though Vajpayee had announced in Parliament during the 1998 confidence vote that he had contested his last elections, he was going to be a candidate in the mid-term polls, the logic being that the Lok Sabha had a truncated term. Despite the NDA's decision to fight the elections as one nation-wide alliance, Mamata's desire to forge a separate agenda for West Bengal was agreed to.

Vajpayee might have expressed the wish to not make Sonia Gandhi's foreign origin an issue, but everybody else did not share this view. There was a revolt in the Congress itself, with Sharad Pawar, Purno Sangma and Tariq Anwar writing to Sonia Gandhi and asking her to step aside from being the prime ministerial face of the Congress. They not only made her foreign origin an issue but also drew attention to her lack of experience. According to them, this country of 980 million could only have 'an Indian, born of Indian soil, to head its government. Our inspiration, our soul, our honour, our pride, our dignity, is rooted in our soil. It has to be of this earth.' The letter also added that the 'person who is to take up the reins of this country needs a large measure of experience and understanding of public life . . . the average Indian is not unreasonable in demanding that his Prime Minister have some track record in public life.' This revolt, while manageable in terms of the members who walked out and joined the newly formed Nationalist Congress Party (NCP), jolted the Congress and gave the BJP extra space in order to project Vajpayee as a tried-and-tested person whose tenure had been unjustifiably curtailed.

Meanwhile, the Supreme Court's quashing of the notification transferring all forty-six of Jayalalithaa's cases back to sessions judge from the three special courts did little to moderate Jayalalithaa's belligerence. People who knew her, or had covered Tamil Nadu politics, explained that Jayalalithaa was just not accustomed to an atmosphere of free-and-frank debate, where somebody could challenge her point of view. That possibly explained her anger at the time of the finalization of the National Agenda of Governance, when Ramakrishna Hegde had questioned her demand to declare Tamil as a classical language. It was clear to everybody that Jayalalithaa had a single-minded personal agenda, and that if events did not go her way, she felt that there was a conspiracy ranged against her.

Sadly, the complete breakdown of governance continued in Bihar, with yet another massacre, which left twelve persons dead. This brought the total deaths in massacres in Bihar to over 300 in the previous two years.

When Vajpayee passed away in August 2018, there was considerable outpouring of grief. For those who were uncomfortable with the BJP's hold on power, this grief seemed to spring more out of a sense that the times had changed, for the worse. There was nostalgia for Vajpayee's moderation and for his ability to keep the 'extremists' on his side of the ideological fence under control. I found such nostalgia misleading as I remembered the hostility and allegations that Vajpayee had to face. The following extract from an editorial of *Frontline* (24 April–7 May 1999), written as an obituary to Vajpayee's government when it fell, is revealing:

> . . . [I]t was communal and divisive with a vengeance. It enabled, and colluded with the RSS's longstanding project of minority-baiting, allowing the most virulent and thuggish constituents of the saffron brigade to unleash a

new level of hate politics and terrorise especially India's small Christian minority. The regime managed to put tremendous pressure on the system's commitment to secularism and the rule of law.

9

The Failed Snare

Politically, the weakest moment in a country's life is when it is run by a caretaker government. What made the situation worse for India was that the caretaker status of the Vajpayee government was going to be a long one. It had lost the vote of confidence on 17 April and mid-term polls would not be concluded till early October, a period of nearly five months. What worried us greatly was that economic decision-making would suffer. An economy that had been in a downward spiral since 1996–97 was finally turning around, or at least the shoots of revival were visible. What impact would a caretaker government have on the emergent growth momentum? Under such conditions, the last thing that Vajpayee and those around him could have expected to worry about was a possible threat to national security which would pull the country into a state of war. But, as fate would have it, that is exactly what happened.

IT WAS MID-MAY, POSSIBLY THE seventeenth, when Brajesh Mishra informed Vajpayee, in my presence, that there were cross-border developments in Kashmir that might become a cause for concern.

The exact nature was not clear, but Mishra seemed anxious and said that the army was soon to provide a detailed briefing about the situation on the ground. The next day, we went to the Ops Room in South Block, where the then director general of military operations, Lt Gen. N.C. Vij, later to be the army chief, conducted the briefing. Apparently, groups of Mujahideen had crossed the Line of Control (LoC) that separated India and Pakistan in the then State of Jammu and Kashmir.[1]

While infiltration of jihadi terrorists from Pakistan had been going on for years, what was different this time was that these groups of Mujahideen were larger in numbers and had occupied the heights of Kargil. At this point, the army had not been able to determine the places where these intrusions had taken place and the numbers of fighters involved. As the story emerged then, two Ladhakhi shepherds had gone up the snow-clad mountains to look for grazing lands when they spotted a group of men in salwar kameez, popularly known as Pathan suits. This was reported to the local army units, which sent up a patrol to investigate. The patrol did not return. However, the situation was not assessed to be very serious, since the army chief, General Ved P. Malik, had proceeded on a ten-day foreign tour and was not cutting it short and flying back. It thus seemed at the time that while the situation may not be normal, it wasn't critical either.

---

[1] In the Jammu sector, the demarcation line where Indian control extends up to the border is accepted as the international border. However, in 1947–48, Pakistani troops disguised as irregulars and Afridi tribesmen, backed and funded by Pakistan, attempted to seize the state for Pakistan, as the ruler, Raja Hari Singh, prevaricated in choosing whom to accede to. This Pakistani invasion happened despite Pakistan having signed a standstill agreement with Raja Hari Singh. The Indian Army subsequently recovered some territory. The two armies also fought two other wars, in 1965 and 1971, and the present LoC was agreed to in the 1972 Suchetgarh Agreement. Both sides committed to respecting this line pending peaceful, bilateral agreement on the final status of the state.

THIS WAS A SHOCK, ACTUALLY, in retrospect the first of many, even more serious ones. After the success of the Lahore visit, the general view was that even if normal, peaceful relations between India and Pakistan would take time to establish, a good beginning had been made. Between the two main parties of Pakistan, Nawaz Sharif's Pakistan Muslim League (PML) was seen as having an Islamic character, as against the more secular-inclined Pakistan Peoples Party (PPP). Sharif and the PML were, in fact, creations of the Pakistani Army, though Sharif had tried to make himself an effective chief executive. So if Sharif was trying to mend relations with India, it could be presumed that Indo–Pak relations would certainly not deteriorate.

From Colombo and New York to Lahore, Vajpayee and Sharif had built a good equation. After the Kargil infiltration, there was anger in India at Pakistan and at Sharif, though there were some doubts right from the beginning about how much the latter was actually involved. In any case, an angry frame of mind could not have been the starting point for decision-making. The orders were clear: the intruders had to be evicted. The initial estimate was that it would be done in a matter of a few days, or at most in a couple of weeks. But, as subsequent developments were to show, these estimates were completely off the mark.

THE MISSION WAS MUCH MORE complicated than just throwing out a group of Mujahideen. Both armies had followed the standard drill of vacating their posts high in the hills when they became snowbound and went back to those altitudes in spring, around mid-to-late-May. What made the Mujahideen narrative a little difficult to digest was the geography of their chosen altitude of attack and their tactics. The Himalayan middle range separates the Kashmir valley from Ladakh; they are connected by a single national highway (NH1), which uses the Zoji La, a high mountain pass, to cross over. The pass is approximately midway between Srinagar and Kargil, now the headquarters of a district of the same name. The Srinagar–Leh NH1, as it comes down the Zoji La, lies quite close to Drass, whose heights, occupied by enemy forces, were perfect for interdicting traffic movement on the highway. Drass and the nearby Mushkoh valley, south-west of the Kargil town, represented the western-most extremity of the Ladakh region.

It was soon clear that the infiltration was substantial. The first intrusion by the shepherds had been in Batalik, north-east of Kargil. The Drass–Leh–Batalik line running from south-west to north-east is about 160 km, and the intrusions were 2–10 km deep, 6–7 km on an average. The question that was bothering us the most was simple: Why would the Mujahideen occupy snowy heights with no habitation, when their supposed strength lies in carrying out hit-and-run/suicide missions in populated areas? A Mujahideen action is normally meant to generate wide publicity and frighten the population, forcing their governments into conceding to the certain demands. But if the Kashmiri Mujahideen were occupying unpopulated areas along the LoC, could it be possible that they were trying to actually win territories from the Indian state? And if this were true, how did the Mujahideen have the necessary logistical capacity to place these many fighters and occupy hundreds of square kilometres of the Indian territory? While these and other related questions did bother us at the time, in retrospect, nothing much was done to seek their answers.

Vajpayee belonged to a tradition that believed India's perceived pacifism had hurt the nation, cost it its independence and allowed invaders to subjugate it. Further, he held that independent India had not done enough to be able to defend itself militarily. This meant, among other things, that the armed forces had to be given a free hand in battlefield tactics. As it is, the priority of the government was to ensure that the intruders were evicted, and this required us to be patient and not distract the army's attention with questions about the nature of the intrusion.

With the return of General Malik, we received another detailed briefing in the Ops Room. This set the trend for the daily meetings of the Cabinet Committee on Security (CCS). Even though the extent of incursion was becoming clearer to us, we were being told that only the Mujahideen were involved. I am still amazed at how we accepted this. There were stories about how intelligence agencies had reported that groups of Mujahideen had collected in the northern areas of Pakistan Occupied Jammu and Kashmir, and how this had actually been predicted in mid-1998, etc. But frankly, these looked like after-the-event media plants— the usual fare in open societies.

Initially, the CCS decided that only the army should handle the situation, as it was not clear until then how the air force could contribute, there being no strategic locations (arms dumps, airfields, railheads, ports, ordnance factories) that could be taken out. The Kargil conflict was an unusual one for the air force, since it lacked conventional battlefields. The possibility of the air force providing the usual tactical support to the infantry was therefore minimal.

THE CCS, AT ITS 26 May meeting, authorized the use of air power after the three service chiefs—General Malik, Air Chief Marshal Anil Y. Tipnis and Admiral Sushil Kumar—came to an agreement on the operational principles. The Indian Air Force (IAF) swung into operations the very next day but faced grief. A MIG-27 suffered a flameout and went down. The MIG-21 that went in search for it was hit by a missile, and the pilot had to bail out. It later came to our attention that while the first pilot Flight Lieutenant K. Nachiketa was taken prisoner of war (POW) after he bailed out, the other, Squadron Leader Ajay Ahuja, who'd parachuted and landed in enemy-occupied area, was tortured, shot and killed, which was a gross violation of the Geneva Convention that governs battlefield behaviour.

But this was not the end of our woes. The very next day, 28 May, an MI-17 helicopter gunship, with four persons on board, was brought down by an American-supplied Stinger missile; there were no survivors. The media reported that the Mujahideen had scored a success in downing an Indian aircraft, with some pointing out that in the Afghan jihad, the Mujahideen had mastered the use of Stinger missiles, which had been accepted as the single-most important factor in changing the tide of war against the Russians. There was speculation that veterans of the Afghan jihad had been inducted into the Kargil sector to support the Kashmiri Mujahideen.

While Sqn Ldr Ahuja and the MI-17 helicopter were brought down on the Indian side of the LoC, Flt Lt Nachiketa was across the LoC. This conduct of the war could not sustain itself, since the media had started grilling the government over the casualties and for overlooking the causes that led to such a situation. It was fortunate that at this stage the army's casualties were also, relatively speaking, low, since the main operation to dislodge the infiltrators had not yet picked up. The only retaliations that the Indian Army had mounted till then were meant to basically identify the enemy positions on the peaks, so that the artillery forces could target them. On the one hand, the IAF went back to the drawing board, while the political leadership led by Vajpayee went into a huddle. Now that it was decided to alter the approach, the results were not far. The IAF modified its tactical approach, and soon, with the induction of laser guided bombs, the ground situation started changing.

Much more important from the point of view of the conduct of the war, the political objective of clearing all intruders from our side of the LoC came with a rider—the military was not to cross the LoC. While my memory may play tricks, I do not recall any objection being made to it. Subsequently, after the war was long over, Vajpayee has been criticized for this caveat, which, it is said, had crippled the ability of the military to regain territory. Much more specifically and with graver consequences, it is said that these restrictions led to higher casualties on our side. These objections are extremely serious and should be addressed, but for that it is useful to understand how the war was progressing and how the world was reacting to it.

Around the end of May, the expectation was that the war would last a few weeks, delayed only by the army's limitations in moving men and material to the battlegrounds. The LoC east of the Kashmir valley was never seen as a weak spot from where infiltrators could sneak in, and rightly so, for there was no local support for them, essential for allowing them to travel and stay undetected. Hence, it was lightly guarded. Further, high altitude warfare requires acclimatization, so there was no question of ramping up numbers at short notice, or even of equipping them with high-altitude gear necessary for survival at these heights. In short, we were caught napping.

The daily meetings of the CCS meant that while the top leadership was in the loop always, the service chiefs could, and did, push through decisions that were necessary and could not wait detailed examination. These meetings were held invariably every evening, in the enclosed veranda of 7 Race Course Road. Vajpayee sat at the head of the table, and on one side were the ministers—Advani (home), George Fernandes (defence), Jaswant Singh (foreign) and Yashwant Sinha (finance). On the other side sat the officers—Prabhat Kumar (cabinet secretary), Brajesh Mishra (national security adviser and principal secretary to PM), the three chiefs, defence secretary and, when necessary, the chiefs of both the intelligence agencies, Shyamal Dutta (Intelligence Bureau) and Arvind Dave (RAW). The discussions were open and frank, with the chiefs in the lead. What brought the war close to the decision-makers was the screening of videos that our planes were recording as they carried out operations. This was first used in an Ops Room briefing and later at CCS meetings, when required. The ski track markings near enemy posts showed that jet skis were being used, hardly something that the Mujahideen would use.

Vajpayee and the other members of the CCS were appreciative of the difficulties the army was facing in trying to climb up steep mountains at that attitude and fighting an enemy who had occupied prominent posts on ridges and could—did—shoot at the Indian Army units downhill. The presence of heavy guns and the strengthened posts meant that it was extremely difficult to dislodge the intruders. The mass movement of troops and heavy guns could only be done using the exposed highway; it was necessarily slow and difficult. At no stage did I feel that Vajpayee had any doubts that the Indian military would succeed, and their resolve and capacity were seen as heroic. Effectively, they were given a carte blanche in operational matters.

This expression of confidence in the services could be seen, for example, in how the navy fashioned its response. The idea that the navy could play a role in helping the army evict the Kargil intruders is itself mindboggling. We all know that the navy played a major part in the 1971 war, but little is known about its role in Kargil, which was a land-based conflict. Admiral Sushil Kumar was quick to understand the precarious nature of the Pakistani economy and India's ability to dominate the waters. After the morale-dipping crash of two fighter jets, the Indian Navy adopted arm-twisting tactics until Pakistan withdrew from Kargil. Immediately after the downing of the Air Force jets, Indian warships were mobilized across the Arabian Sea to Karachi and air surveillance was increased.

As the situation became tense on the battlefields of Kargil during the first week of June, the Indian Navy began deploying more weapons and troops. By the second week of June, the eastern fleet, based in the Bay of Bengal and headquartered at Vishakhapatnam, had reached Cochin and soon joined the western fleet targeting Karachi. With the most important oil ports of Karachi coming within direct range of the naval fleets, Pakistani Navy got defensive and ordered the shifting of their ships from Karachi Port to Omara. The Indian Navy continued to push more ships into the Arabian Sea off the Pakistani waters while firing some missiles on its own waters under weapons testing projects.

The Indian Navy also sent its personnel to the high altitudes of the Kargil area with GPS tracking systems, in order to help the infantry and artillery forces fix enemy positions for attack. Significantly, the amphibious unit based in the Andaman Islands was shifted to the Arabian Sea in order to put off the Pakistanis, who felt that a sea-based attack was imminent. The LoC caveat was not in the public domain, and even those who knew felt that if things did not go well, India retained the right to change it. This was made clear to the three chiefs also by Brajesh Mishra.

THE FIRST CRACK IN THE Mujahideen story was the recovery of pay slips and other standard documents from the bodies of a few enemy dead that the Indian Army recovered. This was in the first week of June. With this, our understanding slightly changed and we now knew that the intruders were Pakistan Army irregulars and Mujahideen—irregulars because they belonged to the Northern Light Infantry (NLI), which was actually commanded by Pakistan Army officers and was later formally made a part of the army. However, the belief that it was still largely the Mujahideen who were responsible for the attack continued to prevail among the media, and even among the decision-makers. I think that Vajpayee and others found it difficult to fathom that the Pakistan Army would push their regulars inside Indian territory and risk an eyeball-to-eyeball confrontation between two nuclear powers, whose nuclear command and control structures were still rudimentary.

In his address to the nation on 7 June, and again as late as mid-June (when Vajpayee visited his parliamentary constituency, Lucknow), he spoke about throwing out the Pakistan Army and 'intruders' from Indian territory. The failure to accept that it was the Pakistan Army alone which was involved was not difficult to understand. Ultimately, this dangerous move by the Pakistan Army went in India's favour in a major way.

WHAT COMPLICATED DECISION-MAKING FOR THE Vajpayee government during the Kargil war, and more so later in the year when it had to handle the hijacking of IC 814, was the media. If the first Gulf War (1990–91) was the world's first televised war, signalled by the rise of CNN, Kargil was India's first televised war. There was a difference though. The Americans had media units imbedded in army units, thereby allowing only such messages to go out as they wanted. But there was no such restriction or organized flow of information during the Kargil war. The media was reporting live from the locations where actual action was taking place, e.g. the firing of Bofors guns, which, many alleged, revealed their locations. Further, reporters had access to junior officers, other ranks and even troops. The reporting ranged from the realistic to the imaginative, putting considerable pressure on the government to act, sometimes even when the time wasn't ripe.

To some extent, this was rectified with the daily joint press briefing at Shastri Bhavan, by the then joint secretary (external publicity, Ministry of External Affairs) Raminder Jassal and Brig. J.J. Singh, who later became army chief.[2] Where necessary, representatives of the air force and navy were present. This was possibly the first time that the Indian government went on a media offensive, with detailed information instead of bland platitudes.

---

[2] Jassal, my senior in Hindu College and an outstanding diplomat, later succumbed to cancer, which cut short a brilliant career.

But this was the public part, important enough as it was; the other part was to keep foreign governments informed. I realized that much as we in India believe in self-reliance and strategic autonomy, India does not live on an island all by itself. Our proactive diplomacy was directed at telling key decision-makers across the world that it was India which was the victim of aggression and that we did not want to change the status quo unilaterally. There is nothing more comforting to an established player than to be told that its position is not being challenged and that its position is actually being respected. But I am going ahead of my story.

To illustrate how ill-informed, or inadequately informed, we still were in the last days of May, just when Vajpayee was telling India that the situation was more serious than previously expected, we were offering the Mujahideen a safe passage. This was not because India was uncertain and wanted an early end to conflict, but because it was expected that the Mujahideen would not have the stomach for a long fight. Thus, while on the one hand, it was realized that the situation serious, it was still unclear as to how serious it would get. Unfortunately, the Pakistanis saw it as a sign of our innate 'defensiveness', and the point of providing a safe passage was rightly not pursued by us. Slowly, the tide would change as the army and the air force would get their act together by marshalling their resources and adjusting the battle plans to suit the geography of the high-altitude war they were fighting.

The pendulum started swinging our way not just because of the battlefield action but, more importantly, because of an intelligence breakthrough that suddenly galvanized India and made the Pakistan Army look devious. Arvind Dave, the RAW chief, came up with two telephonic recordings between the Pakistan Army chief, General Pervez Musharraf, and his chief of the general staff, Lt Gen. Mohammed Aziz. Brajesh Mishra and Dave brought the tape to Vajpayee, and we heard the conversation. There was stunned silence. It was clear that the Pakistan Army was involved, with the Mujahideen playing a minor role, if any. The Indian Air Force aircraft had been brought down by the Pakistan Army, though they got the Mujahideen to claim it. Musharraf was not happy that the helicopter had crashed on the Indian side of the LoC.

Lt Gen. Aziz then said something that indicated his correct understanding of India's resolve to up the ante if things did not go its way. He told Musharraf that a few Indian bombs had fallen on the Pakistani side of the LoC, and that this was deliberate. They did not hit any targets but the point of the strike, as understood by the Pakistanis, was that India could hit targets across the LoC. Though Lt Gen. Aziz mentioned that Nawaz Sharif had been briefed at a meeting on 27 May at his office, it was unclear how much the latter knew. The Pakistan Army's stand, which it wanted their foreign office to propagate, was that while they were located within their side of the LoC, there might have been certain border crossovers due to lack of clarity in the line's actual demarcation.

The Pakistan Army was happy that the Kashmir issue was being internationalized, with the UN secretary-general, Kofi Annan, calling on both sides to exercise restraint. The Pakistan Army was also clear that in his forthcoming negotiations with India, Pakistani foreign minister, Sartaj Aziz, should not accept a ceasefire, since that would allow the Indian Army to use the Srinagar–Drass–Kargil highway to move men and material. It was then expected that the two foreign ministers would meet on 30 May. But the meeting was ultimately held on 12 June, by which time a lot of water had already flowed down the Indus.

Though the CCS was made aware of them, the Musharraf–Aziz tapes were not circulated outside this small group initially. Vajpayee wanted to find a peaceful solution; or to put it differently, he wanted to give Nawaz Sharif a chance to bring the conflict to an early end. R.K. Mishra—a veteran journalist and editor of the

CPI-leaning *Patriot* and *Link*, former Congress MP and head of the Reliance-funded think tank, Observer Research Foundation— was drafted to activate back-channel diplomacy with Pakistan. His interlocutor on the other side was the veteran diplomat Niaz Naik. While the war was on, Mishra made three trips to Pakistan to meet Sharif, with Naik making one trip to India. Mishra carried the tapes and transcripts to Sharif. As Mishra reported to Vajpayee, Sharif had turned ashen while listening to them. Was it because he had been caught red-handed? Or was it because he wasn't fully aware of the extent of the audacity, and adventurism, of Gen. Musharraf?

Subsequent evidence suggests that Sharif was not consulted or informed about Operation 'Koh-i-Paima', under which troops of the NLI were inducted into vacated Indian Army posts; and when Sharif was finally briefed during the first meeting about the operation, the army had refrained from giving him the entire picture. However, his foreign minister, Sartaj Aziz, and defence secretary, Lt Gen. Iftikhar Ali Khan, had caught on and advised Sharif to caution the army, at which point, the army won him over by saying that post the success of their operation, Sharif would be remembered as the 'Victor of Kashmir'.

However, Sharif's position was a tenuous one, and in a later meeting, he indicated to Mishra that they should take a walk in the garden, obviously suspecting that his own house was tapped. When Mishra reported this to Vajpayee, the latter took this as an indication that Sharif was more a prisoner of circumstances than anything else. So Vajpayee continued to pin his hopes on Sharif, counting on his help in de-escalating the situation between the two nuclear powers. Vajpayee must have spoken to Sharif 5–6 times during the one and a half month period from mid-May to 4 July, when the Pakistani PM publicly committed to President Clinton that Pakistan would withdraw its forces to its side of the LoC.

One of these calls was made in mid-June, from Srinagar, after Vajpayee had made a visit to the town of Kargil. Sporadic Pakistani bombardment was on, and we saw from the helipad across the river some shells hitting areas near the highway. On his arrival in Srinagar, Vajpayee asked me to connect him to Sharif. My small team and I tried, but we just could not get through. Then one of the local officers present informed us that dialling Pakistan (+92) from Jammu and Kashmir was barred. The telecom authorities were told to open the facility for a short while, so that the two prime ministers could talk.

Back-channel diplomacy, which generally means using non-officials in developing basic common understanding before formal talks could be held, was not without its peculiar challenges. How do we send across R.K. Mishra at short notice with the tapes and without airport security at either end getting too nosy about what he was carrying? The answer was to make him accompany Vivek Katju, who continued as our point person on Pakistan. Since the legal fiction of Pakistan not being in the picture anywhere in Kargil was accepted, almost till the end of the conflict, normal communications between the two countries continued. Hence Vivek's tour to Pakistan, with diplomatic bags immune to checks, was nothing unusual.

Later, this pretence of normalcy was not required as long as the Mishra–Naik talks were not publicized. It also had its humorous interludes. Once, Mishra rang up very agitated and said that he was suspicious about an Ambassador car, with a few occupants, parked near his house in Vasant Vihar. Since he was carrying out a sensitive assignment, he feared the worst. I was asked to have it checked. The Delhi Police promptly moved in and the car and its occupants were removed. No sooner had this happened than an angry Shyamal Datta rang me up on the government's secured phone system, complaining that some IB personnel, who were keeping a watch on somebody else, had been removed by Delhi Police on instructions from the PMO!

THE NEXT PHASE OF THE efforts at peace was something I could not understand then, nor is the logic clear to me still. I have mentioned Vajpayee's long rope to Sharif, and this seemed to fly in the face of it. Sartaj Aziz's visit was finally fixed for 12 June. Jaswant Singh seemed quite inflexible about allowing any latitude to Pakistan, not even on trying to creating a rift between Pakistan's civilian and military leaderships. A day before Sartaj Aziz's visit, the Indian cabinet was briefed about the Musharraf tapes, which were later played before the media, who were also given the transcripts. The result was that the story of the tapes overshadowed the meetings.

On 12 June, Jaswant Singh went to the Delhi airport to receive his Pakistani counterpart and hosted a lunch for him after the talks, but his whole demeanour was frosty. The agreed boilerplate for us was that complete withdrawal must take place before any substantial dialogue could begin.

Contrary to what Lt Gen. Aziz and Gen. Musharraf had agreed upon during their telephonic conversation, recorded in the tapes, Pakistan now changed its stand and started asking for a ceasefire, using the excuse that since the LoC was 'unclear', some inadvertent transgression might well have taken place. Their plan was that once peace was established, their positions occupied on the ground could be validated. Clearly, believing that causing confusion was good tactics, the Pakistan Army had obviously bargained for our falling for this childish trap. The Suchetgarh Agreement of 1972 had clearly delineated the LoC all the way up to NJ9842, or the southern point of Siachen. The locations of intrusion clearly fell within the demarcated areas along the line, and hence there was no scope for confusion. Further, if the Pakistan Army was not involved in the intrusion and it was the Mujahideen, then why were they asking for a ceasefire? And since when were the Mujahideen bound by India–Pakistan agreement? Their stupidity was breathtaking and audacious. Did they actually think the rest of us were fools?

The anger at the Pakistani deceit was understandable, but was Sartaj Aziz the right person to be facing this onslaught. He was clearly the messenger, not the decision-maker. Therefore, the message had to be conveyed to his principals. Vajpayee, in his address to the nation on 7 June, had made it clear that India would not rest until all the intruders had been evicted. His message to Aziz was measured but clear: How did the Lahore bus reach Kargil? However, the tapes had shown that Musharraf had not kept Sharif in the loop about the extent of involvement of the army, nor about the extent of the intrusion. The tapes had also made it clear that Musharraf and his group were thinking very simplistically and had no idea of the consequences of their dangerous adventure.

Could Aziz's visit be used to widen the wedge that had developed between the military and the elected government of Pakistan? This is what Vajpayee was doing, and continued to do, using the R.K. Mishra–Niaz Naik channel, and ultimately it was this diplomatic chess move which helped end the war. But Jaswant Singh was adamant that Aziz, and by implication his boss, Sharif, were not to be given even an inch.

VAJPAYEE'S VISIT TO THE KARGIL town, in the face of constant bombardment, was a first for an Indian prime minister. It was meant to bolster the morale of the troops and reassure them that the whole country was with them; it was also aimed at convincing Pakistan that India would not rest till victory was achieved. Frankly, I was worried about this visit since the town was within the range of the Pakistani guns, and they knew the lie of the land, having hit an underground ammunition dump there on 9 May. The Pakistanis would not know where Vajpayee was in the town at any given moment of time, and a major mishap or tragedy could always happen. I urged Brajesh Mishra to instruct the director general of military operations (DGMO) to convey to his counterpart to be careful.

This was an unusual war, in that Pakistan did not acknowledge its involvement, due to which normal diplomatic and military communications had continued between the two countries. The two DGMOs talked weekly and more frequently when needed. Diplomats flew to each other's countries, and the train as well as the newly started bus services continued operating. Flt Lt Nachiketa, who was a POW, was handed over to us in early June, as were the dead bodies of the Indian patrol which had disappeared in early May, investigating reports of intrusion across the LoC. Fighting a real war, with heroism, death and causalities, and continuing normal relations at the same time was bizarre to say the least. Both countries had a reason to maintain this fiction. Pakistan, as mentioned, wanted to hide its involvement. Vajpayee had his compulsions. He was afraid that there would be pressure to end the war before India's political and military objectives of recovering the territory had been achieved.

From about the second week of June, the contours of the war started changing, with the army and air force better prepared and equipped to fight the war, which had them placed in extremely disadvantaged positions from the beginning. The deployment of long-range, heavy-duty Bofors guns and the use of laser-guided bombs/missiles by the air force supplemented the brave action of the infantry and turned the war in India's favour, but incrementally. The assaults were better coordinated and the results bore this out. Tololing, near Drass, was secured first, and then, as the engagement intensified on the battlefield, more heights on Tiger Hill fell to the Indian Army. The air force wiped out the big logistics-cum-ammunitions depot at Munto Dhalo and was also able to interdict replenishment efforts by the Pakistan Army.

Against their expectation, the Pakistan Army was pushed into a corner and was now seriously suing for peace. The US had been Pakistan's big brother for over forty-five years, had rescued it out of the hole Pakistan would dig itself into each time, and had equipped and trained the Pakistan Army against the alleged threats from the Communists. Those troops and equipment were now being employed against India. This time, however, Pakistan had dug itself into a hole which was deeper than the US rope could help them out of.

When the Pakistan Army and the country's political leadership both requested the US to intervene and help bring about a ceasefire, Vajpayee, in his telephonic conversations with Clinton, made it clear that the Pakistani adventure was dangerous and could not be condoned. Either they could vacate Indian territory on their own, or India would throw them out the way it deemed best. There would be no ceasefire till the sanctity of the LoC was respected. Surprisingly, Clinton did not have much choice but to eventually publicly rebuke Pakistan and call upon it to withdraw its troops back to the LoC at the earliest.

India's intense diplomatic and media efforts seemed to be paying off. The moniker 'rogue army' to describe the Pakistan Army caught on. Digital media was in its infancy but it played a role, so did full-page advertisements in national and international press. The NRI community rose to the occasion and put their money where their mouth was. Extensive tours of the US by senior leaders like Sushma Swaraj and the then-upcoming BJP general secretary, Narendra Modi, helped increase pressure on US Congressmen. As a result of this lobbying, what followed was the US imposing sanctions on Pakistan, which included blocking all assistance from international institutions like the IMF and World Bank. In fact, the House of Representatives subcommittee, led by Congressman Jim McDermott, had agreed on a far lower level of sanctions, but the thousands of fax messages that his office, and those of the other members, received, thanks to the efforts of Narendra Modi, forced a rethink, to Pakistan's detriment.

WE WERE NERVOUS WHEN THE head of the US Central Command, Gen. Anthony Zinni, visited Pakistan in the last week of June. The US military and the CIA were known to be very close to the Pakistan Army, and Gen. Zinni and Gen. Musharraf were supposedly very close. Zinni met both Musharraf and Sharif. We did not know what transpired in those meetings, but subsequent evidence, in the form of Zinni's book (*Battle Ready*) and Bruce Reidel's writings ('American Diplomacy and the 1999 Kargil Summit at Blair House'), indicates that Musharraf realized that the Americans would not bail him out. The Americans made it clear that they knew there was no confusion about the delineation of the LoC. What did come out publicly was that Musharraf announced at the end of his meeting with Zinni that Sharif would soon be travelling to Washington, D.C. to meet with Clinton. In fact, it was Musharraf who had pushed for the Sharif–Clinton meeting.

Vajpayee politely refused to travel to Washington, D.C. for a trilateral meeting, since we had nothing to offer till the aggression was completely reversed. Despite our scepticism of America's initiative, the latter seemed to understand the reasons for Vajpayee's reluctance to travel to Washington. Sharif's desperate 'flight' to Washington, with his entire family, seemed to suggest that he knew how out of control the situation was. Unusually, Clinton met Sharif on 4 July, which is more than a national holiday in the US. It is this one day when the entire country comes to a complete halt. People abandon their homes, come out with their hampers of food and beverages, and park themselves at strategic locations to watch fireworks done on a grand scale.

We were gathered in the drawing room of 7 RCR around Vajpayee. Jaswant Singh, Brajesh Mishra, K. Raghunath (foreign secretary), Vivek Katju and Prabhat Shukla were all in attendance. Clinton called in between to brief Vajpayee on the progress of the talks. Sharif had agreed to a call back of the Pakistani forces, and this was going to be released in a joint statement. The next morning, when full details of the statement were available, Prabhat Shukla and I were sceptical and could not help but point out the ambiguity in its language.

The statement deserves to be quoted in full:

> It was agreed between the President and Prime Minister that concrete steps will be taken for the restoration of the Line of Control in accordance with the Shimla Agreement. The President urged an immediate cessation of the hostilities once these steps are taken. The Prime Minister and the President agreed that the bilateral dialogue begun in Lahore in February provides the best forum for resolving all issues dividing India and Pakistan, including Kashmir. The President said he would take a personal interest in encouraging an expeditious resumption and intensification of those bilateral efforts, once the sanctity of the Line of Control has been fully restored.

So did Pakistan actually concede that their armed forces were involved, by committing to restore the sanctity of the LoC? What were the implications of Clinton taking a personal interest in moving relations between India and Pakistan further? Vajpayee overruled our scepticism, and as time would tell, he was much more nuanced in his understanding of the shift in global balance that this statement indicated towards. In retrospect, the shift was indeed tectonic, but we were too close to the event to analyse it with the right perspective.

The Pakistani reaction reminded me of Gen. Yahya Khan's famous speech after the Pakistan Army had surrendered to the Indian Army in Dhaka in 1971, which culminated in the creation of Bangladesh as a free country. Yahya Khan told the Pakistanis in his last speech as the head of the government: *'Abhi jang jari hai* [the war is still on].' There could not have been a bigger lie, or so I thought. This time around, after meeting the army chief and other senior commanders, Nawaz Sharif convened a meeting of the defence committee of the cabinet (DCC).

The DCC expressed 'satisfaction' that the Clinton–Sharif joint statement had incorporated the 'main elements' of Pakistan's position. Maintaining the fiction, which I was afraid they would do, the DCC 'decided that Pakistan should appeal to the Mujahedeen to help resolve the Kargil situation' as was mentioned in the subsequent statement issued after a cabinet meeting on 10 July, which said, 'The Cabinet noted that the Mujahedeen have responded positively to the appeal of the Government of Pakistan to help resolve the Kargil situation.' If this was not enough, the cabinet further said that it believed that Sharif's 'peace initiative had helped to internationalise the Kashmir issue in a manner that had never been done before while peace in the region had been preserved'. The proverbial cat was out of the bag, rather slipped out of it, in order to salvage some credit for what was a monumental failure.

TECHNICALLY, THE WAR WAS OVER after the joint statement by Clinton and Sharif was released, but not as far as the larger picture went, because the developments on the battlefield were still unfolding. At the time the agreement was being finalized, Tiger Hill fell to the Indian Army. The air force had played its role in softening the targets, but ultimately it was raw courage, with hand-to-hand combat, that won us this battle, like many others. A few days later, on 7 June, significant progress was made in the Batalik sector, but the area was not secured for another week.

In the meanwhile, the two DGMOs of India and Pakistan met to work out the modalities of withdrawal. But then again, if the Pakistani leadership was withdrawing and conceding at the diplomatic level, the reality at the ground differed. There were fierce counter-attacks still taking place as the retreating Pakistani soldiers would withdraw from some posts but occupy others. Even at the locations they were vacating, they were leaving behind anti-personnel mines. What was more horrifying, however, was that even the dead bodies of Pakistani soldiers were booby-trapped to inflict last-minute casualties on the Indian side. Thus the actual conflict with the retreating Pakistan Army ended only on 26 July, which we now celebrate as the Kargil Vijay Divas.

THE VIDEO FEEDS WE WERE receiving from the battlefield made me feel like I was right there. But of course, I was hundreds of kilometres away, in the safer environment of Delhi, closest to the policy battlefield of decision-making. Though even from this angle, a few things stood out.

One was the bravery of our troops and young officers, some of whom knew that they were never coming back and were yet willing to lead their men. In a world full of avarice and personal aggrandizement, it was sobering to know that such people existed. And their bravery was matched by the courage and determination of their families. Fortunately, these acts of heroism, and these fatalities, were being broadcast and not hidden away. Such levels of transparency had never been seen during the previous wars and helped bring the country together as well as made people appreciate the heroic efforts of our soldiers.

Two, the government's decision to send the remains of the soldiers who'd been killed in Kargil to their respective homes and accord state funeral to them. It was the first time this had been done, so the defence ministry had to purchase the coffins in a hurry. The use of coffins in India was itself limited and procuring them locally was just not possible. Instead of appreciating this gesture for what it was, opponents of the government tried to give

it the spin of a scandal. Much worse, stories were planted that with
the increase in 'body bags' being brought down, there would be
loss of support for the war effort. The use of the term 'body bags'
was itself incomprehensible, and to trivialize a society's gesture of
according public honour, or *samman*, to someone who had made
the supreme sacrifice, was in bad taste.

Vajpayee's understanding was that even a gesture like a state
funeral was not enough. Therefore, he immediately approved a
rehabilitation package for the widows/parents of those who had
laid down their lives. This would not bring back the lost ones,
but at least the families could cope with their lives better. In fact,
the allocation of petrol pumps and gas agencies to the martyrs'
families had started when hostilities were still on, a most unusual
step for a system regarded as slow and unresponsive.

Three, what I found rather extraordinary was the attitude
of the armed forces to the enemy casualties, despite the odd
circumstances and bad faith in which the war had been initiated.
Since Pakistan was not prepared to own up to their involvement,
they refused to collect the bodies of the fallen from the Indian
Army. So the army conducted around 145 funerals, dug graves
at altitudes of 15,000 feet, flew in maulvis and conducted the
last rites.

Four, while on the one hand the war effort was being
monitored and led single-mindedly with no attempt spared to
ensure victory, on the other hand, the routine functioning of the
government continued as before. What made this situation more
impressive was that this was a caretaker government, handicapped
in its abilities to take decisions. No new legislation could have
been contemplated, since Parliament stood dissolved and it was
unprecedented for a caretaker government to try and use the
ordinance route. The routine working of the government meant
that normal functions went on, and new initiatives could be taken
up imaginatively. On 2 June, Vajpayee flew to Mumbai for the

commissioning of the *INS Mysore*. General Malik flew with us on the PM's aircraft, and the opportunity was used to suggest technological upgrade of the army, which would lead to a leaner but more effective force. Admiral Sushil Kumar was the perfect host, though the weather gods' bountifulness meant that we were all drenched.

LATER THAT MONTH, VAJPAYEE VISITED Dhaka, from 19–20 June, to mark the inauguration of the Kolkata–Dhaka bus service. This was a momentous visit, since, unlike the Atari–Wagah border which sees very few people crossing it every day, the Petrapole border is a busy one, both in terms of the people and goods crossing it. But the Indian media and even policymakers are so Delhi-centric that the Atari–Wagah gets a disproportionate amount of publicity, while Petrapole is relegated to the footnotes. (At present, dozens of buses ply on the Kolkata–Dhaka route via Petrapole–Benapole every day.)

At Vajpayee's request, West Bengal Chief Minister Jyoti Basu joined the delegation. He was quite a hit in Dhaka, and the accompanying Indian media credited it to the friendship between President 'Bangabandhu' Sheikh Mujibur Rahman and Jyoti Basu. This seemed improbable, since the two could not possibly have met, other than on some formal occasion. Jyoti Basu's ancestral village was in east Bengal, and having been such a long-serving chief minister (twenty-two years by 1999), he had become a legendary figure in the region.

The visit was not without its share of hits and misses. We were to leave for the airport directly from the last function. As soon as it ended, we were asked to wait a couple of minutes, so that the Bangladeshi prime minister, Sheikh Hasina, could leave for the airport and be there when Vajpayee reached. Being an informal person, Vajpayee suggested that the two prime ministers travel together, which Sheikh Hasina immediately assented to.

Except that it caused chaos. I remember running and shouting loudly, 'She is travelling with the PM!' How do you combine two motorcades into one? How to make sure everybody got into some car, any car, and none was left behind? Somehow, we managed and reached the airport together. All this, despite the fact that our attention was on the war . . .

THERE ARE TWO CRITICAL ISSUES that analysts still debate about. One: Why did the Pakistan Army embark on such a risky gamble that could easily have led to the two countries crossing the nuclear Rubicon? Two: What impact did Vajpayee's diktat on not crossing the LoC have on the war efforts? To me, the two questions are interlinked.

It is often suggested that Pakistan occupied what became known as the Kargil Heights to avenge for what India did in 1984, when it had taken possession of the Siachen glacier, the Saltoro Ridge to its west and important passes of Sia La, Bilafond La and Gyong La. Subsequently, Pakistan made many attempts, including one led by then Brigadier Musharraf. But India not only retained possession, it also took control of some Pakistani posts. In the eyes of the Pakistan Army, this occupation amounted to perfidy and a violation of the Simla Agreement. The Kargil action is explained as Pakistan's revenge for Siachen, a bargaining chip to get Siachen back.

Yet this view is wholly erroneous. Without going into the details of the origin and developments of the ceasefire line (CFL) in Jammu and Kashmir, which broadly evolved into the LoC post the 1971 war, one thing should be clear: While Pakistan was no doubt issuing permits to mountaineering expeditions in the area, the Pakistan Army was never in actual occupation of the Siachen glacier. When the Indian Army moved into Siachen and the Saltoro ridge and passes, it was to pre-empt the Pakistan Army, not to displace it.

Secondly, occupying Siachen did not impact any area outside it, while occupying the Kargil Heights meant that Pakistan could interdict the National Highway 1A, particularly in the Drass–Kargil sector, the vital road connecting Ladakh to the rest of the country. (The alternative, Manali–Leh road via Khardung La was then not in a position to substitute for the Srinagar–Kargil–Leh highway.)

Thirdly, Pakistan could not have seriously thought that India would meekly accept the occupation of its territory and sue for peace without making a full-blown effort to throw out the intruders. It was their mistake to underestimate Vajpayee's resolve. The Lahore Declaration was the extension of the hand of friendship, not a show of friendship.

Why then, did Pakistan embark on this dangerous adventure? Vajpayee was a man of few words, and if he did speak in small gatherings, he was never garrulous. Yet, in the snatches of discussions about what was happening and what India needed to do, it was suggested that Musharraf's risky gamble was linked to Pokhran and the Kashmir imbroglio. Pokhran had made India almost an international pariah. As we saw post-Pokhran, the developed West was using harsh language against India, taking specific steps to humiliate India and its leaders, and painting Pakistan as an unwitting victim of India's deviousness. Suddenly, all past reports of Pakistan as a proliferator, of people going to jail for illegally helping the Pakistani nuclear programme, or of the invidious nature of the China–Pakistan nuclear and missile cooperation were forgotten.

It was well known that neither Pakistan nor India had begun their nuclear programme in 1998, and yet India's test was seen as provocative and a game changer. Clinton, Madeleine Albright and others had literally pleaded with Pakistan not to test, which they said would vindicate India. Don't fall for the Indian trap, Nawaz Sharif was warned. Yet, even after Pakistan's test, the kid-glove treatment continued. The Americans made it clear that the impact of sanctions on both countries should be asymmetrical, obviously to India's disadvantage. The US acquiesced in the release of the IMF loan tranche to Pakistan without lifting sanctions. This was India's weakest moment internationally.

On the other hand, the Pakistani-inspired and -controlled insurgency in Kashmir had run its course. People had seen through it and had started participating in elections in large numbers. Time was running out for Pakistan. The world had forgotten Kashmir, and Pakistan was getting no traction from it. The emerging Vajpayee–Sharif partnership looked promising from the point of view of establishing peace, and if there was one thing the Pakistan Army was afraid of, it was normalcy in India–Pakistan relations.

Peaceful negotiations conducted by civilian interlocutors meant the strengthening of democracy in Pakistan and the end of the army's monopoly over power and resources. This had to be stopped. And what better way to achieve so many objectives than by simply forcing a conflict on India with a sleight of hand? The Mujahideen had taken the initiative, and the only way to stop the situation from deteriorating was through frightening the world into calling on India not to escalate.

Vajpayee understood this and hence took the decision to forcibly oppose the intrusion but without enlarging the conflict by taking it elsewhere. Once the sanctity of the LoC, as the instrument that had maintained peace in the region since 1972, was re-established, Pakistan's game was over. Its leadership had underestimated Vajpayee's determination to not negotiate till the LoC was respected, and to regain Indian territory even if it required the investment of all resources necessary. The strength of Indian deployment in numbers and guns, shocked the Pakistanis who did not expect this robust fightback.

By not crossing the LoC, India demonstrated in action that it understood the dangers of a conflict between two nuclear powers.

Unlike the Pakistanis, who thought that they could get a good deal by pointing a gun at their own heads, India's responsible and mature behaviour won international acclaim. A number of critics today question what such acclaim actually resulted in. The answer is simple: had it not been for the stand India was taking, the US would not have leant so hard on Pakistan and got them to withdraw. It was obvious to us that it would have taken the military months to clear the area. The war was brought to an early end only because of how India conducted itself throughout the war. The danger that the reckless actions of Pakistan posed were becoming obvious, and by contrast, India emerged as a stabilizing force that understood the implications of a wider conflagration. Arguably, the number of casualties would have been far higher had we not taken the decision to respect the LoC. But nevertheless, Vajpayee had indeed indicated that if the situation did not improve, the decision to not cross the LoC would be reconsidered.

What made this decision historic was that for the first time ever, the US had come out in favour of India when dealing with an India–Pakistan issue. Our constant scepticism that the US would tilt against us, whatever the circumstances, proved wrong. It was not that the relations between these two nations had become hunky-dory; sanctions on loans to India from multilateral institutions continued till almost the end of the Clinton presidency. But the die had been cast. India had arrived on the international scene as a responsible power and a potential economic powerhouse.

10

Looking Back

'A bogey is being created in this House that India is moving towards a Hitler type of dictatorship and fascism is raising its head in the country. This sort of fear is being created.'

—Vajpayee, replying to the confidence vote, 28 May 1996

From a study of Atal Bihari Vajpayee as prime minister in his first term, 1998–99, or as a political leader during the 1996–99 span, what can one conclude about him? The problem is that like India, Vajpayee does not fit into easy characterizations. Was he a liberal? But wasn't he associated with the RSS, an organization that is more commented upon than studied? Did he believe in secularism? If he did, why was he so strongly opposed to conversions? Weren't economic reforms of his regime more by oversight than by design? But would that explain his courage in actually going ahead with the privatization of PSUs, a decision that was so revolutionary that the successor government, of Manmohan Singh and P. Chidambaram, who obviously understood its logic, lacked the political will to execute it? In fact, they not only stopped it but undertook to criminally prosecute those who had gone ahead with privatization.

What makes Vajpayee difficult to understand is that he never seemed to have articulated his beliefs in a systematic way. Therefore, if an analyst or a critic, or even a fan, wishes to understand Vajpayee's views on the economy, for example, or on secularism, there are no primers available. It is also Vajpayee's failure that scholars have not made any efforts to study his life, his politics, his words or his actions in a serious manner that would allow a better understanding of the political leader that he was. In fact, but for N.M. Ghatate's pioneering work on collating many of Vajpayee's speeches in Parliament and presenting them thematically, it would have been impossible to even know what Vajpayee's stand was on important issues.[1] Unfortunately, this fate is not limited to Vajpayee only but extends to almost all political leaders of modern India. The result is that there is either hagiography or incomplete accounts.

How then does one better understand Vajpayee's world view? An initial exercise is being attempted here using two approaches. One, a quick look at some economic initiatives of the Vajpayee government would help understand his views, particularly as he never articulated them very clearly in his speeches. Basically, to look if there are any consistencies in these policies and approaches, or if they are simply episodic and ad hoc. Two, examine his written and spoken words on subjects like the nature of the Indian nation,

---

[1] *Four Decades in Parliament* is a three-volume set containing Vajpayee's speeches in Parliament, edited by N.M. Ghatate (Shipra Publications, 1996). It is also available in Hindi as *Sansad Mein Char Dashak* (Prabhat Publication, 2004). Since this work only covers speeches made till 1996, one can also consult *Decisive Days*, also edited by Ghatate, which has speeches made by Vajpayee in Parliament in 1998–99 (Shipra Publications, 1999).

Hindutva, secularism, the communal question and democracy, to take a few key issues.

One can start by looking at his initial choice of finance minister, Jaswant Singh. Rightly or wrongly, Singh was identified as a believer in economic liberalization and the private sector. It is another matter that he could not make it, having just lost the elections to the Lok Sabha. Yashwant Sinha, who actually became Vajpayee's first finance minister, was initially seen as a candidate backed by the swadeshi lobby but whose actions very soon showed him pushing the reforms agenda. Within weeks of becoming prime minister, Vajpayee had reassured the private sector by telling them that he came 'from a political tradition that does not look upon commerce and industry with distrust. When it was conventional political expediency to decry entrepreneurship, we championed their cause.'

As detailed in Chapter 5, 'The Stumble', Vajpayee was all for user charges being paid for services provided by the government, and for the government to be a regulator and not an active player in the economy. But he added that the consumers should get the quality that they paid for. Sinha's first budget tried to rationalize petrol, diesel and fertilizer prices, but in the face of revolt by parties within the ruling coalition, there had to be substantial rollback. Later, the attempt to reduce subsidies on wheat and rice bought by the non-poor went through but contributed to the collapse of Vajpayee's government in April 1999. In fact, when coalition partners objected to this increase, Vajpayee told them that the Coordination Committee must discuss the politics and economics of subsidy.

Two short but powerful examples of policy intervention in Vajpayee's first term (March 1998–October 1999) and a personal example would help clarify Vajpayee's approach to economic reforms. The first, already referred to, was the National Highways Development Project (NHDP), including the Golden

Quadrilateral. For too long, Indian policymakers saw highways as catering to the narrow elite of car owners, even as long-distance cargo increasingly moved out of railways and went to trucks. Initially, the NHDP was seen as a bid to revive the demand for steel and cement, and to create construction jobs, but that was a narrow view. Vajpayee's idea behind it was the creation of one Indian market where logistics would not be a constraint; the time and cost savings would be humongous and could help promote investment and competitiveness in the economy.

Once the rural connectivity component, the Pradhan Mantri Gram Sadak Yojana, kicked in, the effect on rural society, not just on its economy, was almost revolutionary. It allowed small and marginal farmers to find a better market for their produce; lacking holding capacity, they were earlier forced to sell it locally at depressed prices. It allowed agricultural labour to move beyond their villages and find better wages. India's elementary school enrolment increased markedly during this period. A lot of credit for this should go to the launch of the Sarva Shiksha Abhiyan. But would teachers have shown up in rural schools if there were no, or poor, road connections? Going beyond the budget and making users pay part of the costs, including for rural roads, was again an ingenious idea.

Another shibboleth that had to be destroyed was that telecommunications served the rich and the upper-middle classes. The Narasimha Rao government had launched a telecom policy that allowed private players entry in the mobile services market. Possibly due to inexperience and bad advice by consultants, the initial demand was overestimated. Within a short period, the licensees whose bids had been accepted realized that they had all overestimated potential revenue. The massive mismatch between revenues realized and fees payable to the government meant that adequate investment did not take place. This, in turn, prevented licensees from lowering prices to attract more usage. Caught in this vicious cycle, it seemed that the telecom revolution would be aborted and become another case of missed opportunity.

The licensees had a legal obligation to pay up, since they had made the bids and had entered into a contract with the government to do so. It was argued that it was not the job of the government to rescue those whose business models had failed. After all, had they made profits beyond expectations, they would not have shared the windfall gains with the government. The whole logic of economic liberalization was that the government should not be involved in the business, and—as Joseph Schumpeter's theory of creative destruction tells us—those who could not compete should be allowed to die, so that underutilized resources could be released and be better used by somebody more efficient.

But there were two factors that could help one argue for the opposite case. It was not that a few individual companies were doing badly—as it was almost all of them across the country. Many successful bidders did not even begin operations. The Department of Telecommunications, which had to hand-hold the process, was not just a reluctant partner; it mostly worked to sabotage the entry of the private sector in what it saw as its own monopoly. It even stymied the efforts of the regulator who sought to ease the birth pangs of the telecom operators. In short, the issue was not of individual failure but one with systemic issues at play.

The second feature that made the case for a relook at the license conditions was that there was a genuine fear that a single 'knight in shining armour' would emerge, buy up the distressed companies and effectively establish a monopoly. Therefore, if the government was looking at making systemic changes to help sustain the telecom providers, then it had to be done at a time when there were multiple players rather than a monopoly operator.

A participative approach was taken up. The government task force, headed by Jaswant Singh and comprising a large number of people representing different interest, asked for suggestions.

The unanimous suggestion was to move to a revenue-sharing model, but this was not without its difficulties. The telecom minister, Jagmohan, was completely opposed to it, arguing for upholding the terms of the contract. There were lots of articles written against the change, insinuating malfeasance. There was considerable opposition to this move towards revenue-sharing even within the government and in the cabinet. It was Vajpayee's firm conviction and support that allowed the proposal to go through.

But that was not the end, since economic interests looking to monopolize the sector would not give up so easily. A writ petition was filed against the proposal in the Delhi High Court. The court ordered that the government could go ahead with it subject to parliamentary approval, even though in the Indian scheme of governance, it is the executive that determines policies exclusively. It is only when legislative changes are required that parliamentary approval becomes necessary. The telecom policy of 1994, which allowed private participation, did not go to Parliament. Since by now, the twelfth Lok Sabha had been dissolved consequent on the fall of the Vajpayee government, the actual change was affected only in late 1999.

THE INDIA OF 2019 TAKES its telecom revolution and highways as a given, but these did not come about by chance. That Vajpayee was not into the nitty-gritty of economic policymaking was well known; what is less well known was his almost libertarian view of the role of the government in not hindering the economic life of the community.

My in-laws used to stay in a rent-control house in Allahabad. The landlord used specific legal stratagem that allowed the release of such houses for self-use and promptly sold it. When I related this to Vajpayee, his answer was that the landlord, as the owner and investor, should have full discretion in how he uses his property.

MOVING ON TO HIS LARGER world view, Vajpayee comes across as someone quite rooted in the Indian milieu—its culture, civilization, traditions and values. He was a liberal in the Indian sense but very different from the classical Western liberal as defined by John Locke, Jean-Jacques Rousseau and John Stuart Mill. Western secularism arose in reaction to the Church's stranglehold over social life. This was absent in India, where secularism meant equal respect for all faiths. This difference comes out clearly from Vajpayee's writings, speeches and actions.

His literary taste, too, was interesting. He elaborates it in great detail in a biographical note he wrote for *Bindu-Bindu Vichar*[2] as well as in *Decisive Days*. Both of these long essays, though they cover a large span of time, were coincidentally written in the 1996–99 period. Three of his speeches in Parliament—when he moved a no-confidence motion against the Narasimha Rao government on 17 December 1992, after the demolition of the Babri Masjid; his speech on 27 May 1998, when he moved a motion of confidence in his short, ill-fated government; and his reply a day later—present a fairly clear exposition of his views of nationalism, Indian culture and traditions, and secularism and its politics.

The Ramcharitmanas of Goswami Tulsidas had a profound impact on Vajpayee, and he refers to it as his source of inspiration. According to Vajpayee, the comprehensive view of life that it presents has no parallel in the world. The Ramcharitmanas was even translated into Russian when Russia was ruled by the Communist Party. Vajpayee had an eclectic taste in his choice of literary works. However, Indian epics, folklore, patriotism and the tales of heroic figures dominated his reading list. The writers and

---

[2] Edited by Dr Chandrika Prasad Sharma, *Bindu-Bindu Vichar* (Kitabghar Prakashan, 1997) is an anthology of Vajpayee's poems and excerpts from his writings and speeches. *Decisive Days* (Shipra Publications, 1999) is a collection of speeches by Vajpayee, edited by N.M. Ghatate.

works he has cited include Jaishankar Prasad (*Kamayani*), Nirala (*Ram Ki Shakti Puja*), Mahadevi Verma, Ageya (*Shekhar: Ek Jeevani*) and Jaganath Prasad 'Milind' (*Pratap Pratigya*). Vajpayee stressed that Premchand's writing continued to be popular because it was rooted in a realism whose relevance resonated with contemporary readers.

He approved of Jainendra Kumar, who, he said, captured the reader's imagination even as his works created controversies. Vajpayee was particularly drawn to Vrindavanlal Verma and made references to a number of his stories, like 'Jhansi Ki Rani', 'Mrignayni', 'Virata Ki Padmini', 'Gad Kundar', 'Kachnar', etc. The historical settings of Verma's writings and the regional context of Braj drew Vajpayee to him. Surprising for a poet, Vajpayee felt that while poetry captures the angst of an individual, fiction has the potential to capture both the individual and society.

Vajpayee argued that literature and politics need not be two separate compartments and felt that if politicians got interested in literature, it would improve their sensitivities; a poet as a dictator would not shed innocent lives! Authoritarian rulers were cruel because their sensibilities were not developed. Vajpayee was upset that communists had misused the arts to promote their ideologies and hoped that the literary arts would be allowed to flourish without such political interference.

Vajpayee often mentioned in his writings and speeches in Parliament that he should have remained a writer. He wistfully speculated giving up politics and going to a quiet place where thinking and writing was possible, but then realized that this could not happen. In that sense, his life in politics was a dilemma which, as he wrote, he sorted out by expressing his individuality/personality through the medium of his speeches. The writer in him spoke through his speeches, but it was not as if the politician in him was silent. He explained that the politician presented his thoughts to the writer, and the writer reconsidered them and, after study and contemplation, expressed them. The politician had gained a lot from the writer. The writer did not let the politician cross the boundaries of dignity (*maryada*). It is because of this vigilance that the writer was balanced in his choice of words. The politician's speech was bound by the writer's discipline.

Again, for a full-time politician whose career spanned more than five decades, he came across as someone quite critical of politics and political life. He wrote that politics destroyed mental peace, affection (*mamta*) and compassion (*karuna*). Political life created an unusual hollowness in the practitioners as they lived from moment to moment and assumed that their momentary glory was permanent. In politics, idealism had been replaced by opportunism, and differences between 'left' and 'right' had become personal rather than ideological. He was extremely critical of the politics of dynastic succession, which had become all-consuming. Vajpayee lamented that politics had become all about struggle for power, and that this was more so within parties than among opponents. As a loyal party person, he said that he felt happy that these evils were comparatively less in the party that he belonged to, and quoted K.B. Hedgewar, the founder of RSS, who had warned RSS members against seeking self-publicity.

Though Vajpayee did not always agree with his party, he never made his differences public, and once a decision was taken, he went along with it. Reacting to the statement that he was the 'right man in the wrong party', Vajpayee always explained that the fruit was a product of, and drew its qualities from, the tree. Similarly, he always rose to the defence of the RSS when it was attacked. During the 1996 confidence vote, when a lot of negative things were said about the RSS, Vajpayee strongly refuted them, saying:

I regret that during the discussion, the names of such organizations were mentioned here which are independent and are engaged in the task of nation- and character-building.

I am referring to the RSS. One can have differences with the ideology of the RSS but the allegations levelled against the RSS are not warranted. Even the members of Congress and other parties respect and admire the constructive work being done by the RSS and also lend their cooperation for the same. If they go and work among the poor and work for the spread of education in tribal areas, they should be felicitated for their endeavour.

Vajpayee's world view seems to have been profoundly affected by the communal poison that Jinnah and the Muslim League injected into Indian society on the eve of Independence, the resultant tensions and riots, and the Partition. Even in Lahore in February 1999, he publicly spoke against the division of India but added that the reality of Pakistan had to be accepted. During the 1946–47 period, Vajpayee was a student at DAV College in Kanpur, coincidentally along with his father. The city was a stronghold of the Muslim League. The times were traumatic, and as Vajpayee wrote, the more the Muslim League opposed Independence, the angrier people got with them. The result was communal polarization, tensions and riots. He described a function held in his college to discuss the Noakhali riots, when a call was made for volunteers to go to Noakhali to protect the Hindus.[3] Though the call drew lots of support, Vajpayee opposed it at the risk of offending the majority, saying that youth would be

---

[3] Noakhali, in East Bengal (now Bangladesh), saw horrendous communal violence organized by the Muslim League in November–December 1946, marked by mass killings, rapes and forced conversions. This was the result of a paroxysm of violence that had originated in Jinnah's call for Direct Action that saw Muslim League cadres carry out large-scale killings in Calcutta on 14 August 1946. This led to a backlash. Shocked by the violence, Gandhi went to Noakhali and spent four months trying to control the violence.

needed in Kanpur itself to protect people against riots instigated by pro-Pakistan elements. He then gave a specific example of how many, including him, went near a Muslim-dominated area one night and patrolled the area; after that, he said, there was no more violence in that locality.

For Vajpayee, Independence Day, on 15 August 1947, came drenched in blood—a freedom on whose altar the unity of India had been sacrificed. There was both happiness and depression— happiness at the end of 1000 years of dependence; depression at the partition of the motherland. Vajpayee wrote a dark poem to commemorate Independence Day, titled 'Swatantrata Divas Ki Pukar' (The Call of Independence Day). He wrote that Independence was incomplete, that dreams are yet to become reality, and the oath taken on the Ravi was still to be achieved.[4]

With the new situation arising out of Independence and Partition, there were new challenges and new questions. There were fears of the disintegration of India, at the hands of forces inspired by outsiders who sought to remake India on their terms. A massive communist insurgency had broken out in Telangana just after India had to endure the challenge of quashing the Nizam of Hyderabad's bid for independence/joining Pakistan and the consequent massacres of Hindus by the Razakars. This was also the time that India was engaged in defending the then state of Jammu and Kashmir from Pakistani invasion.

Vajpayee quit his studies without completing his legal education and became the editor of a new publication, *Rashtradharam*, based in Lucknow and established by the RSS. This effectively ended his literary career, to his eternal regret. Vajpayee's role model as editor was the noted writer Makhanlal Chaturvedi, who edited

---

[4] It was on the banks of the Ravi River that the Congress, at the Lahore session, declared 'Poorna Swaraj', or complete independence, as its goal on 26 January 1930.

Vishal Bharat. Its publisher was Ramananda Chatterjee, famous for bringing out the *Modern Review.* Chaturvedi was upset when Chatterjee became president of the Hindu Mahasabha and attacked the move in the pages of *Vishal Bharat.* Chatterjee's response was classic. He said that he respected what Chaturvedi had written, explained the circumstances that made him accept the position and requested that his clarification be carried in *Vishal Bharat.* Vajpayee regretted that there were no more publishers or editors like them.

Vajpayee's assessment was that the rising popularity of the RSS, because of the attractiveness of its ideology, irritated the Congress. Gandhi's assassination created an opportunity for the RSS to be banned. The RSS realized that there was no one to speak for it politically. It therefore teamed up with Dr Syama Prasad Mukherjee, who had broken off from the Hindu Mahasabha due to differences with V.D. Savarkar. Dr Mukherjee had been a minister in Nehru's first government but later quit because of what he felt was India's failure to protect the minorities in Pakistan, and especially with the Nehru–Liaquat pact. Dr Mukherjee's wisdom and legislative skills were well known, and it was in their coming together that the Bharatiya Jana Sangh was established in 1951. The Jana Sangh contested the first Lok Sabha elections in 1952, won four seats and was recognized as a political party with the *deepak* (lamp) as its symbol. In April 1998, while inaugurating the Konkan Railway in Ratnagiri, Vajpayee would recall that the Jana Sangh had won the Ratnagiri seat in 1952.

ACCORDING TO VAJPAYEE, THE JANA Sangh believed in nationalism, positive secularism and Hindutva. It made clear to the nation that the word 'Hindu' was not religion-specific (*panth vishesh*); it was not tied to any specific mode of worship. It was a way of life that included different communities, ideologies and modes of worship. The two issues that the Jana Sangh identified with was the adoption of the uniform civil code (UCC), as mandated in the Directive Principles of State Policy, and the complete merger of Kashmir. Speaking on his confidence motion on 27 May 1998, Vajpayee emphasized that it was from the Constitution that the idea of UCC drew strength and that the Supreme Court had ruled in favour of its adoption. The ideal of gender equality could only be achieved by adopting UCC. Vajpayee held that it was up to the leadership of the Muslims to prepare their community for it. Islamic countries had gone ahead with these gender-friendly changes. In India, the Hindu society was dynamic and changes had been made in their personal law.

He was clear that nobody should have a veto over change, and over the adoption of UCC, Vajpayee was profoundly affected by Dr Mukherjee and his supreme sacrifice. Mukherjee had entered Jammu and Kashmir without a permit that Indian citizens required to access this part of their own country. Twenty-two days later, at the age of fifty-three, Dr Mukherjee was dead. Earlier, when he'd parted from Vajpayee and entered J&K, Mukherjee had asked him to go to Delhi and tell the world that he (Dr Mukherjee) had entered Kashmir without a permit. Writing in *Bindu-Bindu Vichar*, Vajpayee could not suppress his anger at, and appreciation of, Mukherjee's sacrifice. Vajpayee called Mukherjee a victim of authoritarianism who died trying to ensure that Kashmir remains the (biological) head of a united body (India). Mukherjee had laid the foundation stone of liberty and democracy, he had fought the forces of darkness and attained eternal light. Vajpayee added that whenever he remembered Dr Mukherjee, Kashmir came to his mind.

A REFERENCE HAS ALREADY BEEN made to Vajpayee's defeat in the 1962 general elections in Chapter 2, 'A Hung Parliament'. Vajpayee attributed his defeat to the communal tension created by his opponents and to the poison being spread about the Jana

Sangh and especially about the RSS. It was insinuated that the RSS founder, Dr Hedgewar, had gone to Germany and, inspired by the Nazis, had started the RSS. As Vajpayee told the Lok Sabha on 27 May, it was not the demolition of the Babri Masjid— or the disputed structure, as he called it—that gave the BJP, or its predecessor, the Jana Sangh, the label of being communal. He explained that in 1991, Opposition parties held rallies to oppose the BJP—rallies where the overwhelming presence was that of Muslims. This tactic actually went in the BJP's favour and helped it win the subsequent UP state assembly elections.

According to Vajpayee, Advani's Rath Yatra in 1990, from Somnath to Ayodhya—which ended in Samastipur, when Lalu's government arrested Advani—had not been organized to bring down the V.P. Singh government but to create awareness and support for the rebuilding of the Ram Janmabhoomi temple in Ayodhya. In this, the Rath Yatra was successful since it touched the sentiments of the majority community. Vajpayee argued that the adoption of policies and behaviour in the name of secularism by the Congress over the past four decades had convinced the Hindus, rightly or wrongly, that they were not being treated well. The Shah Bano case and the attacks on the unity of the country in Punjab and Kashmir had offended them. The use of the minority card by the Congress and left parties upset them. The Rath Yatra symbolized these dissatisfactions.

In May 1998, Vajpayee also referred to the issue of illegal infiltration of millions into India. Though he was careful not to name any country, the non-BJP parties and leaders accused him of being anti-Muslim, presuming that he was speaking about Bangladesh. Despite his clarification that it was not a Hindu–Muslim issue, this accusation was repeated many times. Vajpayee even suggested that no one should be thrown out; rather that illegal infiltrators could enter India utilizing a system of work permits and go back when their contract runs out. Yet he was pilloried. He argued that no country could tolerate large-scale illegal immigration running into millions.

On 27 May, facing the issue of secularism, Vajpayee squarely reminded Parliament that the word did not originally figure in the Constitution. The assumption was that the Indian state can only be a secular one. Though it was thought that the Preamble could not be amended, this had been done during the Emergency, when the Opposition leaders were in jail. Two words, 'secular' and 'socialist' were added to it. Vajpayee said that he agreed with how Sardar Swaran Singh described 'secularism' when the latter moved the Constitutional Amendment Bill in 1976 that added these two words. According to Singh, since India was a multi-religious country, secularism meant that there could not be any discrimination against followers of any religion. The principle that all regions should be treated equally was, for Vajpayee, the quintessence of the Hindu world view.

Vajpayee told the Lok Sabha that the Indian belief was that no one religion or prophet had a monopoly over truth. He quoted the old saying '*Ekam sat vipra bahuda vadanti*', meaning that the truth is one, but the wise know it differently. In other words, all religions and modes of worship were equally valid. Vajpayee said that he was secular and proud of India's culture and civilization. He had, in fact, been moulded by them. In this context, he quoted Nehru at Aligarh Muslim University, shortly after the Partition of India. Nehru told the students that he was proud of his inheritance and that he got a strange thrill from knowing that he was the trustee and inheritor of this civilization. Nehru added that both the Hindus and the Muslims owned this common past. According to Nehru, '. . . the past holds us together whilst the present or the future divides us in a split.'

Vajpayee reminded Parliament that the first mosque in India was built in Kerala with the permission of the local king, as was the first church. The BJP stood for diversity and accepted that India was a multi-religious, multi-lingual and multi-ethnic country. The state should protect life, honour and property of all, and there should be no discrimination. He explained that due to actions of the governments and parties that believed in vote-bank politics, Hindus had developed a minority-like felling, rightly or wrongly.

Vajpayee's alleged role in provoking the kar sevaks to bring down the Babri Masjid has lately gained currency based on his speech to a group of them in Lucknow a day before the demolition, on 5 December. Vajpayee asked them to remove stones and pebbles from the site so that large numbers of people, who would gather there, could sing devotional bhajans together. This call doesn't come across as provocative. On the other hand, as Vajpayee explained in Parliament on 17 December 1992, when he moved the no-confidence motion, if the BJP and RSS had wanted the disputed structure to be brought down, would it have collected almost all its top leadership to be present on the site? Could the demolition not have been done quietly, away from the public glare?

Vajpayee's speech was actually quite defensive, and he was clearly upset that the commitment given by the BJP government in UP to Narasimha Rao—that the disputed structure in Ayodhya would be protected—was not honoured. This rankled him. According to him, people like Arjun Singh—a powerful minister in the Narasimha Rao government and identified as being strongly anti-BJP—prevented a negotiated settlement to the Ayodhya issue. In fact, Vajpayee hinted at a conspiracy to bring down the disputed structure when he said that while most of the kar sevaks were not involved, a small group carried out the demolition, disregarding the pleas made by Advani to remain peaceful.

Vajpayee said that if those devotees of Ram were so keen on constructing the Janmabhoomi temple, they should be prepared to pay the price for bringing down the structure. But he was not defensive about the Hindu claim to the site. He cited the example of how when the Poles recovered their independence from the

Russians, they demolished a church that their rulers had built.[5]
He also quoted the famous historian Arnold Toynbee, who once
said that he was surprised that Hindus had not demolished the
mosques that had been built by destroying temples. Vajpayee
blamed the Indian political leadership for not highlighting that
Hindus and Muslims had been in dispute over the structure in
Ayodhya for over 500 years, and that both communities had been
using it for their prayers. He argued that if more people had been
aware of the complexity of the dispute, the reactions would have
been different. He added that the idols had been placed inside the
structure when there was no Jana Sangh, Vishva Hindu Parishad
or Bajrang Dal.

Vajpayee started his speech in Parliament on 17 December
1992 by saying that the BJP were unhappy with what had happened
in Ayodhya on 6 December. Going back to that fateful day, the
media reported that Vajpayee's first reaction to the demolition was
one of deep sorrow, explaining that the kar sevaks had gone to
Ayodhya for the construction of the temple, not for its destruction.
Continuing in the same vein, he explained that since the disputed
structure was already being used as a temple and housed idols, the
'militancy' of the kar sevaks who carried out the demolition was
not an act of devotion. This 'misadventure', according to Vajpayee,
would make the construction of the temple difficult.

The assumption those days was that the court would soon
rule on the dispute and that it was just a matter of time before
things would be sorted out. But little did Vajpayee, or anybody
else, envisage that the case would reach the Supreme Court, whose
final decision would take another twenty-seven years. Incidentally,
Kalyan Singh resigned as the chief minister of UP on 6 December,

---

[5] Vajpayee was referring to the Alexander Nevsky Church in Warsaw,
built by the Russians and completed in 1912. The Poles recovered their
independence from Russia in 1918. The Church was demolished in 1924.

since he had failed to protect the disputed structure. So the BJP then had an absolute majority in the UP assembly. (It would not be till 2017 that the BJP was again able to form a majority government in UP.) The demolition in Ayodhya would affect the BJP and the Ram Janmabhoomi temple far more fundamentally than was imaginable in 1992.

THE TEMPLE ISSUE LED TO further controversy over whether Vajpayee was a liberal in the classical nineteenth-century sense. But his critics were forgetting the fundamental values of Indian traditions. The first problem, in this context, arises conceptually from the meaning of the word 'religion'. The Abrahamic faiths have an in-built exclusiveness that sees only themselves as the one true path. Therefore, if you are not with me, you are damned. Worse, the concepts of blasphemy and apostasy strengthen this exclusivity.

Unlike Gandhi, who had detailed exposure of living in a non-Hindu milieu and extensive conversations with Christian theologians, Vajpayee was very much rooted in the larger Hindu traditions. Hence, for him, discrimination based on faith was completely no-go, and the ruler was not to be concerned with the belief systems of his subjects. This worked fine conceptually when boundaries between faiths are fluid and faith is not seen as all-pervasive. But can belief systems be equated with religion? Can Shaivism, Vaishnavism, Nath Sampradaya or even Kabir Panthism be categorized as separate religions? Going further, do marriages take place between Jains and non-Jains? Vajpayee strongly argued for Vijayadashami to be a national event since it symbolized the victory of good over evil and was, in his eyes, was non-sectarian. The same logic would apply to Holi and Diwali too.

These assumptions would obviously not be acceptable to most believers of Abrahamic religions, as the following incident makes clear. As cited above, while moving the confidence vote

on 27 May 1996, Vajpayee had said that India was inherently
secular, since Indians did not believe that any faith or system of
worship had a monopoly over truth. This, for Vajpayee, was self-
evident. Syed Shahabuddin, the diplomat turned politician and a
prominent voice articulating a Muslim point of view, disagreed
with Vajpayee's description of the Indian philosophy. According
to Shahabuddin, it was his belief as a Muslim that his was the only
true path. So could Vajpayee say that Indians accept all faiths as
true and equally valid? I showed Shahabuddin's letter to Vajpayee
and asked him if a reply had to be sent. He read the letter carefully
and gave it back to me. His body language suggested that no
action was necessary. It was early days and our comfort levels were
not too high, so I did not ask him anything. I would hazard that
Shahabuddin's logic would not have appealed to him. Nor would
he have really understood why many would see Vijayadashami as
sectarian and not a national event.

Religious conversions deeply offended Vajpayee's sensibilities.
He saw it almost as a humiliation, a continuation of foreign rule,
with the weaknesses of Indians being exploited. It wasn't that he
was not aware of social evils within Hindu society. In fact, when
the former sarsanghchalak of the RSS, Balasaheb Deoras, passed
away, Vajpayee quoted him as saying that if untouchability was
not a sin, then nothing was a sin. This distaste with conversions
did not make him communal or discriminatory against those
belonging to other religions. In fact, he was very sympathetic to
the converted, accepting in his mind that it was economic or social
desperation that led to conversions.

A case had come to him as prime minister to cancel the
appointment of a young lady from Tamil Nadu who had been
selected into the IAS as a candidate belonging to the scheduled
caste (SC). A complaint had been received that she had written
the civil services examination earlier as a general candidate. The
inquiry revealed that many members of her community, who were

Dalits, had converted to Christianity, while others had not. The law was clear: if she was a Christian, she could not claim SC status. However, Vajpayee decided to overrule the recommendation, understanding that the motives for conversion often have to do with economic and social gain. That, however, did not make him a proponent of extending the reservation of the 'Dalit Christians' as a community, something he'd made clear when a similar move was being made under the United Front government. Vajpayee also wrote that conversion does not mean giving up one's culture and traditions. His ready acceptance of Nehru's and Swaran Singh's logic would fit into this world view—a world view that the Western liberal, with multiculturalism up the sleeve, would have difficulty reconciling with.

It was not that Vajpayee was ambiguous about what he stood for; rather, he was not an ideologue, which meant his world view was not rigid or dogmatic. The context was always a factor, whether it meant dissolving the Jana Sangh in the larger corporate identity of the Janata Party to rescue democracy, or making Gandhian socialism the slogan of the newly formed Bharatiya Janata Party, in order to distinguish it from the Jana Sangh and widen its appeal. It also meant temporarily shelving three controversial issues—abrogation of Article 370; establishment of the uniform civil code; and the Ram Janmabhoomi—when the National Agenda for Governance was negotiated in 1998, so that several non-Congress parties could come together on the common platform of the NDA. In fact, when he was taunted during the 1998 confidence vote for having dropped these issues from the NAG, Vajpayee said that this was done because the BJP did not have a majority. He never disowned these fundamental issues. He laughed away the Opposition's charge by saying that they seemed upset that the BJP did not include these issues in the NAG.

The trouble was not in Vajpayee's world view but in what the observer wanted to see in him. Many who saw him as communal, as a polarizer and a cover for saffronization when he was in power, changed their view by 2014—when the Modi government came to power—and began to regard Vajpayee as a genuine 'liberal', a person who was accommodative and carried people with him. To quote Cassius from *Julius Caesar*, 'The fault, dear Brutus, is not in our stars, but in ourselves . . .'

VAJPAYEE WROTE THAT HE WAS not afraid of death, and he demonstrated this in real life at least twice. On 22 January 1993, the Lucknow–Delhi Indian Airlines flight, IC 810, was hijacked, with Vajpayee on board. Vajpayee negotiated with the hijacker and got him to surrender. Later, it was established that the hijacker's threat to blow up the plane was hollow, since he did not have any explosives on him, but this fact was not known when Vajpayee was singly persuading the hijacker to surrender. There was real fear, but that did not deter Vajpayee. On another occasion, he was quite calm, even joked about a state funeral, when the small plane he was on, flying to Dharamshala, lost its navigational aid and got enveloped in fog. The plane somehow reached Kullu, over the Dhauladhar range. It was a providential escape, but at no stage was Vajpayee frightened, while his fellow passenger, Balbir Punj, was in a panic.

So when in the context of his cancer, Vajpayee wrote that he could not understand how one could be afraid of death, which was as certain as the North Star, this was no idle boast. In fact, his prose became almost lyrical when he said that if death came to his door, he will leave without even waiting for a moment; but if it wanted to play around, like a cat does with a mouse, then Vajpayee would fight hard, till his last breath. After his bout with cancer, Vajpayee did not suffer from any life-threatening diseases, and though he was afflicted by a paralytic stroke when he was past eighty, with his cognitive abilities slowly deteriorating, his innate strength ensured that he did not yield easily, just as he'd predicted.

It was therefore not a surprise that his poem about death was a declaration of war, not a song of the defeated. It was not a cry of hopelessness, but a call of one brimming with self-confidence:

Haar nahin manunga, raar nahin thanunga,
Kaal kay kapal pe likhta-mitata hoon,
Geet naya gata hoon.

Acknowledgements

I would never have written this book but for Milee Ashwarya's persistent efforts. The idea was hers to begin with, which she quickly followed up with a contract. In effect, I was presented with an offer I could not refuse. Over the last two years or so, she has kept the project under her control. Her encouraging push, very polite but persistent, was always there when I felt that I had hit a dead end. So, thank you, Milee.

I gained a lot from reading the books and articles listed at the end, and even though I may not have interacted with the authors personally, I acknowledge my gratitude to them, like Eklavya.

I wanted to get my facts right as memory can play tricks. At the Nehru Memorial Museum and Library (NMML), Sonika Gupta was a big help in locating the microfilms I was looking for, loading them on to the reader, and frequently helping out by sorting technological problems associated with an inept user and old tapes. In addition to Sonika, my thanks also to Dr Pankaj Chaurasia and to their bosses, Dr Narendra Shukla and Dr Ajit Kumar. NMML provided me with just the right environment to work in, and I must thank everyone there for their efforts and support.

I also spent a week at the *Indian Express* archives in Chandigarh, and this week was a very productive one, thanks to Raj Kumar Srivastava, who ensured that everything I needed was made available to me. His courtesy went beyond formality, and he made that extra effort to ensure all the creature comforts, little things that actually matter so much. Thank you, Raj Kumarji.

Initially, two young researchers, Ratika Gaur and Abhinand Srinivas, helped me by researching specific topics that I wanted to understand better. Abhinand then found more productive employment, working on an NMML project that involves getting together all the speeches and writings of Vajpayee, which I hope would soon be made available to the public at large. It is surprising how little Vajpayee is studied. We at NMML were grateful to draft Vajpayee's long-term Boswell, Dr N.M. (Appa) Ghatate, to lead this project. I gained immensely by interacting with Appa and reading his edited volumes on Vajpayee. Thank you, Appa. You have been, and continue to be, a big source of information and support.

Abhinand's notes, especially on the telecom policy of 1999, really helped me understand the nuances so much better. His reflexes are very quick. I wish he had hung around longer on this book! Thank you, Abhinand.

Ratika continued working with me and has been most helpful, especially with her editing skills, particularly after I left NMML. A first-time writer, unconsciously, makes a lot of assumptions when describing any incident or circumstance. Facilitated mostly by email, Ratika's meticulous comments on names, acronyms and flow really helped make the narrative understandable for someone who might not be very familiar with the 1998–99 period. Being next-gen, her questions and doubts made me explain things with much greater clarity. I realized the virtues of not making assumptions. She did the first-round editing of all the chapters, sometimes more than once, contributing greatly to the book. Her hard work remains unseen but was invaluable. Thank you, Ratika.

At Penguin Random House, Vineet Gill proved to be a hard taskmaster. The text changed visibly in the few weeks that he worked on the manuscript. A lot of redundancies, general statements and irrelevant information was weeded out. The language became tighter and the flow more coherent. Working with Vineet, I realized the value of professional editing. I was happy to accept his suggestions, mostly, as I could see how much better it read with the changes. Thank you, Vineet.

This book is unusual because I do not list too many names outside the main actors. Lest an impression is created that I was working alone with Vajpayee during these years, particularly the 1998–99 period, I must mention that we had a very good team at the prime minister's house, with V. Anandarajan, the additional private secretary, who, after I left, became the private secretary along with Ajay Bisaria. Anand and I shared responsibilities, and without him by my side, I would have collapsed with exhaustion in a few months. We were ably supported by a number of persons—Venkat, Dilip Kumar, Shanker and others.

At the PMO, besides Brajesh Mishra, about whom there are a lot of references in the book, there was Ashok Saikia, who, as someone who knew Vajpayee for decades, was able to convey the complexities and undercurrents that people at the top are often not told. Ashok Tandon very ably dealt with the media and conveyed feedback to the boss effectively. One cannot forget Kanchan Gupta and his writing skills backed by a formidable political brain. Sudheendra Kulkarni brought Mumbai and the business world so much closer to political decision-making. He was ably assisted by the IIM graduate Harsh Shrivastava. At a later stage, N.K. Singh, or Nandu Babu, joined the PMO and brought his grasp of economic policymaking and wide network, something that the PMO had missed till then.

The PMO had very solid foreign-policy bench strength, what with Brajesh Mishra himself heading it. The erudite

Prabhat Shukla and Satish Mehta, whom I mention in the book, in the context of organizing the Lahore visit, were always available to help me understand the nuances of diplomacy. Regrettably, Brajeshji and Ashok are no more with us.

Interacting with friends and colleagues in external affairs—the redoubtable Hardeep Puri, Vivek Katju and Rakesh Sood, to take only three names—was always an intellectual treat. I must say thank you to all of them, many of whom I have not listed here. I learnt a lot from them, which decades later helped me write this book. I may not have always agreed with their assessments, but I definitely gained a lot from them.

Discussions over decades with close friends Pradeep Puri, Pradeep Chhibber and Subhash Misra, particularly on political trends, have shaped my own mental make-up. This actually requires a paragraph, but you will understand. Thank you.

We have this terrible Indian English expression, 'last but not the least'. In fact, often, as in this note, the most important is reserved for the last. This book, and a lot of what we take for granted in contemporary India in terms of quality of life, India's increasing importance to the world, etc., would not have been the same without the vision and efforts of Atal Bihari Vajpayee. He did what many cannot achieve, which is make the transition from a successful politician to a statesman. Do I uncritically accept what he believed in or did? Far from it. As I said before, Vajpayee deserves to be studied a lot more. Vinay Sitapati (*Jugalbandi*) has made a start, even if I do not agree with a number of his propositions. Vinay's effort must be appreciated. I have learnt a lot while interacting with him. So thank you. I hope others pick up the baton.

So much of my life and my learning would not have been possible but for my professionally joining Vajpayee in 1996. 'Thank you' seems a small phrase compared to what I have gained. But I shall nevertheless say it: Thank you, Atalji.

In fact, I would not have joined Vajpayee in 1996 but for a person, my mother-in-law's elder sister, Bibi Masi to us, and Kaul Aunty to the world. She radiated love and went out of her way to make me feel at home. She was an immense source of support, far more than what words can describe. Thank you, Bibi Masi.

Namita (Gunu) and Ranjan remain not just family but much more. I did not tell you I was writing this book, but I had to pay my tribute to Baabji. Thank you for your love and support, especially at difficult moments.

P.G. Wodehouse once thanked his daughter, Leonara, without whose help 'this book would have been finished in half the time'. My experience has been the opposite. My long hours at the table all evening, and on holidays, were not just tolerated but encouraged. Surabhi, Kartikeya and Suhasini ensured that I had the space to work. One could not have asked for anything better. And yes, Surabhi read the manuscript after the first proof, and found many errors. Erich Segal, in his epic novel *Love Story*, had this beautiful line, 'Love means not ever having to say you are sorry.' He had nothing to say about not ever having to say thank you. So, thank you, Surabhi, Kartikeya and Suhasini.

List of Sources

'Watch: When Atal Bihari Vajpayee Spoke of "Levelling the Ground" in His Speech to Kar Sevaks in 1992', Scroll.in, 30 September 2020, accessed on 24 April 2020, https://scroll.in/video/882331/watch-when-atal-bihari-vajpayee-spoke-of-levelling-the-ground-in-his-speech-to-kar-sevaks-in-1992

Indian Express (New Delhi), 1 March–3 April 1998

Times of India (New Delhi), 1–3 April 1998

'Jayalalitha vs the BJP', *Frontline*, 9 December 2019, accessed on 22 July 2020, https://frontline.thehindu.com/politics/article30161298.ece

'The Arrival of Western Economic Aid Brought AIDS to India: Murli Manohar Joshi', *India Today*, 18 March 2013, accessed on 22 July 2020, https://www.indiatoday.in/magazine/indiascope/voices/story/19980504-the-arrival-of-western-economic-aid-brought-aids-to-india-murli-manohar-joshi-828077-1998-05-04

'We Can Only Pity the Left and Feel Sorry for the Congress: M. Venkaiah Naidu', *India Today*, 25 March 2013, accessed on

22 June 2020, https://www.indiatoday.in/magazine/indiascope/voices/story/19980706-we-can-only-pity-the-left-and-feel-sorry-for-the-congress-m.-venkaiah-naidu-763203-2012-08-27

Harinder Baweja, 'M.L. Khurana's Outburst Embarrasses BJP, Allies Demand Party to Rein in Sangh Hardliners', *India Today*, 27 February 2013, accessed on 22 July 2020, https://www.indiatoday.in/magazine/nation/story/19990215-m.l.-khuranas-outburst-embarrasses-bjp-allies-demand-party-to-rein-in-sangh-hardliners-780159-1999-02-15

'Back from the Brink', *Hindustan Times* (New Delhi), 4 February 1999

'The Joint Statement', *Frontline*, 9 December 2019, accessed on 22 June 2020, https://frontline.thehindu.com/cover-story/article30159219.ece

Indian Express (New Delhi), 1 March–3 April 1998

India Today, 24 August 1998

India Today, 11 January 1999

India Today, 18 January 1999

ParliamentofIndia.nic.in, accessed on 24 June 2020, https://parliamentofindia.nic.in/ls/lsdeb/ls11/ses1/4312069613.htm

India Today, 8 February 1999

India Today, 18 February 1999

India Today, 4 May 1998

India Today, 6 July 1998

Frontline, 2–15 January 1999

Times of India (New Delhi), 7 April 1998

Frontline, 16–29 January 1999

Frontline, 27 March–9 April 1999

Hindustan Times, 3 May–5 July 1998

Hindustan Times, 16 March 1998

Hindustan Times, 2 June 1998

Hindustan Times, 9 May 1998

Hindustan Times, 28 May 1998

AIR 1997 SC 2725, 1997 (1) BLJR 110, 1996 (9) SCALE 680, (1997) 1 SCC 444, 1996 Supp 10 SCR 925

Inder Malhotra, *Sunday*, 21 February 1999, p. 11

'Advani, Joshi, Uma Bharti Must Resign', Rediff.com, accessed on 29 April 2020, https://www.rediff.com/news/1998/apr/27swamy. htmAtal Bihari Vajpayee, *Four Decades in Parliament*, Shipra Publications, 1996'Indian's Letter to Clinton On the Nuclear Testing.' *New York Times*, 13 May 1998, accessed on 22 July 2020, https://www.nytimes.com/1998/05/13/world/nuclear-anxiety-indian-s-letter-to-clinton-on-the-nuclear-testing.html

Aditi Phadnis, *Sunday*, 21 February 1999, pp. 40–41

Priya Sehgal, *Sunday*, 26 February 1999, pp. 6–19

Amit Baruah, *Frontline*, vol. 6.5, 27 February–12 March 1999

Sukumar Muralidharan, *Frontline*, vol. 6.5, 27 February–12 March 1999

Vinod Mehta, *Outlook*, 8 March 1999

'Laloo Yadav Splits Janata Dal, Sets up Rashtriya Dal', accessed on 24 July 2020, https://m.rediff.com/news/jul/05laloo.htm

Kanti Bajpai, *Outlook*, 8 March 1999

Najam Sethi, *Outlook*, 8 March 1999

S. Gajrani, Shiri Ram Bakshi and Sita Ram Sharma, *Sonia Gandhi: The President of AICC*, APH, 1998

Manoj Joshi and Shahzeb Jilani, *India Today*, 1 March 1999

'Kargil War Reiterated India's Supremacy Over Pakistan', Aviation Defence Universe, 26 July 2020, accessed on 20 September 2020. https://www.aviation-defence-universe.com/kargil-war-reiterated-indias-supremacy-pakistan/

Kuldip Nayar, 'The RSS Game Plan', *Hindustan Times* (New Delhi), 9 May 1998

Abu Abraham, 'The Deterrence Myth', *Sunday*, 31 May 1998, p. 3

Rajni Kothari, *Hindustan Times*, 1 June 1998

'Downside Legacy at Two Degrees of President Clinton', Indian Defence Forum, accessed on 22 July 2020, https://defenceforumindia.com/threads/downside-legacy-at-two-degrees-of-president-clinton.41269/

Frontline, 24 April–7 May 1999

Frontline, 8–21 May 1999

Amulya Ganguly, 'Politics of . . .', *Hindustan Times*, 1 June 1998

S. Ubaidur Rahman, 'Vajpayee Is as Much Sanghi as Sudarshan and Advani', *Milli Gazette*, accessed on 20 November 2020, https://www.milligazette.com/Archives/15052002/1505200269.htm

Sunanda K. Datta-Ray, 'Vajpayee: An Unsolved Riddle', *Telegraph India*, 4 September 2018, accessed on 20 April 2020, https://www.telegraphindia.com/opinion/unsolved-riddle/cid/1531985

Times of India, 10 March 1998

Hindustan Times, 5 May 1998

Hindustan Times, 8 May 1998

Indian Express, 7 May 1998

Hindustan Times, 20 June 1998

Hindustan Times, 7 February 1999

Hindustan Times, 17 February 1999

Hindustan Times, 5 February 1999

Hindustan Times, 18 February 1999

Hindustan Times, 23 February 1999

Vasantha Surya, 'Vajpayee's Poetic Voice', *Frontline*, 4 November 2004, accessed on 20 May 2020, https://frontline.thehindu.com/other/article30225170.ece

'Clinton, Nawaz, Vajpayee and a N-war', Ministry of External Affairs, 4 July 1999, accessed on 29 April 2020, https://www.mea.gov.in/articles-in-indian-media.htm?dtl/15419/Atal   Bihari Vajpayee, *21 Poems*, Viking, 2002

Ullekh N.P., 'How Vajpayee Straddled Two Worlds and Made Hindutva Palatable to the Masses', UllekhNP.com, 22 August 2018, accessed on 20 July 2020, https://ullekhnp.com/2018/08/22/how-vajpayee straddled-two-worlds/

India Today, 13 April 1998

India Today, 26 April 1998

'Atal in His Contradictions', HardNewsMedia.com, 21 August 2018, accessed on 20 July 2020, http://www.hardnewsmedia.com/2018/08/atal-his-contradictions

Bibliography

Books

A.B. Vajpayee, *Bindu-Bindu Vichar*, edited by Chandrika Prasad Sharma, Kitabghar, 1998

A.B. Vajpayee, *Decisive Days*, edited by N.M. Ghatate, Shipra, 1999

A.B. Vajpayee, *Meri Sansadiya Yatra*, vol. 4, Prabhat Prakashan, 1999

A.B. Vajpayee, *Towards a Developed Economy: Defining Moments*, Publications Division, Ministry of Information and Broadcasting, Government of India, 2004

Admiral Sushil Kumar, *A Prime Minister to Remember: Memories of a Military Chief*, Konark Publishers, 2019

C. Raja Mohan, *Crossing the Rubicon*, Viking Publication, 2003

Jaswant Singh, *A Call to Honour: In Service of Resurgent India*, Rupa Publications, 2006

Kingshuk Nag, *Atal Bihari Vajpayee: A Man for All Seasons*, Rupa Publications, 2016

Raj Chengappa, *Weapons of Peace: The Secret Story of India's Quest to be a Nuclear Power*, HarperCollins India, 2000

Strobe Talbott, *Engaging India: Diplomacy, Democracy and the Bomb*, Viking Penguin, 2004

Sumit Ganguly, *Indian Foreign Policy*, OUP, 2015

Ullekh N.P., *The Untold Vajpayee: Politician and Paradox*, Penguin Random House, 2018

Vijay Trivedi, *Haar Nahi Manungam*, Harper Hindi, 2016

Articles

A.B. Vajyapee, 'One of Us', *Sunday Times*, vol. 26, issue 8, February 1999

B.R. Nayar, 'India and the Super Powers: Deviation or Continuity in Foreign Policy?', *Economic and Political Weekly*, vol. 12, issue 30, pp. 1185–1189, 1977, available at https://www.jstor.org/stable/4365798

Ejaz Ghani, Arti Grover Goswami, William R. Kerr, 'Highway to Success: The Impact of the Golden Quadrilateral Project for the Location and Performance of Indian Manufacturing', *Economic Journal*, vol. 126, issue 591, 2014, available at https://dash.harvard.edu/bitstream/handle/1/13135314/ghani,goswami,kerr_highway-to-success.pdf?sequence=1

Jayant Prasad, 2018, 'India's Deterrence and Disarmament: The Impact of Pokhran-II', Institute for Defence Studies and Analysis, vol. 42, issue 3, available at https://idsa.in/strategicanalysis/42_3/indias-deterrence-and-disarmament

R. Prasanna, 'POKHRAN2@20: When India went full blast', *Week*, 1998, available at https://www.theweek.in/news/india/2018/05/08/pokhran-2-20-india-full-blast.html

Rahul Mukherji, 'Regulatory Evolution in Indian Telecommunications', Working Paper No. 7, Institute of South Asian Studies, National University of Singapore, 2006, available at https://www.isas.nus.edu.sg/wp-content/uploads/media/isas_papers/ISAS_Working_Paper_7.pdf

Shakti Sinha, Ratika Gaur, 'Atal Bihari Vajpayee: Deshbhakt-Rajneta', *Sahitya Amrit Masik*, December 2018

Sreeram S. Chaulia, 'BJP, India's Foreign Policy and the "Realist Alternative" to the Nehruvian Tradition', *International Politics*, vol. 39, pp. 215–234

Webpages

Abhijnan Rej, 'The Foreign Policy Legacy of Atal Bihari Vajpayee', LiveMint, September 2018, https://www.livemint.com/Opinion/kZI9uaKnH41oM9d7HJdfZO/The-foreign-policy-legacy-of-Atal-Bihari-Vajpayee.html

Abhishek De, 'Atal Bihari Vajpayee Passes Away: 10 Defining Moments of His Political Career', *Indian Express*, 16 August 2018, https://www.google.co.in/amp/s/indianexpress.com/articles/india/1--defining-moments-of-atal-bihari-vajpayees-political-career-5310378/lite/

Jayanth Jacob, 'Atal Bihari Vajpayee's Deft Foreign Policy Helped Forge Stronger Relationships', *Hindustan Times*, 17 August 2018, https://www.google.co.in/amp/s/m.hindustantimes.com/india-news/atal-bihari-vajpayee-s-deft-foreign-policy-helped-forge-stronger-relationships/story-y898kQrb03v!TU7dwXvjQK_amp.html

Shakti Sinha, 'A Master of Details, He Gave Everyone a Free Hand to Speak, but Took Final Call', *Mint*, 17 August 2018, https://www.livemint.com/Politics/ILwFosJVS0x8oDd3mzMcZP/A-master-of-details-he-gave-everyone-a-free-hand-to-speak.html

Shakti Sinha, 'Atal Bihari Vajpayee, a Normal Person with Infinite Patience', *Economic Times*, 17 August 2018, https://economictimes.indiatimes.com/news/politics-and-nations/atal-bihari-vajpayee-a-normal-person-with-infinite-patience-shakti-sinha/articleshow/65433125.cms

Shakti Sinha, 'Atal Ki Banayi Hui Sadake Par Hi Kulanche Bhar Rahi Desh Ki Aarthik Raftaar', *Dainik Jagran*, 16 August 2018, https://www.jagran.com/politics/national-atal-will-be-remembered-for-his-infrastructure-projects-and-diplomacy-18319713.html

Shakti Sinha, 'Pokhran Anniv: Vajpayee's Secretary Recalls Moments of Tension & Tears on Nuclear Test Day', ThePrint, 11 May 2018, https://theprint.in/opinions/pokhran-anniv-vajpayees-secretary-recalls-moments-test-day/57218/

Shakti Sinha, 'The Uncompromising Patriot: Shakti Sinha on Working Closely with Atal Bihari Vajpayee', *Hindustan Times*, 16 August 2018, https://www.hindustantimes.com/india-news/the-uncompromising-patriot-on-working-closely-with-atal-bihari-vajpayee/story-s34gPStkpp4jf04Pvn KF6L.html

Shakti Sinha, 'Vajpayee and India's Foreign Policy: Early Articulation', *India and World*, vol. 2, no. 1, special edition, TGII Media Private Ltd, 2018

Shakti Sinha, 'Vajpayee Was Popular Even among Citizens Who Didn't Vote for Him, Writes His PMO Aide', ThePrint, 16 August 2018, https://staging2.theprint.in/opinion/vajpayee-was-

popular-even-among-citizens-who-didnt-vote-for-him-writes-
his-pmo-aide/99644/

Shakti Sinha, 'Vajpayee . . . Orator, Economic Reformer, Affable
Politician', Rotary News, vol. 69, issue 3, pp. 42–45, September 2018